CAMBRIDGE LIBRARY COLLECTION

Books of enduring scholarly value

Egyptology

The large-scale scientific investigation of Egyptian antiquities by Western scholars began as an unintended consequence of Napoleon's invasion of Egypt during which, in 1799, the Rosetta Stone was discovered. The military expedition was accompanied by French scholars, whose reports prompted a wave of enthusiasm that swept across Europe and North America resulting in the Egyptian Revival style in art and architecture Increasing numbers of tourists visited Egypt, eager to see the marvels being revealed by archaeological excavation. Writers and booksellers responded to this growing interest with publications ranging from technical site reports to tourist guidebooks and from children's histories to theories identifying the pyramids as repositories of esoteric knowledge. This series reissues a wide selection of such books. They reveal the gradual change from the 'tomb-robbing' approach of early excavators to the highly organised and systematic approach of Flinders Petrie, the 'father of Egyptology', and include early accounts of the decipherment of the hieroglyphic script.

Pyramids and Progress

This highly illustrated 1900 work on Egypt old and new by John Ward (1832–1912) seeks to guide the visitor to the ancient sites while also remarking on the radical changes to the economy and development of the modern state since the intervention of the British government in 1883 and the appointment of Lord Cromer as consul-general and effective ruler. This blending of ancient and modern can be seen in discussions of Port Said ('not an Egyptian town at all') alongside the abandoned and silted-up delta ports of the Egyptians, Ptolemies and Ottomans. Thebes is discussed both as a city of the living and a city of the dead, and Ward notes approvingly the flattening of the ancient town of Assouan (Aswan), to form the foundations for new public buildings, on the orders of Lord Kitchener. Ward's subsequent book, *Our Sudan* (1905), is also reissued in this series.

T0381672

Cambridge University Press has long been a pioneer in the reissuing of out-of-print titles from its own backlist, producing digital reprints of books that are still sought after by scholars and students but could not be reprinted economically using traditional technology. The Cambridge Library Collection extends this activity to a wider range of books which are still of importance to researchers and professionals, either for the source material they contain, or as landmarks in the history of their academic discipline.

Drawing from the world-renowned collections in the Cambridge University Library and other partner libraries, and guided by the advice of experts in each subject area, Cambridge University Press is using state-of-the-art scanning machines in its own Printing House to capture the content of each book selected for inclusion. The files are processed to give a consistently clear, crisp image, and the books finished to the high quality standard for which the Press is recognised around the world. The latest print-on-demand technology ensures that the books will remain available indefinitely, and that orders for single or multiple copies can quickly be supplied.

The Cambridge Library Collection brings back to life books of enduring scholarly value (including out-of-copyright works originally issued by other publishers) across a wide range of disciplines in the humanities and social sciences and in science and technology.

Pyramids and Progress

Sketches from Egypt

JOHN WARD

CAMBRIDGE
UNIVERSITY PRESS

University Printing House, Cambridge, CB2 8BS, United Kingdom

Cambridge University Press is part of the University of Cambridge.

It furthers the University's mission by disseminating knowledge in the pursuit of
education, learning and research at the highest international levels of excellence.

www.cambridge.org
Information on this title: www.cambridge.org/9781108081986

© in this compilation Cambridge University Press 2015

This edition first published 1900
This digitally printed version 2015

ISBN 978-1-108-08198-6 Paperback

This book reproduces the text of the original edition. The content and language reflect
the beliefs, practices and terminology of their time, and have not been updated.

Cambridge University Press wishes to make clear that the book, unless originally published
by Cambridge, is not being republished by, in association or collaboration with,
or with the endorsement or approval of, the original publisher or its successors in title.

PYRAMIDS AND PROGRESS.

ROYAL SCARABS.

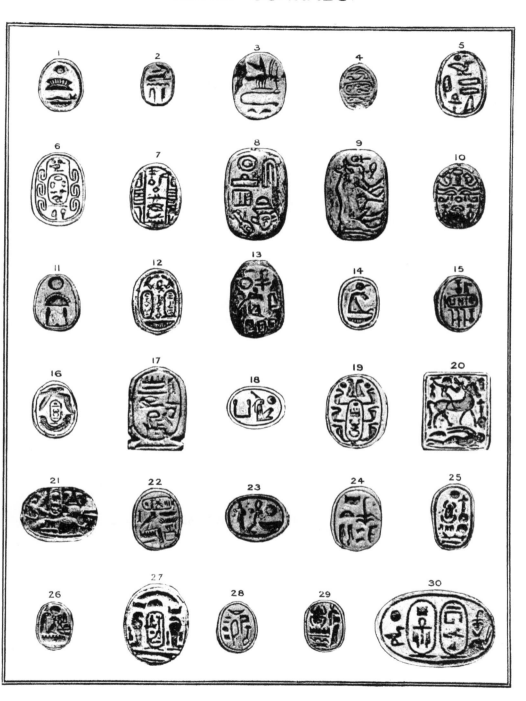

From the Author's Collection.

KEY TO THE PLATE OF ROYAL SCARABS

(FRONTISPIECE).

					B.C.
1.	KHAFRA	IV. Dynasty	.	.	3908–3845
2.	UNAS	V. ,,	.	.	3536–3503
3.	TETA (?)	VI. ,,	.	.	3503–3473
5.	SHESHA	(?)			
4.	RA-EN-KA VII.–VIII.	,,	.	.	3230–3220
7.	S-KHA-EN-RA IX.–X.	,,	.	.	3050–2821
8–9.	AMENEMHAT I. XII.	,,	.	.	2778–2748
10.	USERTESEN I. XII.	,,	.	.	2758–2714
11.	USERTESEN III. XII.	,,	.	.	2660–2622
12.	KHENZER XIII.	,,	.	.	
6.	KHYAN —	Hyksos ? .			2098
13.	APOPA —	Hyksos .			1587
14.	AAHMES I. XVIII.	,,	.	.	1587–1562
15.	THOTHMES I. XVIII.	,,	.	.	1541–1516
16.	THOTHMES II. XVIII.	,,	.	.	1516–1503
17.	HASHEPSU (Hatasu) —		.	.	1516–1481
18.	,, ,, —		.	.	,,
19.	THOTHMES III. XVIII.	,,	.	.	1503–1449
20.	,, XVIII.	,,	.	.	,,
21.	,, XVIII.	,,	.	.	,,
22.	AMENHOTEP II. XVIII.	,,	.	.	1449–1423
23.	AMENHOTEP III. XVIII.	,,	.	.	1414–1379
24.	TYI, Wife and Queen of Amenhotep III.			.	,,
25.	AKHENATEN (Khu-en-aten) XVIII. Dynasty				1400
26.	SETI I. XIX. Dynasty	.	.	.	1327–1275 ?
27.	RAMSES II. XIX. Dynasty (The Great)	.			1275–1208 ?
28.	NEFERT-ART-ERY, Wife of Ramses II.			.	,,
29.	SETI II. XIX. Dynasty	.	.	.	1189–1184 ?
30.	TIRHAKAH (Ta har ka) and PIANKHY, XXV. Dynasty	.	.	.	750 ?

The dates on this page are taken (as far as possible) from Petrie's *History of Egypt*, published by METHUEN & Co.

PYRAMIDS and PROGRESS:

SKETCHES FROM EGYPT

BY

JOHN WARD, F.S.A.

WITH AN INTRODUCTION
BY THE
REV. PROFESSOR SAYCE, D.D., LL.D., &c.

" Signs and wonders in the land of Egypt unto this day."
JEREMIAH xxii. 20.
" There is no country that possesses so many wonders."
HERODOTUS.
" Age cannot wither her, nor custom stale her infinite variety."
SHAKESPEARE.

LONDON
EYRE AND SPOTTISWOODE
Her Majesty's Printers
GREAT NEW STREET, FLEET STREET, E.C.
EDINBURGH, GLASGOW, MELBOURNE, SYDNEY, AND NEW YORK
MDCCCC.

DEDICATED TO

VISCOUNT CROMER, G.C.B., &c.

WITH DEEP RESPECT

AND ADMIRATION FOR HIS WORK

IN EGYPT.

Cairo

June 19. 1899

Dear Mr Ward.

I shall feel

greatly honoured

if you will dedi-

cate your forth-

coming work true...

Cromer

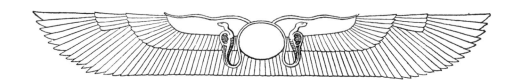

AUTHOR'S PREFACE.

❧ ❧ ❧

WHEN poor old Egypt was sick unto death, not so many years ago, a wise physician was called in to give advice in a case well nigh hopeless. This specialist was Lord Dufferin, who recommended certain remedies, in his masterly reports from Cairo, for the consideration of his Government at home. Many of these remedies were carried out *au pied de la lettre* : for some of them the patient's "constitution" was not found fit, at least it was well to wait. Lord Dufferin's advice, however (the part that was instantly acted upon), saved the country. Lord Cromer was placed at the head of affairs and backed up by being given every help he asked. Ever since he has been devoting his life to old Egypt's regeneration. The splendid selection of Indian officers, experts in all that the country needed, men like Sir W. Garstin, Major Hanbury Brown, Sir John Scott, Mr. Willcocks, Mr. W. J. Wilson, and many others—I only name those whom I have met (other great men of Lord Cromer's noble band had left Egypt before my time), working like heroes for small reward beyond their well-earned pay —have saved the ancient country. It is still "a land of wonders unto this day"; but the greatest marvel is a new one for Egypt— it is now worth visiting as a model of good government. Under British guidance its credit is restored; by great engineering works its income will be doubled. There are still magicians in the land, wonder-workers as of old.

Then the hidden treasures of antiquity have not been neglected; what Mariette and De Morgan left incomplete has been disinterred from the desert and the rock by Dr. Petrie, Messrs. Naville, Griffith, Grenfell and Hunt, and Quibell, and many more, whether working for the Egypt

(vii)

b 2

Exploration Fund or for other societies. Professor Sayce quietly makes his own researches, and is always ready to afford his scholarly help. He and his excellent library on the "Istar" are generally at hand when wanted.

To all of these great men, whether statesman, engineer, lawyer, or antiquarian, and to their friends and helpers at their work, I beg to tender my deep sense of gratitude for much kindness during my many visits to this old land, the cradle of all ancient civilisation and now once again the land of progress. The poor cowardly fellah, the dusky Nubian, the warlike Soudanese, have all been taught how to defend their native land from the brutal slave raider. A people who were enslaved for six thousand years are now as free as ourselves. Even the men engaged at this modern wonder-working, Lord Kitchener (and his shadow, Major Watson), Sir F. R. Wingate, Colonel Macdonald, and many others, have to be thanked for much politeness and assistance. By the help of these kind friends, I have travelled much up and down the banks of old Nile, finding none to make me afraid.

Egyptian literature is somewhat heavy. The volumes I have studied in order to learn a little about Egypt are too weighty to carry about, and so I thought a portable volume, describing something of my wanderings, and with a little historical knowledge introduced, illustrated by my own sketches and photographs, might be interesting to folks at home, or might tempt a visit to Egypt, and when there to go up the Nile farther than Cairo.

Dr. Petrie and the Egypt Exploration Fund have allowed me to make use of copies of some of the excellent illustrations of their various publications, for which I tender my grateful acknowledgments, while Sir Benjamin Baker, Mr. John Aird, M.P., Mr. Maurice Fitzmaurice, and Mr. G. H. Stephens have generously supplied information regarding the great engineering work of our times, which rivals the deeds of ancient Mena.

JOHN WARD.

CONTENTS.

(ix)

LIST OF ILLUSTRATIONS.

TOMBS OF THE CALIPHS.

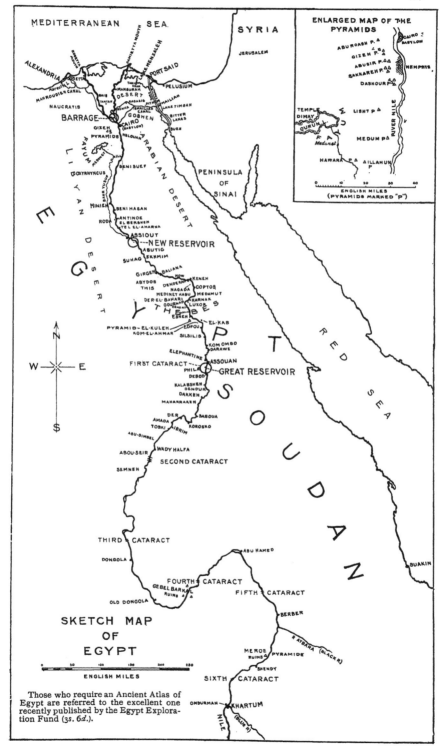

ENLARGED MAP OF THE PYRAMIDS

SKETCH MAP
OF
EGYPT

ENGLISH MILES

Those who require an Ancient Atlas of
Egypt are referred to the excellent one
recently published by the Egypt Exploration Fund (3s. 6d.).

KEY TO THE PLATE OF ROYAL SCARABS

(FRONTISPIECE).

							B.C.
1.	KHAFRA	IV. Dynasty	.	.	.		3908–3845
2.	UNAS	V. ,,	.	.	.		3536–3503
3.	TETA (?)	VI. ,,	.	.	.		3503–3473
5.	SHESHA	(?)					
4.	RA-EN-KA VII.–VIII.	,,	.	.	.		3230–3220
7.	S-KHA-EN-RA IX.–X.	,,	.	.	.		3050–2821
8–9.	AMENEMHAT I. XII.	,,	.	.	.		2778–2748
10.	USERTESEN I. XII.	,,	.	.	.		2758–2714
11.	USERTESEN III. XII.	,,	.	.	.		2660–2622
12.	KHENZER XIII.	,,	.	.	.		
6.	KHYAN —	Hyksos ?	.	}			2098
13.	APOPA —	Hyksos	.	}			1587
14.	AAHMES I. XVIII.	,,	.	.	.		1587–1562
15.	THOTHMES I. XVIII.	,,	.	.	.		1541–1516
16.	THOTHMES II. XVIII.	,,	.	.	.		1516–1503
17.	HASHEPSU (Hatasu) —		.	.	.		1516–1481
18.	,, ,, —		.	.	.		,,
19.	THOTHMES III. XVIII.	,,	.	.	.		1503–1449
20.	,, XVIII.	,,	.	.	.		,,
21.	,, XVIII.	,,	.	.	.		,,
22.	AMENHOTEP II. XVIII.	,,	.	.	.		1449–1423
23.	AMENHOTEP III. XVIII.	,,	.	.	.		1414–1379
24.	TYI, Wife and Queen of Amenhotep III.		.	.			,,
25.	AKHENATEN (Khu-en-aten) XVIII. Dynasty		.				1400
26.	SETI I. XIX. Dynasty	.	.	.	.	.	1327–1275 ?
27.	RAMSES II. XIX. Dynasty (The Great)	.	.				1275–1208 ?
28.	NEFERT-ART-ERY, Wife of Ramses II.		.	.			,,
29.	SETI II. XIX. Dynasty	.	.	.	.	.	1189–1184 ?
30.	TIRHAKAH (Taharka) and PIANKHY, XXV. Dynasty						750 ?

CYLINDER OF KING
NEFER-AR-KA-RA,

KING OF V. DYNASTY
(3680–3660 B.C.).

May have been his own royal signet. This remarkable Cylinder is probably unique. No scarabs are known of this king. His pyramid is supposed to be one of those at Abusir. (Petrie, *History of Egypt*, vol. i., p. 73.)

The dates on this page are taken (as far as possible) from Petrie's *History of Egypt*, published by METHUEN & Co.

SCRIBES OF ANCIENT EGYPT.

INTRODUCTION.

By PROFESSOR SAYCE, D.D., LL.D.

BOOKS upon Egypt are numerous, but for good ones there is still plenty of room. The country and its people are changing rapidly; even the climate, it is said, is sharing in the general movement, and writers are needed to record not only what is passing away but also what is taking its place. Nowhere else in the world can we find the past and the present ranged as it were so closely side by side or so incongruously mingled together. The newest agricultural steam engine from Europe is driven by a *fellah*, whose brother works the neighbouring field with the mattock of the Pharaohs, and the electric tram in Cairo hurries past street corners and scenes of life which transport us to the days of the "Arabian Nights." The Pyramids look down upon one of the most comfortable and luxurious of modern hotels, and the fragment of a vase that was made in the reign of Khufu lies in the desert sand by the side of an empty sardine tin. The soil and climate of Egypt are more conservative than its inhabitants; the latter are beginning to change, at all events outwardly, under the influences of the English Occupation, but the monuments of the past retain all their pristine freshness and colouring, in a land where there is neither frost nor rain, if only the friendly sand conceal them from the destructive hand of man.

A voyage up the Nile is still a revelation to the traveller who has eyes to see and ears to hear. If he is a historian and archæologist he

finds himself brought face to face with monuments which carry us back
to the earlier days of civilisation, and with a history, varied and romantic,
which can be traced continuously through unnumbered centuries; if it is
the present rather than the past which claims his interest, he can watch
one of the most single-minded attempts that have ever been made to
engraft what is best in Western civilisation upon the decrepit East, or
can appraise the doubtful blessings of international control. If he is
an engineer he can study the works of irrigation, to which Egypt owes
its very existence, and criticise the endeavours that are being made to
bridle the Nile; while, should he be interested in theological disputations
and ecclesiastical antiquities, he will have in the Coptic Church a Christian
community which has survived twelve centuries of persecution, and still
retains rites and beliefs that carry us back to the first ages of Christianity.

But the traveller who would learn all that a voyage up the Nile can
teach him must have the seeing eye and the hearing ear, and possess,
moreover, the understanding mind. It is for such that Mr. Ward's book
is written. Mr. Ward is no mere tourist, who, after a month among
the gaieties of Cairo and a voyage of three weeks on a Nile steamer,
believes himself qualified to instruct the world concerning Egypt and the
Egyptians, on the strength of a few conversations in broken English
with waiters and donkey-boys. He has, on the contrary, lived with the
natives and travelled in native boats; he has visited tombs and temples
far away from the tourist's track, and he has gone for his information
to the best authorities, European or native, archæological or political.
He has got together one of the best existing collections of historical
scarabs, and can speak at first-hand on their value and genuineness.

In one respect Egypt is like Japan, and that is in the rapidity and
far-reaching character of the changes through which it is passing. But
in Egypt this is true not only politically and socially, but also archæo-
logically. The soil of Egypt is a veritable treasure-house, but it is a
treasure-house that is being despoiled with feverish activity. Each year
brings with it a discovery more startling and revolutionary than those
that have gone before. The world of the past has risen up from its
grave of centuries and is even speaking to us in modern tones. The
latest discoveries have drawn aside part of the veil which hides the

beginnings of culture and civilisation, a veil which seemed folded over them for ever. The age of the Pyramids is no longer the beginning of history as it was but three or four years ago ; we now know that it really was the bloom and climax of long periods of growth; that long before the days of Khufu and Khafra books were written and read, that portrait statues were carved out of the hardest stone, that landscapes were painted in delicate colours, that great engineering works were executed, and that the political organisation of the country was complete. The first event in Egyptian history that has been handed down to us was the stupendous achievement of diverting the Nile from its old channel, under the Libyan hills, into the one through which it has flowed ever since, and Mr. Willcocks tells me that borings he caused to be made a few years ago between Cairo and Beni Suef proved that the statement was founded on fact. It was fitting, however, that the reign of the king who first united Northern and Southern Egypt, should have been signalised by such a work. Habitable Egypt was created by the engineers and their irrigating labours, and the dykes and canals, the basins and escapes, which transformed the Delta from a pestiferous swamp into fertile ground and rescued the banks of the Nile from the annual flood, went back to days of which we are but just beginning to have a glimpse.

The restoration of Egypt to its ancient prosperity and the gift to its people of justice, such as they have never before enjoyed, have been intimately bound up with the works of irrigation that have so preeminently marked the epoch of British rule. The water, which centuries of oppression and neglect had allowed to run to waste, has again been utilised and is equitably distributed between rich and poor, the powerful and the weak. If the English Occupation had done nothing more, this alone would have justified its continuance.

Those who knew Egypt in the days of Ismail Pasha, or the Dual Control, find it difficult to realise that it is the same land as that to which the tourist is transported to-day. The change has been gradual, though with each successive year the rate of progress has been increasingly rapid. It is only when we contrast the Egypt of to-day with the Egypt that we remember twenty years ago that we understand how great the change has been. We may, perhaps, regret the loss of the oriental flavour it has brought with it, but along with the oriental flavour has gone the tyranny, the squalor and the misery of the past.   There is equal justice between man and man, a prosperous peasantry, and a high standard of education.   The dark corners of the land have been cleansed, and comforts have been placed within the reach of the poor which wealth formerly could not purchase.   Much, doubtless, still remains to be done; but the work that has been achieved, in despite of international complications and obstacles, is a guarantee of the future.   And in one section of the Egyptian population at all events—the Christian Copts, whose blood is uncontaminated by inter-marriage with Arabs or negroes—the reformer has a race which inherits all the ability and quickness of its Egyptian forefathers, and can be trained to carry out English ideas of justice and morality,

A. H. SAYCE.

PROFESSOR SAYCE'S DAHABEAH "ISTAR"
MOORED OFF ELEPHANTINE.

PYRAMIDS AND PROGRESS.

CHAPTER I.

THE DOORWAYS OF EGYPT.

FROM THE PORTRAIT BUST OF ALEXANDER THE GREAT.
(Found at Alexandria ; now in the British Museum.)

PORT SAÏD—THE SUEZ CANAL—TANIS—ISMAILIA—PITHOM—
TEL-EL-KEBIR—ZAGAZIG—
ALEXANDRIA—NAUCRATIS—SAIS—CAIRO.

PYRAMIDS AND PROGRESS;

SKETCHES FROM EGYPT.

CHAPTER I.

THE DOORWAYS OF EGYPT.

CLEOPATRA'S NEEDLE,
LONDON.

ROSETTA and Damietta, in modern days good Mediterranean harbours, have silted up, as in ancient times still older ports on other mouths of the Nile had done. Several of the old branches of the river have disappeared by the same process. There were in olden times seven arms of the Nile. Now only two remain, and they do not occupy their ancient channels. As the river bed rises three or four inches in a century, owing to its annual deposit of mud, and the canals and embankments were neglected for more than a thousand years, the face of the country and the outlets of the Nile flood have undergone continual changes. Egypt must now be entered from the north by Port Saïd or Alexandria. There is not very much in either place to interest the tourist or to tempt him to make any prolonged stay. Port Saïd is not in fact an Egyptian town at all; it is a port on the Suez Canal, a mere station on the highway to India, China, or Australia. In ancient days, a great city existed on the coast, some twenty miles to the east of the northern outlet of the Suez Canal. In the days of the prophet Ezekiel it was known as Sin, and being called by him "the strength of Egypt," it was possibly an important frontier fortress. In classic times it was known as Pelusium. An arm of the ancient Nile supplied it with sweet water to give it life. But the Pelusiac branch of the river was lost by the neglect of Mohammedan rulers; it was allowed to silt up, and the city became uninhabitable. Its site is now a pestilential swamp, but immense mounds covering the ancient ruins testify to its former extent and

(3)

PORT SAÏD : THE HARBOUR,
Looking south over the Suez Canal and eastern desert.

importance.　The Suez Canal effectually cuts off the old connection with the Nile, the water of life, and Pelusium can never rise again.　It was the frontier fortress of Egypt, and here the great Roman general Pompey met his death ingloriously.　The site of Pelusium is utterly deserted ; neither human beings nor cattle can exist in the neighbourhood owing to the want of fresh water.

The numerous vessels going to the Orient offer temptations to the Egyptian tourist to enter the country by the Suez Canal, and as no direct line of steamers yet connects London with Alexandria, ninety out of a hundred visitors to the Nile every year enter Egypt by Port Saïd, where passenger ships, bound for distant lands, arrive almost every day.　So some description of that remarkable port should be given.　It was, a few years ago, the most rowdy and undesirable seaport in the world, as Rudyard Kipling has graphically told us.　But it has mended its ways, and to the passing stranger has outwardly a most respectable appearance.　There is now a good hotel—The Eastern Exchange—clean, moderate, and excellent.　The rooms are not encumbered with furniture, but this is rather an advantage than otherwise.　The building is very lofty, but there is a "lift" to every floor, and the view from the top storey is wonderful indeed.　From that point the Suez Canal can be seen for miles, and the melancholy desert, which it intersects, seems spread out like a great map.　The piers and lighthouses which guard the entrances to the canal lie far below—the whole thing looks unnatural, impossible, Utopian.　Far away, on the

western horizon of Lake Menzaleh, can
be seen the mounds which mark the
sites of long-lost cities, now drowned
out by the neglect of ancient canals or
the banks that may have confined the
river to its channel. Most of the wide
expanse of Lake Menzaleh, now covered
frequently with picturesque fleets of
fishing-boats, and teeming with aquatic
fowl of many species, was a wide stretch
of cultivated land, intersected by numerous canals, and full of towns and
villages. (Some day, when reservoirs
and barrages have doubled the wealth
of the banks of the upper Nile valley,
British engineers may teach the Egyptians how to reclaim Lake Menzaleh,
as is being done with Aboukir Bay on
the other side of Alexandria.) M.
Mariette was fortunate in discovering

ANCIENT SUEZ CANAL USED BY SETI I.,
As depicted on the walls of Karnak (Thebes).

in some of those far-off mounds the ancient site of Zoan * of the Bible,
the Tanis of the Greeks.† They were afterwards again excavated by Professor
Petrie for the Egypt Exploration Fund. Later discoveries of Tahpanhes
or Tehaphnehes,‡ the Greek Daphnæ, in the Delta, not far from the lake,
were also published. I am permitted to give some reproductions from this
excellent society's volumes which may be interesting; but ordinary travellers
are not likely to visit the locality, which is rather a pestilential one. The
enormous ruins show what a vast city stood here, and the terrible destruction
that has fallen upon it is difficult to understand. The prophet Jeremiah was
a prisoner here, and Petrie's discoveries included the finding of " a great

---

* Zoan, on the Tanitic mouth of the Nile, was about 30 miles distant from Sin or Pelusium,
at the W. end of a rich plain of pasturable marshes, watered by four branches of the Nile,
which, perhaps, was called the "Field of Zoan" (Ps. 78. 12, 13).

† Messrs. Eyre & Spottiswoode have recently issued an admirable illustrated volume by
the Rev. C. J. Ball, *Light from the East*, which adds much information to the Biblical mention
of this wonderful old city.

‡ Tahpanhes in Jeremiah (43. 7–9), Tehaphnehes in Ezekiel (30. 18); the Pelusian Daphnæ
of Herodotus (ii. 30, 154; *see* 107), who describes it as the Eastern frontier fortress of Psammitichus, the founder of the xxvith dynasty of Pharaohs, who garrisoned it with Greek mercenaries encamped on each side of the Pelusiac mouth of the Nile

open-air platform of brickwork," which may be the very pavement at the entry of Pharaoh's house in Tahpanhes to which Jeremiah pointed, foretelling that Nebuchadrezzar as conqueror should set his throne and spread his royal pavilion over it. The greatest statue of Ramses II., a hundred feet high, was at this city; nothing now remains but fragments—it is pulverized. When entire, this must have been a wonderful object, seen all over the level Delta, asserting the visible power of this great king, the Sesostris of the Greeks.

The ground floor of The Eastern Exchange contains a bazaar, where every possible want of the traveller—clothing, food of all sorts, liquors, sweets, litera-ture, crockery, everything—can be had as cheap and as good as in London. In fact, Port Saïd is not half a bad place to pass a day in—waiting for your ship —but two days would be too long. The canal is a mere ditch cut out by dredges through the level sandy desert, or through the marshes of the great salt-water lagoon of Lake Men-zaleh. Yet, though monotonous, the passage through the fifty miles of artificial channel from Port Saïd to Lake Timseh should be made once, for there is nothing like it in the world.

PITHOM: ONE OF THE STORE CITIES
Built for Ramses II. by the Israelites; discovered by Dr. Naville.

Lake Timseh is a pretty sheet of blue water: here a steam launch conveys passengers from the steamers to Ismailia, about a mile from the line of the canal. Lake Timseh was formerly fresh water, and its name implies that it was the abode of crocodiles. These creatures have now deserted Egypt, and are only occasionally seen in Nubian waters; they do not understand steamboats, which disturb their gentle nature. Ismailia was designed, by the first Khedive who gave it his name. to be a great city, and the unbuilt streets cover a large space. But its time has not yet come, and at present it is a most desolate place, which one leaves as soon as possible. For those who are compelled to remain a few hours, there are the beautiful gardens of the Khedive's palace, where orange and lemon trees, palms, bananas, and all sorts of fruit flourish exceedingly. Lovely roses and every flower will grow here luxuriantly; for Ismailia is supplied by the "Sweet Water Canal," which brings health and life from the great Nile to make the desert blossom as the rose. This channel was made to supply the

workers on the Suez Canal, and Port Saïd, Ismailia, and Suez, with fresh water. While it was being made the engineers came upon the ancient course of the Canal of the Pharaohs which connected the Nile and the Red Sea. This great work was in full operation four thousand years ago, but had been forgotten for ages; many doubted if it had ever existed, though it was mentioned by ancient authors. But a plan of the canal, engraved by King Seti I. on the temple wall at Karnak, is still to be seen there. Seti only claims to have used it; it existed long before his time. It is represented as full of crocodiles, to show that it was a fresh water channel, and there were locks, bridges, and barracks along its banks. The surrounding country

COLOSSAL HAWK, PITHOM.
(*Now in the Park, Ismailia.*)

—now desert and deserted—was the once fertile Land of Goshen, where the Hebrews lived for centuries, and reared their flocks and herds, developing from a poor wandering tribe into a rich people, the founders of an important nation. This canal also, like everything else under Moslem rule, was neglected, and the whole of the once fertile Land of Goshen went back to desert. The treasure cities of Pithom and Raamses, which the Bible tells us were built for Pharaoh by the Hebrews, were in this neighbourhood. Pithom was discovered in 1883 by Dr. Naville for the Egypt Exploration Fund.* The exact site of "Raamses" has not yet been found. The mounds of grey rubbish beyond the railway station of Zagazig mark the site of the ancient city of Bubastis.† The mounds were well explored by Dr. Naville some years since, and his researches fill one of the volumes published by the Egypt Exploration Fund. Some interesting carved

TRIAD.
(*Now in the Park, Ismailia.*)

---

* The results of this wonderful discovery, and the proof of the line of flight of the Israelites towards the Red Sea, were published in the first volume of the Egypt Exploration Fund in 1885. I give reproductions of some of Dr. Naville's very interesting plates.

† The Pi-Beseth of Ezek. 30. 17, now *Tel Basta;* the Egyptian Pi-Bast, *i.e. house of* the goddess *Bast*, on the Tanitic Nile, about halfway between Pelusium and Memphis, was the key to the route to Syria. On the national religious festivals held here see Herod. ii. 59, 60.

stones from Pithom and Tanis are preserved in a little park at Ismailia.   The

sweet-water channel is now being extended by the British engineers into a wide canal, large enough to supply Nile water to the whole district, and in a few years the Land of Goshen may recover its ancient fertility.*   As fast as our engineers supply water, there are fellaheen ready to undertake its reclamation.   It takes several seasons to wash the salt out of the soil, during which time no taxes are charged, and rent only begins after a crop has been raised.   The railway from Ismailia to Cairo runs through this territory.   The first station is Tel-el-Kebir, where our soldiers crushed Arabi's rebellion in 1882.   The little graveyard, beautifully tended and walled round, contains the bones of many of our soldiers who fell on that day.   After Zagazig we pass Benha, now celebrated for its oranges and grapes.   Near this we see, close to the railway, the mounds which mark the site of the ancient city of

HEAD OF AMENEMHAT I.
He erected great buildings at
Tanis and Bubastis.

Anthribis.   Soon the Pyramids of Gizeh come into sight on the horizon, and we run into the station of Cairo.   _____

But, if selection can be made, Alexandria is the proper doorway of Egypt. But there is little to be seen of the works of the Pharaohs, for the city can boast no great antiquity ; as its name implies, it was the creation of Alexander the Great.   Before his time the Egyptians had no great ports on the Mediterranean, and no desire for any.   Their policy was to exclude foreigners from their country.   As long as this seclusive policy was carried out strictly and literally they had been safe from invasion, and their wonderful civilisation went on developing for many thousand years, unseen and unknown by the outer world. The Persian conquest gave them a rude awakening, and undoubtedly retarded the progress of their ancient civilisation.   Thenceforth they had to keep up standing armies on their frontiers, and to enlist from Europe and Asia Minor mercenaries skilled in the peculiarities of foreign warfare.   Thus the Greeks got a footing in Egypt, at least in the northern part, for they were excluded from Thebes and Upper Egypt for a lengthened period.   Herodotus was enabled by this partial intercourse with Greece to travel in Egypt, but he never got any

---

* Major Brown, R.E., has just published (Stanford) a very interesting little volume on the "Land of Goshen."   He, as the Chief Director of Irrigation, is much interested in the recovery of the fertility of this district.   An antiquarian as well as an engineer, he is the highest authority on the subject.

farther than the Delta, Memphis, Pyramids, and Fayum. His account of what he saw took the European world by surprise; they had never before heard of the wonders of Egypt, which had been a closed land to them. The Hebrews

CLEOPATRA'S NEEDLE.
(Now in Central Park, New York.)

had had dealings with the Egyptians about 1,000 years before, when a Semitic race known as the Hyksos or Shepherd Kings* had held the land in bondage for some 600 years. These Hyksos were expelled, and this was how a new Pharaoh came into power, who had no sympathies with the Hebrews, and "knew not Joseph." Besides, in those days the Hebrew records, telling of the wonderful adventures of the Patriarchs in Egypt were probably not accessible to the Greeks and quite unknown to them. Alexander vanquished the Persian conquerors of Egypt, seized the country, and at once determined to make a great port in Egypt to intercept all the trade of Asia and Africa. He is said to have himself laid out the ground plan of the city. His power was short-lived, but Alexandria was a great city when Alexander died and his general, the first Ptolemy, became sovereign of the country. Alexandria was the finest port in the world, and during several centuries the city grew in splendour. It tapped all the riches coming from the far East, until the whole commerce of the world seemed to pass through it. The early Ptolemies possessed enormous wealth, as their plentiful gold coinage testifies. The number of temples rebuilt by these Greek rulers, which are computed to have cost many millions sterling, show their politic protection of its ancient faith. Half of the temples now existing in Egypt were built by

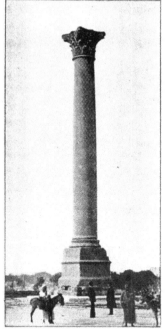

POMPEY'S PILLAR, ALEXANDRIA.
Made from an Egyptian obelisk.

* So named from a fragment of Manetho; *cf.* Herod. ii. 128. See the Article and series of Illustrations of these invaders in Ball's *Light from the East*, pp. 78–81 (Eyre & Spottiswoode, 1899).

the Ptolemies.   They were restorations mainly of older structures, copied in
a coarser style of work.   Many temples that were re-built by the Greek rulers
have been destroyed in this century under Moslem rule.   Under the Romans,
Alexandria was an enormous city, full of splendid buildings.

With the decline of the Roman power trade seems to have left the
place; its great schools of philosophy, art, and letters languished, and in
the midst of this decadence the great library was neglected and dispersed,
some say maliciously burnt.   Alexandria, when the Roman empire was divided,
came under the rule of Byzantium and its inglorious succession of weak
emperors, Christian only in name, and its fortunes waned under their influence.

THE PORT OF ALEXANDRIA: THE MODERN HARBOUR.

Then came the blighting rule of the Moslem.   The canals were allowed
to silt up, Alexandria no longer got water from the Nile, became a heap
of ruins, and was fast becoming another Pelusium.   But Mehemet Ali's
genius saw that this was the proper site for the port of his regenerated Egypt.
Accordingly in one year the tyrant made the Mahmoudieh Canal, thirty miles
long, but at an enormous outlay of human life, 25,000 souls having perished at
the work.   But the canal saved the city, and Alexandria, restored to life by
the Nile, again became the great seaport of the East and West.   Modern
engineering skill restored the harbour to usefulness, and once again it became

the important seaport for which it was founded more than 2,000 years before. In Egypt old things become new with wonderful rapidity. The splendid harbour we see to-day was that which the Romans called the "old port." Their new port has silted up, and is now only used for fishing-boats. A modern lighthouse replaces the ancient Pharos of Alexander's days, which has disappeared utterly. In fact, it seems as if all the old city has vanished—a por-

COIN OF ALEXANDER.

tion beneath the waves, by encroachments of the Mediterranean, and perhaps by earthquakes having altered the coast line. No ancient city has been so utterly lost; nothing remains above ground but "Pompey's Pillar," as it is called. Possibly modern Alexandria is built over the Greek and Roman ruins. When new houses are being constructed ancient foundations constantly come to light. There is a good Græco-Roman museum in the town, under the skilful charge of Dr. Botti, full of fragments of classic times—statues, capitals, and inscriptions. Of the ancient Museum, however, the greatest the world ever saw, not a trace remains. Such a disappearance of a whole city is very wonderful and inexplicable indeed.

Pompey's Pillar is a noble shaft of Assouan granite. Dr. Mahaffy has proved that it was made undoubtedly from an Egyptian obelisk. There were till recently two obelisks in Alexandria in their original condition. One of these is now on the Thames Embankment, the other is in New York. Both were possibly brought from Heliopolis to adorn Alexander's magnificent city. Pompey's Pillar stood in the centre of the Serapeum. Dr. Botti has excavated round its base and found great remains of foundations, but nothing to indicate the former magnificence of the temple described in glowing terms by classic writers. He, however, discovered great subterranean corridors in which the Mysteries of Serapis were celebrated, proving that the buildings he found

PTOLEMY II. AND BERENICE. | PTOLEMY I. AND ARSINOE.
Gold coin struck to announce the deification of Ptolemy I. and his wife.

were actually part of the celebrated Serapeum. Anything found of any value has been taken to the local museum, which is admirably arranged and well worth visiting. Pompey's Pillar rests on a foundation composed of remains of a temple of Seti's time, the granite blocks of which bear his cartouche. This beautiful

MAHMOUDIEH CANAL,

Connecting Alexandria with the Nile (50 miles).   It was entirely made in one year by
forced labour, 1820.

structure had been destroyed to make a foundation for a Roman monument,
itself made out of an Egyptian obelisk a thousand years older than Seti !
Although containing little to interest the antiquary, Alexandria is a magnificent seaport, and the approach to it or the retrospect from the vessel on
leaving Egypt, is one of the finest in the world.   The Mediterranean everywhere is remarkable for its wonderful colour, but the hues of the water off
Alexandria are bewilderingly beautiful.   Such blues and greens, violets and
purples, especially in morning and evening effects of sunlight, are seen nowhere
else.   The busy harbour is full of shipping of all nations, but the greater part is
British.   Hundreds of well-found fishing-boats give life to the waters, and the
picturesque caiques which convey the pilots several miles out to sea add to
the beauty of the scene.   After twelve centuries it has become even more than
the Great Alexander meant it to be, an *entrepôt* for trade between East, West,
and South, and one of the most interesting seaports of the world.   Under British
rule it cannot fail to become one of the most prosperous African cities.   It will
be the port of Egypt, and the principal depôt of the great trade which will
undoubtedly result from the pacification of the Soudan.   Alexander meant it for
the trade of India, but Africa, for the first time in the history of the world
having freedom from the curse of slavery, and opened up by steamboats and

by railways, will require all its capabilities for the great resources of the vast continent, and the imports as well as the exports of this new trade must find their development through Alexandria. The canal dues at Port Saïd are excessive. Alexandria is virtually a free port. It has been well termed "the most characteristic monument of the life and work" of Alexander the Great. In pursuance of his main object, viz., "to wed the East and West in a just union," he designed the city to be the metropolis of his Western Empire.

About 50 miles from Alexandria, on the way to Cairo, the great mounds which mark the ruins of Naucratis can be seen, five miles west of the station of Tel el-Barûd. This city was founded by the Greeks in the age of the Twenty-sixth Dynasty, but sank into insignificance after the rise of Alexandria. Dr. Petrie's eagle eye soon detected the importance of these mounds, and may be said to have re-discovered the site which had been unidentified and forgotten for 1,500 years. He excavated here for the Egypt Exploration Fund, in 1884–1885.* The volume containing his discoveries can still be had, and shows what important factors for Egyptian cults the Greeks had become. This year (1899) the excavations have been resumed, and Mr. Hogarth announces his

CAIRO: DISTANT VIEW OF THE CITADEL.

---

* Naucratis, now *Nebireh*, on a canal still partially in use "outside" (*i.e.* to the W. of) the westernmost mouth of the Nile, the Canopic. The result of these excavations indicates that a Greek colony, probably from Miletus, was established here, perhaps about the middle of the seventh century, B.C., while Egypt was broken up through the Assyrian invasions; but that Amasis, the Phil-Hellene, officially founded and reorganized the colony as related by Herodotus (ii. 178, 179); granting a monopoly of trade to Greek settlers there.

discovery of the Hellenion. It is to be hoped that he will publish an account of his recent discoveries, which are of a most interesting character. About 60 miles from Alexandria lie the mounds which mark the site of Sais, the seat of government of Psamtek (called by the Greeks Psammitichus) and other royalties of the short but brilliant Twenty-sixth Dynasty, when a wonderful effort was made to restore the ancient faith and works of a bygone greatness. This was about 600 B.C.; but although the beautiful artistic works they have left show that the people still possessed the genius of their ancestors of 3,000 years before, their efforts were of short endurance. Considering the elaborate description of the extent of Sais given by Herodotus, one would have expected great remains of it would be discovered, but Mariette's researches gave but a poor result. The very site of the ancient buildings could not be discovered, and none of the great monuments described by the historian. There is no railway or station near Sa-el-Hagar (the village near the ruins); it can be reached only by boat or donkey from Tanta, but there is not much to reward the visit. Tanta is an important station, and a busy place of modern trade. A native town on a market day is a very interesting scene of busy, successful commerce, showing how British guidance has benefited the agricultural classes.

We now run through a well-cultivated country; in an hour's time the everlasting Pyramids come into sight; and, winding round Cairo, we find ourselves among the mounds of old Babylon, and enter the station of Cairo, the hotel touts saluting us in many languages.

THE BRITISH GUARDSHIP AT ALEXANDRIA.

CHAPTER II.

CAIRO, THE CARAVANSERAI OF THE WORLD.

ENTRANCE TO
THE MOUSKI.

CAIRO—STREET SCENES—THE MOUSKI—
THE MOSQUES—THE UNIVERSITY—THE CITADEL—MENA HOUSE—
THE DRIVE TO THE PYRAMIDS.

THE TOMBS OF THE CALIPHS.

CHAPTER II.

CAIRO : STREET SCENES—MOSQUES—THE CITADEL.

CAIRO is the caravanserai of the world; all nations seem to meet in this wonderful cosmopolitan centre. Formerly there was only one good hotel—Shepheard's—but now there are several excellent establishments. Still, there is nothing like the terrace of Shepheard's; it is always the most interesting rendezvous for the well-to-do folk of London, Paris, Berlin, Vienna, St. Petersburg, New York, and everywhere else. Then when we leave this fashionable and rather expensive hostelry, and plunge into the town, with its dirty, ill-paved streets, and visit the bazaars, we find ourselves among a crowd of Turks, Bedouins, Greeks, Nubians, Negroes, Jews, Persians, and Hindoos. The colours and costumes vary so much that it is like a scene from the "Arabian Nights"—we could fancy ourselves living in the time of Haroun-al-Rashid. Stately camels plunge along the dirty streets, bearing heavy burdens; one with a cartload of fresh clover from the country, another mounted far aloft by a richly-dressed Arab gentleman, a third bears the belongings of a household piled up, with the pots and kettles suspended

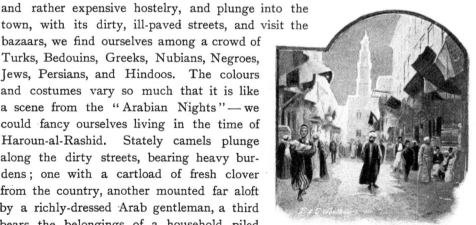

STREET SCENE IN CAIRO.

(17)

from every point of the furniture, and the cargo filling up the narrow roadway. Then a company of British Grenadiers or a Highland regiment, with now and then a troop of Lancers. Blue-uniformed Soudanese soldiers march gallantly along. In the distance we hear a crack Egyptian band playing in the Esbekieh Gardens. Flocks of shaggy goats crowd up the thoroughfare, stopping to be milked when wanted and utterly impeding the traffic. Veiled women pass on carts, rolled up in blue bundles of drapery, generally the numerous wives of a native household, with an assortment of babies of all sizes. Then strings of donkeys, and here and there a rich native merchant on a handsome Arab pony. All the motley throng is swept aside, when several gaily-dressed saices, with bare feet and legs, running before the carriage of a native gentleman, shout and clear the way, with free use of their wands if necessary. It is impossible to describe the bazaars; they must be seen. But the quaint street, The Mouski, that leads to them, more than a mile long, is one of the most interesting thoroughfares in this motley crowded city. To tell the wonders of modern Cairo would need a volume to itself, but this I will leave to someone better fitted for the task. I will content myself with giving some peeps at ancient Cairo before visiting the Pyramids. Modern Cairo (the city of Mehemet Ali and of Ismail), with its ex-

cellent hotels, wide, well-paved streets, electric tramways, smart victorias, gas and electric light, and a-bundant supply of water, is a nine-teenth century revival of the grandeur of Old Cairo, the city of the Ca-liphs and Ma-melouks, with its splendid mosques and the citadel

THE PROCESSION OF THE EMBROIDERED TENT CONTAINING
THE HOLY CARPET.

Every year an embroidered carpet is sent to Mecca, the procession through Cairo being several miles long. Everyone pretends to be going with it, but only a few hundreds actually make the journey.

founded by Saladin. The tombs of the Caliphs and those of the Mamelouks, in the outskirts of the city, are the finest specimens of Arab art. In their perfect state they must have been magnificent gems of Saracenic architecture. The mounds once surrounding Cairo contain the broken pottery and porcelain of generations of families, and cover a thousand acres of ground. The walls of the Roman stronghold of Babylon are close to Old Cairo, and there are the remains of a Roman theatre. It is difficult to say whence they were brought, but many of the mosques contain hundreds of pillars of classic origin, with almost every capital of different design, stolen from ancient temples. Ancient Egypt no doubt could have shown several villages on or near the site of modern Cairo; but of these all traces, above ground, have disappeared. Memphis, the capital of the " Ancient Empire," was not far off, but the Nile has swallowed it up, and little remains to be seen save two gigantic statues of Ramses the Great, lying on their backs among palm groves on the opposite side of the Nile and bathed by the waters at the time of the annual inundation. Hero-

COURT OF UNIVERSITY, CAIRO.

dotus records the tradition that Mena, whom he calls Menes, the first historical king and the first to unite Egypt under one sceptre, turned aside the ancient course of the stream, and built this great city, surrounding it with the river. Possibly some enemy hastened its ruin by cutting the dykes, or it may be, as modern observers reckon, that the bed of the Nile is ten to twenty feet higher than in Mena's time—6,700 years ago, and that the land has of course risen by the annual deposit of mud. In any case, Memphis has disappeared, but we must believe in its former extent, for part of its great enclosure remains.

SCHOOL SCENE
IN A CORNER OF THE
UNIVERSITY.

Boys only are allowed to have any teaching; the little girl is only a
spectator of her brother's studies.

The ancient cemeteries, marked out by the Pyramid groups, extend for forty-five miles along the margin of the Libyan desert. The common idea is that the only pyramids are those of Gizeh, about seven miles from modern Cairo, but these three, the greatest of all and those best known to the ancients, are but the burial places of one dynasty. Before visiting them it is well to drive, by the native town, through the picturesque streets of Cairo. We pass many splendid mosques, with their elegant, fairy-like spires, all different and all most picturesque. One has two lovely minarets, forming the towers of a handsome gate, part of the ancient fortifications. Near this we find the great university, El Azhar, which should be visited. The instruction is old-fashioned enough as to astronomical knowledge, for the 2,000 students are taught that the sun revolves round the earth! The teaching may be bad, but the designers of these beautiful mosques were great architects, and it is pleasant to see that many of them which were falling to ruin are undergoing thorough repair. This is due to Lord Cromer, who greatly admires Arab art, and recently, since he has had some little rest from his arduous government duties, has taken the matter in hand with his characteristic energy. He has succeeded in recovering many of the ancient native bequests which had been misapplied, and he has got the leading Mahometans to join heartily in the work. Twenty thousand pounds were spent in this way, and funds have been found from other sources, so that the good work of restoration goes on apace, and is very popular with the intelligent native population. There are several hundred mosques and funerary Moslem buildings in and about Cairo, and many of them were built of stone stolen from the Pyramids! It is a wonder how so much of the Pyramids has been spared. After a drive round the vast city, and a visit to some of the finest mosques,

FOUNTAIN AND SCHOOL, CAIRO.

These are pious endowments, and to most of them a free school (carried on above the fountain) is attached.

(From a Water-Colour Drawing by John Varley.)

it is well to mount up to the citadel. On a high platform of rock, it is conspicuous from afar by the great dome and two slender minarets, 200 ft. high, of Mehemet Ali's mortuary mosque. This is a modern erection, and, though it has a certain impressiveness and is entirely built of Egyptian alabaster, is vastly

SCENE IN THE COURT OF THE UNIVERSITY.

inferior to the ancient architecture of the Caliphs. Its designer was a Frenchman, it occupied thirty years in building, and is internally a reduced copy of Santa Sophia at Constantinople. The most impressive of all the ancient mosques is at the foot of the ascent to the citadel. This is the mosque of Sultan Hasan, and is one of the finest buildings of the kind in the world. It was built in A.D. 1360, and was entirely constructed of stones robbed from the Great Pyramid. It is indeed a masterpiece of design, compared with which the modern building adjacent looks poor and tawdry. The great mosque in the citadel is built within the fortress of Saladin, the Moslem prince whom Richard Cœur de Lion regarded as a hero. It has a remarkable well of great depth, which the Arabs say was sunk by the Patriarch Joseph. From the great terrace on a clear day a magnificent view of the whole pyramid-plateau is obtained. Before studying the wonderful panorama let us look round the fortress. It bristles with fine modern cannon—all pointed upon Cairo, showing whence danger is expected. This terrace is well worth visiting on the last day of Ramadan, when the dark-skinned Nubian gunners fire twenty-one guns at noon and the echoes

SIDE DOOR OF THE UNIVERSITY.

give an effective return of the cannon's roar thrice repeated as they reverberate from the Mokattam Cliffs. The regularity of the firing is excellent, and it is really a magnificent spectacle. This stronghold dominates Cairo, and the great city which is spread out at our feet for miles in every direction could be utterly destroyed by its artillery. The city was in imminent danger during Arabi's rebellion in 1882. The citadel was held by rebellious Egyptian troops—there was not a British soldier in Cairo. Tel-el-Kebir was fought and Arabi's army conquered one fine morning, and a small body of our cavalry galloped all the way from the battlefield, arriving at the fortress before the news could reach Cairo. The sentinels at the gate were despatched, the defenders arrested, and the first tidings of victory made known to the citizens by the Union Jack being hoisted on the citadel. The whole army was supposed to be close behind; there were really but a hundred men.

The army, under Lord Wolseley, marched in next day, the cannon of the fortress being turned on the city, now held by the gallant century of heroes.

On a clear day we look away across the wide valley to the vast desert fringed with its groups of pyramids. This is the necropolis of the magnates of ancient Egypt.

Now let us get a good glass and study the distant pyramid-fields. Near

MOSQUE OF SULTAN AMR.
This Mosque is entirely built with columns from destroyed Greek and Roman temples; nearly every capital is different.

at hand, apparently, are the three great pyramids of Gizeh. Beyond them those of Abu Roash; seven pyramids, much ruined, and evidently of enormous antiquity —they have never been properly examined. Then the pyramids of Abusir, of which we are told there were fourteen, but only a few now remain. Next, the pyramids of Sakkarah, the greatest of which is built in steps, and may be the oldest of all. Four here, and then further on again towards the south there are the pyramids of Dahshur; four more, two of them interesting, having been explored; two still await scientific investigation to determine their owners. Nearly all can be seen on a clear day. But the travellers are few who will leave this splendid point of view without wishing to study the pyramids close at hand.

Almost all these wonderful monuments — seventy-six have been enumerated—were built of the stone from the hills on the eastern side of the Nile. The quarries of Masarah are well worth visiting. The great works of the giants seem to have been carried on here. Many inscriptions still exist in the quarries, recording the Pharaohs who worked them for 5,000 years, both here and in the Tourah cliffs, further north, where the fine white limestone used for casing the pyramids was obtained. The great blocks seem to have been floated across the river on rafts at high Nile, and the causeways made to convey them from the western bank to the pyramids existed till lately. Until the opening of the Suez Canal there was no road from Cairo to the pyramid platform of Gizeh. Visitors from Cairo generally crossed the river in boats from Old

DOORWAY OF THE MOSQUE OF SULTAN
HASAN (1360 A.D.).
Near the ascent to the Citadel.

Cairo near Rodah, getting donkeys on the other side for paths along the embankments. The Khedive had invited the Empress Eugénie to inaugurate the Suez Canal. To do her honour he hurried on the great Kasr-el-Nil Bridge, and not only made a straight road all the way to the Pyramids, but planted it with shady sycamores. It was all done in a few months by forced labour. In this work at any rate, Ismail emulated the deeds of the ancient

MOSQUE TOMB OF
KAIT BEY.
The most perfect in style of all
the Mosques.

CAIRO: EVENING SCENE, RODAH, OLD CAIRO, NEAR THE NILOMETER.

(From a Water-Colour Drawing by John Varley.)

(25)

Pharaohs.   Whether all their great buildings were done by forced labour we know not.   Dr. Petrie thinks the workman- ship of the early

GENERAL VIEW OF CAIRO, FROM THE TOWER OF THE MOSQUE OF TULUN.

pyramid times is too good to have been done by slaves.   But the great public
works of the modern tyrant were done by labourers torn from their fields, and
under terror of the task-master's whip.   Now, under an enlightened British rule,
all the forced labour is banished for ever.   We have, however, thanks to Ismail,
a level, well-shaded roadway all the way from Cairo to the Pyramids.   The
Kasr-el-Nil Bridge is a handsome structure, and the busy scene that it offers is
really one of the sights of Cairo.

At the end of the bridge the road turns to the right, leading to the richly
decorated Gezireh Palace, one of the most extravagant erections of Ismail.   It
is now a hotel, well managed and much frequented.   Its apartments are richly
furnished, and the shady palm groves in which it stands are a
great attraction.   The race-course is
just at hand, and the military polo
ground and grand
stand.

MOSQUE OF SULTAN TULUN.
One of the most ancient in Cairo, now undergoing restoration.

The road on
the left, after cross-
ing the bridge,
leads to Mena
House Hotel, un-
der the very sha-
dow of the Great
Pyramid.   Mena
House is a delight-
ful place of stay

for those who wish to study the Pyramids and breathe the glorious desert air, and for such as can endure quiet and comparative loneliness. The climate is far more healthy than in Cairo, the food is excellent, and the charges are reasonable. Some think it the best hotel in the world, well worthy of a stay of some weeks or months. Its origin is due to an English gentleman, Mr. Head, who had derived great benefit to his health by a winter passed in a cottage that had been erected on this spot at the time of the visit of the Empress Eugénie. This led to its purchase by Mr. Locke King, who subsequently built this hotel, employing Mr. Favarger, the eminent English architect, of Cairo, and giving him *carte blanche* as to style of architecture, etc. He said the hotel should not be built without a constant supply of good spring water. Using native labour only, they bored and found a constant supply of purest water, between twenty and thirty feet below the desert level. This spring has never failed, and gives abundant supply to the great establishment, which frequently, with visitors and servants, contains several hundred persons. There is even a large marble swimming bath, from three to ten feet deep, supplied with water clear as crystal. This water and the pure desert air render the place a per-

GATE OF THE CITADEL, CAIRO.
The Tomb-mosque of Mehemet Ali, with its delicate minarets in the distance.

fect sanatorium. The dairy is worth visiting; it is like a first-class English establishment, and supplies any quantity of excellent milk and butter. Fresh vegetables are produced in the kitchen garden in plenty. There are golf links provided on the desert, and abundance of space for other sports.

The interior of the building is well worthy of notice. The architectural features of the exterior are simple in the extreme, but the wooden vestibule, open to the air, is very attractive—of Moresque style, admitting abundant air but carefully excluding all sunshine. Part of this is glazed off to give shelter in a sand-storm, or to give cool air by shutting out the oppressive "khamsin" wind from the Western desert. The entrance hall is beautiful, and is lit from above

MENA HOUSE, WITH THE PYRAMIDS OF GIZEH.

through an octagonal well; a wide marble staircase leads upwards with steps so easy that the ascent is almost unfelt. The large reception room is a lofty and spacious apartment, well lit, yet the burning sun never shines into it. All the furniture is in Cairene style, made by native workmen. Beautiful Oriental rugs are on the floor, and all the curtains and upholstery are of native material. But the architectural gem of Mena House is the dining room. It is without doubt the finest of its kind in the world. The roof is lofty—about forty feet or more in the highest part. About two hundred can dine comfortably in it. A raised daïs runs all round the room, behind four great Saracenic arches. Round this the private tables are placed, while in the centre of the room three great tables afford accommodation to ordinary guests. The kitchens are completely isolated, and the odour of cooking is never discernible. All the openings and the entire architectural treatment of the great dining hall are adapted from the details of the ancient mosque of Kait Bey, in Cairo, the gem of Moslem architecture, and one of those that has been recently restored by the Commission presided over by Lord Cromer. An electric tramway has just been completed from Cairo to the great terrace on which the Pyramids stand. Verily "Progress" is here associated with the "Pyramids."

DINING ROOM, MENA HOUSE.

CHAPTER III.

THE GREAT PYRAMID-PLATFORM.

KHAFRA'S TEMPLE—THE SPHINX—THE GREAT PYRAMID.

THE GREAT PYRAMID OF GIZEH—
THE PYRAMIDS OF ABU ROASH—KHUFU—KHAFRA—MENKAURA—
THE GREAT SPHINX.

(29)

THE PYRAMID-FIELD OF GIZEH: THE SPHINX, FROM THE SOUTH.
(From a Water-Colour Drawing by the Author.)

CHAPTER III.

THE PYRAMID-PLATFORM OF GIZEH.

There is a general notion that the Pyramids can be seen in an afternoon. The usual practice is to go out by the Mena House coach, lunch in the handsome dining-room of the hotel, ride round the Great Pyramid, paying a passing visit to the mysterious Sphinx; then a cup of tea on the hotel terrace, dinner, and a drive back to Cairo, by moonlight when possible. But the proper way is to make some stay in the Mena House establishment, and to get up early now and then to see the wonderful effects of sunrise from and near the Pyramids. The gorgeous sunset effects, never twice alike, are more available, however, to most mortals. When the moon is at the full, the Sphinx should be interviewed at moonrise and waited upon till the beams gradually light up the countenance of this great mystery of the past 6,000 years. Its poor scarred visage loses its mutilated aspect, the lips seem to smile, the eyes seem almost to flash in the clear air, as the light increases and seems to give it life. Then, when you can tear yourself away, descend into Khafra's superb temple of rose-granite, close at hand, and see how it lights up as the moon climbs the sky. Do not refuse the excellent cup of coffee, the tall, handsome guardian will gladly make for you. And should you see this wonderful corner of the desert under such circumstances I think you will want to see it again, and as often as you can. I have seen it hundreds of times, and always "ask for more," and I shall want to go back to it every year! But then I am hard to satisfy, and the Sphinx has, perhaps, fascinated me. Let us now mount the pyramid-platform. We can walk to the

Great Pyramid from Mena House in fifteen minutes.
As we approach, it seems to grow larger and larger.
The base covers actually the space of Lincoln's Inn
Fields—775 feet on each side—and it was originally
480 feet in height. Now in steps, it was once covered
with a smooth casing of white Tourah stone, and in
its original perfect state, in the strong sunlight, must
have been a most beautiful object, visible from a great

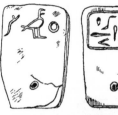

PLUMMET OF KHUFU.

distance. The glistening surface of the vast monument must have been a
wondrous sight in bright moonlight. The king who planned it (Khufu, called
by the Greeks Cheops, of the Fourth Dynasty, about 3910 B.C.) certainly
succeeded in erecting a monument that has handed his name down to posterity
for over five thousand years and seems likely to endure as long as the world
lasts. Col. Vyse proved it to be Khufu's, by finding the king's name written
in red paint on the blocks inside. Subsequently Dr. Petrie found a plummet
with Khufu's name, in the *débris*, which had possibly been buried with
him. The pyramid's beautiful casing has been stolen, but Dr. Petrie discovered part of the lower courses buried in the sand. This greatest living
Egyptian explorer, when quite a young man, spent three seasons here, and
made a masterly survey of the entire pyramid-field of Gizeh. He published a
most exhaustive volume on the subject—a perfect work of its kind. The work
is now out of print. It is a pity that its gifted author should not publish a
reprint; but he wants to go over the ground again before he does so. The

KHAFRA'S TEMPLE, NEAR THE SPHINX.

jealousy of the French direction of the
Cairo Museum has hitherto prevented this,
and Dr. Petrie has never been allowed to
complete his great survey. No doubt the
entire platform is full of wonders awaiting
discovery. It would be a costly task to
remove hundreds of millions of tons of sand.
But in these days, when the sandy bar of
Liverpool has been pumped out, science
could possibly adapt a sand-pump to the
purpose. When Lord Cromer has time, no
doubt some of his engineers, such as Major
Hanbury Brown, or Major Lyons, could
advise how it could be done. As both of
these excellent engineers have archæological
tastes and knowledge as well, they could

be safely trusted to clear the ground for Dr. Petrie's completion of his greatest and, at the same time, his first Egyptian work. In his volume, Dr. Petrie works out the mysteries of the construction of the Great Pyramid, and shows that the number of labourers stated by Herodotus (100,000 men, working three months at a time for 20 years) was pro-bably correct, but he sug-

ONE OF THE MASTABAS NEAR THE GREAT PYRAMID.

gests that they were employed thus at the time of high Nile, when no labour could be done in the fields. Dr. Petrie found the foundations of the barracks where the skilled workmen were quartered during the work. These are still uncovered, and can be seen behind the Second Pyramid, on the high ground. There are three deep trenches on the east of the Great Pyramid which may have been made to contain water. Beyond, and on the same side, are the three smaller pyramids of the king's daughters. These were beautifully cased with white stone, and many of the casing blocks are in their original position, only hidden by the sand, if we know where to look for them. We can dismount and crawl into passages under each pyramid, whence we emerge into chambers whose walls are engraved and painted with the whole story of the life and parentage of the princess who was interred in the deep shaft beneath

ALI GABRI AND HIS BOY, THE HADJI.

the tomb. The numerous small erections of masonry called mastabas, with sloping sides and flat tops, cover the tombs of Khufu's kindred, and many of them bear his name or *cartouche*. But all that Dr. Petrie discovered in this region can be learnt from the best guide in the place, who was Petrie's trusted servant and friend during his three years of hard work. His name is Ali Gabri. His little son has been to Mecca and is therefore a Hadji, and always follows his father about, making himself useful.

Everyone who is young or active enough should climb the Great Pyramid. The view from the top is magnificent. The several

c

groups of pyramids can be seen for forty miles on one hand and seven miles on the other. The green cultivated flat which the Nile covers at the inundation and the rocky, illimitable Libyan desert (the plateau extends on the west for 2,000 miles) are very impressive. The great city of Cairo seems to lie at our feet and behind it the grand barrier of the eastern cliffs, whence came the stone of the artificial mountain on which we stand. The silvery Nile threads the wide valley, flecked with its picturesque sail-boats like gigantic birds with expanded wings.

Nor should a visit into the interior of the Great Pyramid be missed. It is best done in the early morning : each person should have two attendants, who are now licensed and better looked after. They provide candles, but visitors should have their own magnesium wire, and indiarubber shoes should be worn. The interior shows the most perfect workmanship, the joints being almost imperceptible. The guide books describe the various chambers and provide the measurements from Dr. Petrie's book. There is now an official guardian, who provides tickets and trusty guides for the ascent and also for the interior of the Great Pyramid.

The Second Pyramid stands on high ground, and from some points looks more lofty than its older neighbour, but it is considerably less in height, and its workmanship is not so perfect. Part of its casing remains near the top. Belzoni opened it, and found within the remains of the king for whom it was built (Khafra, Dynasty IV., 3900 B.C.). The scarabs of this king are amongst the earliest known. I am fortunate in possessing one of them, and the hieroglyphics are the same as were used on the Rosetta Stone 3100 years later, proving the great antiquity and continuity of the Egyptian written language. In early times every king had his own pyramid, which was in progress during his life, so all the pyramids themselves were sepulchres, but only for the kings. Their sites were chosen with great care ; the sides always face the four points of the compass. At the east side of each pyramid there was always a temple where worship

PORTRAIT STATUE OF KHAFRA,
Carved in Diorite, found in his Temple. (*From the Cairo Museum.*) was carried on by a body of priests

THE PYRAMIDS OF GIZEH: VIEW LOOKING EASTWARDS TOWARDS THE CULTIVATED LAND.
(From a Sketch by the Author.)

who were supported by landed estates and endowments. The hierarchy of several of these early monarchs' memorial services seems to have existed down to Greek and Roman times. But the temples here have nearly all disappeared; only their foundations exist and fragments of sculptured walls and of the votive treasures they once contained—morsels of broken marble, granite, alabaster, diorite, and basalt, many of them showing traces of polish or sculpture. The entrance to the Pyramids was always on the north side.

The authorities of the Cairo Museum issue no licences for excavating on the pyramid-fields, and no proper researches have been made for many years. Dr. Petrie was only permitted to examine the pyramids here and those of Medum and the Fayum. All around the various groups of pyramids are thousands of tombs, mastabas, and monuments, which for fifty years have been unscientifically rifled by the Arabs in search of treasure. There are still no official custodians. This is a great disgrace, and it is to be hoped that the Government will soon give attention to the matter.

The Third Pyramid (that of Menkaura, 3800 B.C., the Mykerinos of Herodotus) is much smaller than the others, but is very interesting. It is easily entered and ascended, and, Petrie thinks, was perhaps never finished. It was cased with red granite, but apparently only in the lower part, and there the stone is left rough, the blocks retaining the knobs used for lifting into place. Possibly

MACE-HEAD OF KHAFRA.
Found by Dr. Petrie in his Pyramid-Temple.

C 2

THE DOOR OF A MASTABA.
The Tomb of the Architect of Khafra's Pyramid. (*British Museum.*)

the king died before it was completed. He certainly was buried in it, for his body was found therein about fifty years ago, and part of his wooden coffin and some of his bones are in the British Museum, the rest having been lost at sea. There was a large and evidently splendid temple attached to the Third Pyramid; the remains show excellent architectural skill. There are three small pyramids at the north side of Menkaura's pyramid, which were built for his daughters. So there are nine pyramids in all at Gizeh. Each of the three large ones had its enclosing wall, which can still be traced, and the royal family and dignitaries of the court were the only ones permitted to be interred in the region allotted to each sovereign. It is well worth while to walk or ride over the rocky desert to the west of the pyramids. The ground rises, and about a mile back, the view, looking down on the Gizeh cemetery, is very fine. We can see over the pyramids and they appear in a setting of brilliant green, the fruitful wide valley which is covered with the inundation. The great city of Cairo lies beyond, its towers and minarets catching the sun. The yellow eastern hills, whence came the stone of the vast monuments we have visited, close in the landscape, and gleams of the mighty Nile show themselves at intervals among the lines of tall date palms that border its course.

There are many charming excursions from the Mena House Hotel, many interesting carved and painted tombs to explore, and, if Ali Gabri's help can be obtained, days, and even weeks, can be pleasantly spent in this wonderful neighbourhood. Dr. Petrie had his home for three seasons in a "nice dry

ABU ROASH: Central Tomb-Chamber of the Great Pyramid.

comfortable tomb," which he says is by far the best abode, when it can be found, for the living as well as for the dead! In those days there was no Arab village at the pyramid, and he and his devoted Ali Gabri lived in the tombs cut in the cliffs near the pyramid causeway. I have gone all over the Gizeh platform hundreds of times, and always found something I had never seen before. I had often wished to explore the little-visited group of pyramids, or rather their ruins, at Abu Roash, about six miles north of those of Gizeh, and recently we rode there across the desert behind Mena House, along the crest of the hills. The excessive purity of the air had caused it to seem quite close to us. The grand

DISTANT VIEW OF THE PYRAMIDS.

THE SPHINX.
(From the Picture by D. Roberts, R.A., 1840.)

terrace on which the ancient pyramids once stood has a most commanding situation. The rich green meadows and dark groves of palms extend close to the steep, white cliffs like a great sea, and, like an island of palaces, far Cairo spreads itself in the centre.

On the western side the great Lybian desert extends for 2,000 miles. Here, a century ago, were many pyramids. The Dynasty for whom they were built is unknown, but they are of far older date than the Pyramid of Gizeh. They have nearly all been quarried away, and when I saw them this year (1899) a busy trade in carrying away the stone for building and road-making was going on. The whole site should have Lord Cromer's attention and be put under State protection. There are hundreds of quarries around that could be used where no pyramids exist. The great pyramid of Abu Roash must have been a grand one. The whole country round is red with chippings of granite from far Assouan; all the pyramid was cased with it, but not one block remains. The rapacity of the quarrymen has cleared out the vast central chamber cut in the solid rock and lined with white stones of enormous size. We took a photograph; this chamber now resembles the central chamber of Khufu's Pyramid, but is very much larger. No doubt there are many such chambers among the mountains of worked-stone rubbish all around which are the sole remains of this pyramid group. The ride to Abu Roash is delightful, but the homeward journey is even more charming, returning under the palm groves' shade in the heat of the day, among richly-cultivated meadows stocked with many heads of cattle.

SOUTH SIDE OF THE SPHINX. (Present state.)

Let us now return to the Gizeh platform.   There is a well-defined ancient causeway leading, for about half a mile from where the river flowed in ancient times, towards each of the three pyramids on the great platform.   This road to the Second Pyramid is angled off so as to avoid touching the Great Sphinx, a proof that it was a venerated ancient object when Khafra was building his tomb.   He had two temples; one at the pyramid, and another at the eastern end of this causeway.   The lowermost structure is the beautiful mortuary temple of Khafra, and a number of fine statues of this king were found in a deep well within it, which were of remark-ably fine sculpture, the material being diorite, possibly the hardest stone known. The tem-ple was probably meant as a sepulchre for his family, and it is the most impressive mauso-leum in Egypt.   The blocks of polished As-souan granite are often 18 feet by 7 feet, and are quite perfect, as freshly polished as when the temple was built, but all that survives is the lower storey of the temple.   The desert sand being piled round it gives it the appear-ance of a cellar.   The style of its architecture

THE SPHINX IN 1899, SHOWING HOW THE SAND IS AGAIN ENCROACHING.

is simple and massive.   There are several chambers whose uses are unknown, lined with blocks of transparent alabaster.   No doubt much more of this superb temple remains under the sand awaiting discovery.   What is now un-covered was found by the indefatigable Mariette.

In 1840, the Sphinx, as we see from Roberts's drawing, was buried up to the neck in the sand, and this temple was also entombed in the then level desert.   This would soon happen again, and the sand has to be cleared away every few years. The Great Sphinx must be numberless years older than even the Pyramids;

Mariette, Maspero, Petrie, Sayce, and many others, consider it to be pre-historic. The enormous creature is cut out of the living rock, and the same strata appears a short way off to the south, and at almost a similar elevation. All the stone between has been excavated for building tombs and temples, long subsequent to the carving of the Sphinx, which was carefully left as a venerated monument. This alone is enough to prove its great antiquity. It was much admired and protected in Greek and Roman times, and even the early Mahometans seemed to have respected it. But the fanatical Mamelouks regarded it as an Afreet, or evil spirit, and used it as a target for their matchlocks, and even battered its features with cannon shot. Even now there is much need for this venerable relic to have the consideration of the Government. There should be trustworthy guardians appointed to take charge of it. The Bedouins from the adjacent village crowd about the place, running all over the crumbling stone, climbing to the top and capering like monkeys, to earn baksheesh. Now the neck is all worn away owing to the softness of that part of the stone, being acted upon by the sand-blast of the desert, while the head remains intact, being of hard rock. These wild creatures dancing on the top may actually loosen the head so as to endanger its breaking off altogether. With all that it has suffered, though ruined and battered by wanton violence, it is, perhaps, the most wonderful monument in the world. In certain lights we do not notice the battered countenance, and the earnest eyes seem to glow like those of a faithful dog, trying to express what it cannot utter.

I had often tried to take its portrait, and one day recently I tried again. I mounted the hillock of sand which commands the view of the Great Sphinx itself, opened the sketching apparatus—the faithful Arab holding the big umbrella over me to exclude the burning sun—and began to sketch the once lovely countenance. The Arabs of bygone times made a target of its head, with the result that only in certain positions of the light can its original expression be even imagined, much less caught by camera or by the draughtsman. As I puzzled over this part of the work, I heard my Arab friend say, " Sar, if you saw what she was like when she was made, you would be glad, would not you ? " I said, " I should be glad indeed. I am sure she was beautiful ; but how horribly spoiled now." " I once found a little sphinkes, a nice little model, and, I think, as old as the big one." " What became of it ? Could I see it ? " He waited till all the Arabs standing round had disappeared, and from the folds of his voluminous mantle produced a little sphinx, about five inches high, broken away below, but with a lovely face, quite perfect as to head and features, and of beautiful workmanship. The modelling and carving was exquisite. The stone was green basalt, so hard that it could barely be marked with a sharp penknife ;

SPHINX IN GREEN BASALT.

Size of the Original in the possession of the Author.

This beautiful little object was found among the ruins of Khafra's Pyramid-Temple, and had been possibly one of the votive offerings at the shrine. The carved portion is quite perfect. The broken surface underneath shows by its "weathering" that it was exposed to the atmosphere for an immense period of years. It possibly had been uppermost, and the carving preserved by being buried in the sand, downwards, for ages.

whilst the expression was sweet, there was a mysterious, far-off look in the eyes. It might have served for a model of the great monument itself. This pretty little relic is now in my possession. Professor Sayce considers it to be a work of the Third or Fourth Dynasty. Dr. Petrie said that as it was discovered in the ruins of Khafra's Pyramid-Temple, it was possibly of that period, for no later work has ever been found there. One may, however, looking at this little model, account for the extravagant praise given to the countenance of the Sphinx by ancient writers.

The whole body of the Great Sphinx is perforated by a shaft opening from the centre of the back, which leads doubtless to a tomb at a great depth which has never been scientifically explored. Perhaps careful excavation properly carried out around might explain something of its mysterious origin. It was decayed and repaired by Thothmes IV. about 1415 B.C., as an inscription of his time on the *stele* of granite which is placed between the paws testifies. The king says that one day, after the fatigue of hunting, he fell asleep in the shadow of the image of his father Harmachis, and the god spoke to him and promised him long life if he would "clear away the sand which swallowed him up, and would restore his image in every part." And so, says Thothmes, he carried out the orders of his lord given him in his dream. The paws, of solid rock,

had, however, again become decayed, and were several times renewed with built
work in Greek and Roman times. Then again the desert sand "swallowed him
up," and when the French re-discovered it in 1799 only the head was visible.
They cleared it out, but in so poor a manner that it soon filled up again.

The head was originally painted; some of the colour can still be seen on
the cheeks. The classic writers praised its beauty. This is hard to trace
now, for how can any face be beautiful without a nose? The eyes are, however,
still most expressive. In Pliny's time (A.D. 40) it was perfect, and he was much
struck with its beauty. He said a king had been buried in it. In this Pliny
may be correct, for the shaft of a tomb is undoubtedly within it. An Arab
geographer, Abd-el-Latîf, describes (in A.D. 1200) its face as being very beautiful,
the mouth graceful and lovely, as if smiling graciously, and still bearing
freshly its red paint. It seems to have been forgotten for centuries, till the
French publications, after Napoleon's expedition to Egypt, drew attention to
it. The face appears to have been much in the same state as at the present day.
Still, whether with its ancient beauty, or with its present battered visage, it
has always had a weird and wonderful effect on the beholder's mind.

Here are some modern quotations regarding the Sphinx :—

" Science, regarded by ignorance as a monster."—*Lord Bacon.*

" Comely the creature is, but its comeliness is not of this world."—*Kinglake.*

" There is something stupendous in the sight of that tremendous head. . . .
If it was the giant representative of Royalty, then it fitly guards the greatest
of royal sepulchres."—*Dean Stanley.*

" Look up into those eyes, so full of meaning, though so fixed."—*Miss Martineau.*

" Nature ! the Sphinx, its emblem, shows also the claws of a lioness."—*Carlyle.*

" Its calm, majestic expression of countenance."—*Kenrick.*

DEEP SHADOOFS, NEAR THE PYRAMIDS, GIZEH.

CHAPTER IV.

THE FURTHER PYRAMID-PLATFORM.

THE PYRAMID OF MEDUM.

Near view from the West, showing the immense heaps of stone chippings.

MEMPHIS AND ITS CEMETERIES—
SAKKARAH—ABUSIR—THE APIS MAUSOLEUM—
DAHSHUR—MEDUM.

(43)

PYRAMID-FIELD OF SAKKARAH: MARIETTE'S HOUSE.
(From a Water-Colour Drawing by the Author.)

CHAPTER IV.

LOST MEMPHIS—THE GREAT CEMETERIES OF SAKKARAH— ABUSIR—DAHSHUR—MEDUM.

WE have visited the pyramids on, and north of, the platform of Gizeh. The horizon seen to the south showed us still more royal cemeteries—those of Abusir, Sakkarah, Dahshur, and (on a very clear day) even the far-distant Medum. But, till people get fond of pyramids (and in this case—to change the copybook metaphor—familiarity generally breeds respect), let us visit them by a roundabout journey by way of Memphis. The site is not far off.

The ruins of this once great city are buried underneath the long undulating mounds of black earth which lie near the village of Bedrasheen, a station on the railway from Cairo. They are now covered with shady groves of picturesque date palms. Green fields and pools of stagnant water lie between, which we are asked to believe were once the Sacred Lakes of the buried Temples of Memphis. The only remains of the once powerful city are two colossal statues of Ramses the Great, lying on their backs among the palm trees. These formerly stood before the great temple of Ptah, but the temple and the whole city have been partially swallowed up by the Nile mud of twenty centuries, for the river-bed rises several inches in every hundred years. One of the huge statues is of granite, the other of fine limestone. The latter is the finest portrait of Ramses. It has a tranquil expression and great nobility withal. To prevent any doubt as to the person represented, the sculptor has carved the king's name on the shoulder and on the belt which carries his dagger. He now lies placidly looking up to heaven, like a great warrior taking his rest. He looks like what he was—the greatest king of his age. Although a tyrant, his works proclaim his power.

There are huge mounds of rubbish here, under which may some day be found buildings and monuments; and some antiquarians see here traces of the vast dyke by which old King Mena reclaimed his city from the waters of the Nile.

A pleasant ride from Memphis through richly-cultivated fields brings us in an hour to the pyramid-field of Sakkarah. The great Step-Pyramid is the central attraction of this wonderful necropolis, and has the character of being the earliest of all structures of the kind. It is possibly the tomb of a king of the First Dynasty, or even earlier. It consists of six courses or steps, and is constructed of small stones and is much more rudely put together than the other pyramids. It is not square, but is oblong in shape—a rude parallelogram. It seems to have been added to from time to time, as, at the corners, where broken away, complete faces of earlier construction are seen underneath. It has an indescribable look of hoary antiquity, but has never been properly excavated so as to determine its date or origin. The ruins of several other very ancient pyramids are in its vicinity. One heap of ruins is known to have contained the tomb of Pepi I., and another to be that of Teta; a third the pyramid of Unas, of the Sixth Dynasty (3530 B.C.). The last was recently excavated at the expense of Mr. John Cook. It is carefully guarded and easily visited. The king's sarcophagus is still in the central chamber, which also has the finest inscriptions found in any pyramid, the hieroglyphs being beautifully carved and painted in pale blue. Although now mere heaps of loose stones, the excavation of all these sites of pyramids has afforded most interesting results. No doubt a systematic survey would discover the substructure of many more similar royal tombs. The tombs that have been opened contained many extraordinary religious inscriptions most

PALM FOREST ON THE SITE OF MEMPHIS, NEAR BEDRASHEEN.

beautifully execu-
ted. The earlier
pyramids contained
no inscriptions
whatever.

The rest-house
provided for travel-
lers near this,
known as "Mari-
ette's House," is a
mere wooden shed
resting on frag-
ments of carved
stones, the dwelling
of the great Egyp-
tologist, and was

GRANITE COLOSSUS OF RAMSES THE GREAT, MEMPHIS.
The finest one, made of marble or fine limestone, being enclosed in a wooden
hut for protection, cannot be photographed.

the scene of his wonderful discovery of the Apis Mausoleum.

Mariette was a wonderful man, a Petrie of thirty years ago. He was determined to explore the wonders of Sakkarah, and so he built himself this hut
in the desert sands of the great cemetery. There he dwelt several seasons,
making his famous discoveries all round. One day he saw that the sand had
blown away and disclosed a line of small stone sphinxes. Several of such had
been brought into Cairo for sale—before his time—and two of them guard the
doors of Shepheard's Hotel to this day. But they were found to have been
brought from Sakkarah, and this made Mariette decide to search there for
more. A passage in Strabo told him that they had formed part of the
"dromos" or avenue leading to the burial-place of the Apis-bulls. He
excavated on the spot, and discovered the lost Apis Mausoleum. It had been
known to the classic writers, but the sands of the
desert had entombed it for 2,000 years. It proved to
be an avenue 600 feet long, and hundreds of sphinxes
or their pedestals still remained to guide the way.
The sand had obliterated the entrance to a vast subterranean hall 1,200 feet long and to vaults in which
the Sacred Bulls were buried on each side. The
animals were enclosed in granite coffins, some of which
will hold five persons, each of one block of Assouan
syenite. Twenty-four such coffins are now to be seen,
and this hall is only a part of the vast collection of

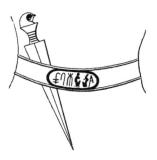

DAGGER AND BELT, WITH
TITLE OF RAMSES.

PORTRAIT OF THYI, HIS WIFE, AND SON.
(From the Tomb of Thyi, Sakkarah.)

the Apis Mausoleum. The avenue of sphinxes is again covered with sand, but a gate and a custodian have been placed to preserve the entrance and the subterranean cemetery of the sacred animals. The worship of the Bulls was no part of the simple cult of the First Dynasty. According to Manetho it was introduced by the second king of the Second Dynasty, and it lasted till the time of the Ptolemies. But most of these holy beasts seem to have been interred at Sakkarah with as much pomp and circumstance as if they had been kings. At Sakkarah there are many beautiful ancient tombs of the great men of old Egypt, far older in date than those of animals, and many of the oldest monuments crowd the whole of the wide cemetery. Doubtless all the designers and occupants of these tombs, or the greater part, were inhabitants of the lost city of Memphis. There are several interesting

tombs that must have taken years to build, carve, and decorate. The greatest "mastaba" in Egypt, the "Mastabet-el-Faroon," is in the centre of the great city of the dead. It seems a royal tomb, and older than any pyramid, but its royal owner has never yet been identified. There are also many painted sepul-

PEASANT WOMEN BRINGING TRIBUTE.
(From the Tomb of Thyi, Sakkarah.)

chres of private persons and of officials of the court. Every spot of the cemetery seems to have been occupied during several thousand years. Only a comparatively few tombs have been scientifically explored, and these are now provided with gates and have trustworthy custodians. Some that had been rudely dug out left behind dangerous pitfalls for the unwary; the Government have now taken charge of them and these pits have been filled up again.

THE MAYOR OF A VILLAGE BROUGHT TO ACCOUNT.
(From the Tomb of Thyi, Sakkarah.)

The painted tomb of Thyi is well worthy of careful examination, and gives a series of pictures of ancient life in Egypt 5,000 years ago, so vivid and realistic as to carry us back to comprehend the very life of the people. Thyi was a sportsman, and the fishing, shooting (with arrows), hunting, and pursuit of "big game" are most vigorously represented. Crocodiles, hippopotami, and other monsters are shown as drawn out with hooks. The sowing, reaping, and storing of grain is depicted. Herds and flocks of cattle are shown, and then the best of the animals are selected and brought

PYRAMID-FIELD OF SAKKARAH,
From the cultivated ground beyond the site of Memphis.

for sacrifice. Thyi was also a gentleman farmer, and had a great stock of rare animals at his establishment in the country and a rich mansion, a plan of which is shown. Antelopes, ibexes, gazelles, and rare birds from Nubia were kept alive. Many portraits of the owner himself are given, and his statue is preserved in the Cairo Museum.

The tomb of Meri is also well worth visiting; it was the discovery of M. de Morgan. It is remarkable in having three complete dwellings, so to speak; one for the owner, one for his wife, and one for their son. The statue of Meri is still in its place, and the whole of the sculptures and paintings are very interesting as showing the ancient industries of Egypt, pictures of ships and boats, agricultural and mercantile transactions of all sorts. Not

REMAINS OF THE PYRAMID OF PEPI, THE PYRAMID OF TETA, AND THE STEP-PYRAMID, SAKKARAH.

D

TOMB OF MERI, SAKKARAH.
The statue is that of the owner of the tomb.

only are we shown how they lived, but the deceased ones are shown after death as being purified for their entrance into heaven. The art is not as good as in the tomb of Thyi, but it is more interesting. Meri lived during Dynasty VI., about 3400 B.C. There are many other tombs of the wealthy classes; but the ordinary mortals were mummified and buried together in rows and on the shelves of great pits provided for the purpose, many of which, being now open and unprotected, are unpleasant reminders of poor mortality, the whole ground being strewn with fragments of coffins, bones, and mummy cloth. The air is so dry that nothing decays here, and the ghastly relics are everywhere around. They should be returned to earth and buried beneath the kindly desert sand that has so long preserved them.

The pyramid-field of Sakkarah seems to join that of Dahshur, though it is actually five miles off. It is well to leave a visit to Dahshur to another day, and, turning the camel's (or donkey's) head northward, to return to Mena House, but this time by the desert track. The sun has gone round now, and we do not feel the glare of the sand so much. This route leads us past the pyramids of Abusir. These pyramids have never been properly explored, and should have their mysteries unveiled. They are said to be those of Dynasty V. or VI., but

THE GREAT PYRAMID OF ABUSIR,
Half-way between Gizeh and Sakkarah.

are probably much older. No doubt each was the mausoleum of a king, whose remains, or at least a proof of his name or title, are still hidden beneath or within. Although very ruinous now, no doubt their tomb-chambers exist intact and should be properly investigated. Granite of Assouan must have been largely used in their construction, for the ground is covered with its fragments. The ride over the hard desert in the evening air is delightful. We soon come nearer the giant pyramids of Gizeh, crossing some well-cultivated land, fed with water by very deep shadoofs. Ploughing is going on briskly, for the beneficent Irrigation Department has formed a small reservoir to store up water at high Nile, and the land is rapidly returning to cultivation by its use. But it takes longer to reach Mena House than we expect. We ride by the desert path over the great necropolis extending for miles, the sand and rocks being everywhere perforated with tombs. Hundreds of thousands of human beings must have been carefully buried in this wondrous rocky desert, and the skulls and bones and fragments of mummy cloth often show through the pebbly surface. In the summer, when they have the place to themselves, the Arabs rifle every tomb they can find in search of beads, scarabs, and "antikas" to sell to the tourists. At length we arrive at Mena House, rest under the shady verandah while the refreshing tea is enjoyed, and compare each others' beads and scarabs collected by the way from the Arab plunderers.

SAKKARAH: PTAH-HOTEP'S SON.
(From the Volume published by Petrie, " Egyptian Research Account.")

Sakkarah is worth even several visits, but everyone has not time for this. But from Sakkarah we have seen the pyramids of Dahshur, and so much has been heard of the jewellery found thereabouts, that most people will want to visit them. Therefore, if an excursion to the cemetery of Dahshur be contemplated, it is well, as I elsewhere suggest, to give it another day, taking fresh camels or donkeys for the journey. When I first went there I was under the guidance of M. de Morgan, then the Director for Antiquities in Egypt. He had just made some wonderful discoveries, and, like his predecessor Mariette, he expected to find so much more, that he had built himself a comfortable house, and he and his wife dwelt therein for nearly two years. There are remains of two or three brick pyramids at Dahshur, and two stone ones in

KING HOR.
(Head of his Wooden Statue, found at Dahshur.)

a perfect state. One of the stone pyramids has two different angles of outline, the other is much more flat in its angles than any other pyramid. The brick pyramids had been cased with white stone, but it was stolen from them long ago and only the interior structure of sun-dried bricks remains. They are most un-attractive-looking mounds, like Scotch or Irish peat stacks on a large scale. Yet each was the tomb of a great king. One of them was cer-tainly that of Usertesen III. (2650 B.C.), and the other that of one of the same dynasty. The denizens of the two stone pyramids have yet to be identified; they are no doubt of very much earlier date, belonging to the early em-pire, when only stone pyramids were built. M. de Morgan found that the north side of the northern brick pyramid had many tombs of the royal family arranged outside it. The whole of the rock underneath was pierced with shafts and hori-zontal tunnels running east and west, and having chapels and sepulchres on each side. The entrances to these were hidden till found by De Morgan, and have been since closed again. I give a photograph of their state during my visit. Every tomb had been rifled in ancient times, and in clearing out the shafts several thieves' entrances were discovered, tunnels by which the despoilers had entered the cata-combs. But the robbers had done their nefarious work hurriedly, and M. de Morgan's eye detected several tombs that had only been partially opened. The treasure was found intact in one of those which the discoverer showed me himself. I was lowered by a stout rope slung from under my arms into the shaft—about 40 feet cut in the solid rock. At the bottom we found a tunnel leading westwards. With lanterns, we walked upright along this passage for about 200 feet. There were openings on either side, each containing an empty stone coffin. Opposite each was a smaller chamber which was devoted to the four "canopic-jars" for the viscera of the deceased. The floor was flagged, and underneath one tomb, that of a royal princess, a wooden coffer was found containing £40,000 worth of jewel-lery, gold, and precious stones. The ornaments were beautifully designed and of perfect skill in workmanship and in the most exquisite taste. Another tomb also had a somewhat similar treasure, but not quite so rich. The jewellery, or some of it, had belonged to King Usertesen, and bore his cartouche, in gold inlaid with sapphire, lapis-lazuli, turquoise, carnelian, and other precious stones. These treasures are now preserved in the Cairo Museum. M. de Morgan also found the tomb of Hor,

Pectoral of Usertesen III. (Twelfth Dynasty).

Pectoral of Amenemhat III. (Twelfth Dynasty).

SOLID GOLD PECTORALS, INLAID WITH SAPPHIRE, CARNELIAN, TURQUOISE, AND OTHER
PRECIOUS STONES, CHAMPLEVÉ LIKE ENAMEL (FULL SIZE).

(These are part of the treasures discovered by M. de Morgan at Dahshur, and are now in the Cairo Museum.)

(53)

PYRAMID-FIELD OF DAHSHUR.
The two Stone Pyramids on the right, the remains of the Brick Pyramid on the left.

a king hitherto unknown, containing his wooden coffin and a statue of himself (or his double), nearly life-size, beautifully sculptured in wood, doubtless some rare and valuable kind more costly than stone at that period. This fine statue also is to be seen at the Cairo Museum. All the monarch's wands of office and the royal sceptre and other insignia were found, and are also exhibited. The statue is evidently a portrait; the king seems to have died young. M. de Morgan found many other rich antiquities in this district, and he intended to devote several years to it, but he was recalled from his post, or resigned his office, to be succeeded by a less-gifted antiquarian. De Morgan is now excavating in Persia, I believe. He was an able engineer, a most accomplished man, and courteous and obliging to everyone who came in

NORTH BRICK PYRAMID OF DAHSHUR.
Near which De Morgan discovered the tomb of King Hor (Twelfth Dynasty).

contact with him. He presented me with a beautiful volume, with illustrations of his great Egyptian discoveries, all from drawings by himself. M. de Morgan's ancestors were of British origin, and he spoke English fluently. No doubt much is yet to be found at Dahshur; those stone pyramids should be made to unfold their records, which without doubt are yet safely concealed within their recesses. I rode round the entire circuit of the cemetery. The western portion is of vast extent, and seems never to have been opened or searched for thousands of years, and yet doubtless it is as populous of the dead of 3,000 or 5,000 years ago as the more northern pyramid-fields. Where can all the cities have been, whose teeming population gave their dead by millions to all these places of sepulture? Long before Memphis was

SOUTH PYRAMID OF DAHSHUR,
With shaft sunk by M. de Morgan, by which he found the treasure (now closed up).

founded, and long afterwards, densely peopled towns must have been along this valley. Their names are lost, their sites unknown, naught is left to us but the relics of their aristocracy; of their common people no trace is left.

I devoted more time than most tourists could afford to these ancient repositories of the past, but all I saw of one pyramid-field made me desire to see the next one. In this way I had been led from Gizeh to Abusir, then to Sakkarah, and from Sakkarah to Dahshur. And as I rode away in the declining day I reined up and rested on the highest point of the plain to take a survey of the wonderful scene of vast, illimitable desert. From where I sat the thin green strip of cultivated land which margins the wide Nile was invisible. Northward extended the dunes of the desert and the pyramids of Sakkarah, Abusir, Gizeh, Abu Roash, and others, as far as the eye could reach from those of Dahshur around me. To the west the Libyan Desert was illimitably lost in the warm clouds and rich haze of approaching sunset. Next to the Dahshur Pyramids come those of Lisht, but they do not show in the view from this point. They are on lower ground. Great discoveries were made recently at Lisht—a king's tomb, with

DAHSHUR: BOAT WHICH CONVEYED KING USERTESEN'S
MUMMY TO THE PYRAMID. *(Now in the Cairo Museum.)*

ten fine statues larger than life, now in the Cairo Museum. They are all portraits of Usertesen I., who was buried there. It was he who erected the fine obelisk at Heliopolis, which we describe in Chapter VI.

Far away to the south there towered up in solitary grandeur the great perpendicular mass of the Pyramid of Medum. Here the distant Nile appeared in serpentine windings, and in one of these bends the great Medum Pyramid stood enthroned on a platform of rock some 250 feet above the river, rising out of the white mound that surrounded it. I had often seen this imposing object from the Nile. It seems to dominate everything for a whole day as one slowly sails up or down the river. As the Nile winds, the great Medum Pyramid seems now on the left, now on the right hand, sometimes near at hand, then twenty miles off, and then again close to the river bank. But never did this mysterious " Ultima Thule " of pyramid plateaux look so grand as now, and I decided to visit it without loss of time. So I slowly wended my way back to Cairo, securing the services of my faithful Arab

PECTORAL OF USERTESEN II.
(Found at Dahshur.)

guide for the arduous journey of a future day. I inquired everywhere as to the best route. Nobody had ever been to Medum. Everyone, of course, had seen it from the Nile; no pyramid advertises itself like Medum. Petrie had spent several months here, and had written a book about it, but nobody in Cairo had the book, and Petrie could not be found. My guide truthfully avowed that

PAINTED OAR.
(Found with Boat at Dahshur.)

VIEW OF THE PYRAMID OF MEDUM: THE VILLAGE TO THE RIGHT.
(*From a Water-Colour Drawing by the Author.*)

he had been to the Fayum from Sakkarah with a party of sporting English "officers" and passed by the pyramid, but had not visited it. My guide is a good man for finding game, but he is not the least bit of an antiquarian, and therefore I always take him when I can get him, for he is utterly unbiassed. Of course he knows his way about, and speaks Arabic. He is a gentleman, and is nice looking, very particular in his dress, and as clean as an Englishman is expected to be. So we started by rail for Wasta, where it was supposed camels or donkeys could be got. But camels were not to be obtained. One awful humped animal appeared, a beggarly account of shreds and patches, all skin (where there were no holes in it), and bones stretching out everywhere. We could not both ride on one camel, and such a camel! Then we inspected the donkeys. They were about the size of goats, and as skinny and bony as the ancient camel. We selected two of the least appalling skeletons, and we then demanded saddles, innocently. Then we were told that a saddle had never been seen in Wasta. The word for saddle, "berda," seemed unknown here. So we had to start on bare-backed, angular-sectioned donkeys, so small that our toes could almost touch the ground. To ride a lean, bare-backed donkey without stirrups is painful in many ways. After ten miles of this purgatorial procession we seemed almost at our pyramid, when, lo! a canal came in our way, and we had to make a long detour, and after numerous zigzags and advances by parallel lines at right angles to the pyramid, we found ourselves at the foot of the enormous white mounds from which it seems to rise when seen from a distance. These are entirely composed of chippings of the beautiful white Tourah stone, of which the courses of the outer casing were composed. All this casing has disappeared, but in 1891, during his masterly survey of the district, Petrie discovered, deep down under the banks of the débris, and twenty feet outward from the present almost vertical sides, a number of the ancient casing blocks in their original position, and I had the pleasure of seeing these. The original slope of the completed pyramid had the same angle as that of the Pyramids of Gizeh. Now we see only the great core of nearly perpendicular masonry in several tiers, beautifully built without mortar, and of huge blocks fitting so closely that a knife-edge would scarcely be admitted into the joints. The work is as good as in the Great Pyramid of Gizeh, though the principles of construction are entirely different. It is believed to be much more ancient. Dr. Petrie advances several theories as to its possibly being one of the earliest of such structures, and others that it was a sort of experiment in pyramid-building. He supposes it to be a glorified and enlarged "mastaba" made into a pyramid by adding successive stages. Whether these theories be right or wrong, the result is grand. Even in its present ruined state it is by far the most commanding and imposing of all the pyramids. Seen from a distance, it seems to dominate the whole country and hold itself aloft on the finest situation for such a monument in all the land of Egypt. When one is close to it or under it, its vast sides seem to tower up to the skies, inaccessible. No one has climbed to its summit. It is the eyrie of a brood of eagles. The utter loneliness of the old-world monument, never visited by mankind, suits the solitary king of birds for the dwelling of himself and his secluded family. Dr. Petrie thinks that it is the tomb of Sneferu, a king who reigned 3990 B.C., but it is probably much older. But, if this be No. 1 of good pyramid-building, how did masons arrive at such perfection, for it is a masterpiece? No "'prentice hand's" attempt is here. It is the perfection of strength and wise construction. Not a crack or "settlement" of any kind in the whole work. It is as strong and sound as when it left its builders' hands 5,000 or 6,000 years ago.

The Temple of the Medum Pyramid was on the east, contrary to later usage. It was found by Petrie, and was nearly perfect. It had been used and restored during Dynasty XVIII., but, unfortunately, Ramses the Great, of the Nineteenth Dynasty, began to destroy the splendid pyramid, stealing the stone for his own buildings. Spoliation has gone on from that day to this, and the mounds of stonecutters' chippings, forty feet deep, show the wicked work, and the little temple was buried underneath them. The door Dr. Petrie found on the north side was also buried beneath the ruins, but is now accessible. The

FROM MEDUM: THE OLDEST PICTURE IN THE WORLD. (*Now in the Cairo Museum.*)

name of Sneferu was found in various places in the internal passages, and also in the little temple on the east side, and its discoverer is confident it was his pyramid.

Evidences were not wanting to prove that the old thefts of stone still go on, and the Government have no officer on the spot to prevent this spoliation. So Petrie buried his discoveries again, as Mariette had done. But visitors to the Cairo Museum can see the wonderful statues of Rahotep and his wife Nefert (the beautiful), which were found at Medum. He is a handsome, dignified gentleman, and the lady well deserves her name. She is a good—

and sweet—looking woman. The limestone is beautifully painted, and the eyes, being of glass, are wondrously lifelike. The whole is as fresh as when executed 6,000 years ago. Rahotep's tomb was beautifully decorated, and is one of the oldest known. The very hieroglyphics were painted in the natural colours of the animals and objects represented, and thus have contributed largely to identify their meaning. The artist must have been an adept in natural history. A tomb found here by Mariette had for its background a marvellous painting of a flock of geese, which is the best thing of its kind in this Museum and the oldest picture in the world. The wooden carved portraits of Hesy, far older than the time of Sneferu, and yet of even better work, are also from Medum and are worth attention. There is a wonderful wooden statue of a man, which may be called a speaking likeness. It is named " The Sheikh," as it resembled the head man of the village, near Medum, where it was found. Medum is forty miles from Cairo, thirty from ancient Memphis. Whether the great folk buried there were citizens of Memphis

"THE SHEIKH EL BELED."
Wooden Statue found at Medum.

or of some other lost city we cannot say. Perhaps many of them lived before
Memphis was founded. One at least of these men was lieutenant over the
Fayum oasis, about twenty miles away. Among other trophies of sport, two
servants are shown bearing an enormous fish between them. The finny monster
has a pole thrust through his snout, and is so heavy that the stout pole bends
beneath its weight. I have myself seen in the Fayum similar fishes which
were caught in the lake in the Libyan Desert. They were more than five feet
long and about twenty inches deep. I could tell more of the wonders of Medum,
but I might weary my readers. I remained on the great terrace of the pyramid
till the day began to wane. My guide and I were the only human beings on
the scene. A wretched village some miles off seemed deserted; it rises up
like an island from the plain, and it is actually surrounded with water at high
Nile. It is, however, a striking object, with its drab mounds and the minaret of
its little mosque, rising up out of the dark green grove of date-palm that surrounds
the islet. The Nile was low and far off at this time; the only water at hand was
a very dark, greasy-looking pool. The villagers use this as a bath (I saw the
urchins bathing), as a washing-place, for washing-day was being celebrated,
and also for drinking purposes, for the women were carrying on their heads
the jars filled for the evening meal. Fortunately we had brought good water
with us, and brewed our own tea in a tomb before descending from the pyramid.
We had another agonising ride on our serrated donkeys, but in due time we
reached the railway station, after a fatiguing day, but one of the most interesting
experiences of Egyptian travel. The next time I visit Medum, I shall provide
myself with saddles beforehand and supply my own donkeys from Cairo. I
shall take a tent, and encamp in the desert for a week at least. I mention
this as my advice to future pilgrims to Medum.

Dr. Petrie's magnificent book on the wonders of Medum is out of print.
He should reprint it; there would now be a greater demand than when he
published it in 1892. His work at this place was
one of the great explorer's chief successes. Fortunately his Egyptian History, vol. i., supplies much
information regarding this rarely-visited spot.
Some day a decent inn may be established in
Wasta, for the journey is too much for one
day. Saddle donkeys may be
obtainable in time, and the
Government may re-open the
tombs and place them under
reliable guardians.

Mastaba, with succes-
sive tiers of masonry
added till the stepped
outline was attained
to carry the smooth
outward casing.

DR. PETRIE'S SUGGESTION OF CONSTRUCTION OF
PYRAMID OF MEDUM.

CHAPTER V.

THE OASIS OF ROSES.

MEDINET-EL-FAYUM.

SCENE ON THE BAHR YUSUF, IN THE CENTRE OF THE TOWN.

THE FAYUM—THE PYRAMIDS OF ILLAHUN AND HAWARA—
MEDINET-EL-FAYUM—BIAHMU—
BEGIG OBELISK—LAKE QURUN—ROMAN CITIES—
THE LIBYAN DESERT.

OLD ILLAHUN REGULATOR AT THE POINT WHERE THE BAHR YUSUF ENTERS
THE FAYUM. ILLAHUN PYRAMID IN THE DISTANCE.

(Major Brown believes that this was the site of the sluices which in ancient times controlled the canals so as to act as a Reservoir for storing the Nile's surplus waters.)

CHAPTER V.

THE FAYUM: THE OASIS OF ROSES.

THIS wonderful oasis—an emerald isle of fertility far away in the surrounding wastes of the Libyan Desert—is seldom visited by tourists.* Now and then in spring small parties of young English military men run down for a few days' quail-shooting. Several times in the season—that is, from January to March— a German or Russian prince, a rich American citizen, or a sporting British nobleman may organise an expedition with camels, tents, and the orthodox accompaniment of Arab attendants for a bit of desert life. These generally take the desert route, starting from the great pyramid-field of Gizeh. Thence they journey by the desert, passing the pyramid groups of Abusir, Sakkarah, Dahshur, and Medum, and cross the cemeteries where sleep the kings and nobles of ancient Memphis. They then strike across the wild waste of billowy sand, till at length the green Fayum gladdens the sight. The trip requires a fortnight, at least, and the camping out at night under the glorious starry sky is not the least part of the pleasure. The air is dry, and no dew falls. It is safe to sleep in the open, the Arabs say, but the nights are very cold, and the shelter of the tent is welcome. The Arab merely rolls himself in his blanket and

---

* Dr. Petrie published several volumes on the Fayum, but they, like so many of his monumental works, are out of print and very scarce. His *History of Egypt*, vol. i., however, gives much of their information. But for the tourist, Major Brown's book is best of guide books for the Fayum, having admirable maps, classic lore, the essence of Petrie's discoveries, and the modern experiences of a great engineer who has restored fertility to the province, all combined in a most interesting manner. (Stanford, London, 10s. 6d.)

My friend Major Brown, R.E., now Director-General of Irrigation, gave me his admirable work on the Fayum, of which province he was Irrigation Officer for several years. I was so fascinated with his history of the strange old province, and interested in his description of its modern aspect and his account of the antiquities recently discovered there, that I immediately determined to visit the place, and found his book a perfect guide. Major Brown tells in his book that modern inventions for raising water were found to be more costly and quite inferior to the ancient methods. He accordingly adopted the old systems in almost every case, restoring the old works. The Bahr Yusuf was cleared out and deepened, the sluices were

HIGH LIFT SELF-ACTING WATER-WHEEL.
(Photo. by Major Brown.)

rebuilt on the ancient foundations, and the result is that the Fayum has become, as of old, one of the richest provinces of Egypt, and has a constantly-increasing revenue. The area under cultivation increases every season as ancient canals are restored, and there seems to be no limit to the extension. Many ruins of cities, their names forgotten, remain far away in the desert, marking out the great highways which led to cultivated tracts.* These cities were about ten miles apart; a canal had supplied them with water, and the land had been richly cultivated. All around now is drifting sand. Once bring the blessed sweet water back and all the desert will become amenable to cultivation. This dream of future richness is likely to be realised. The waters of the old Bahr Yusuf will soon be doubled in volume, and will then pour their fertilising flood round the sites of the ancient cities, and they, after 2,000 years of ruin, may again be habitable. The great dams in process of construction at Assouan and Assiout will raise the Nile after the time of flood, impounding its waters which are now allowed to run waste to the Mediterranean.

---

* Dr. Petrie discovered, far away in the desert, a well-made Roman road, leading northwards from the Fayum to the Delta, marked out with milestones. It is now buried in the sand, but could possibly be restored to use, or made to carry a line of light railway.

E

VIEW IN MEDINET EL-FAYUM.
Bahr Yusuf Canal passing through the town, a rapid stream.

This great engineering feat will do what natural barriers did, many of which have been swept away since the ancient days. Possibly the planners of the ancient Lake Moeris may have had artificial dykes or dams to perform the same office ; in any case they had more control of the flood of the Nile than now exists, and they certainly turned its surplus waters to more account. The great reservoirs now being constructed at Assouan and Assiout will, however, remedy all deficiencies, will add millions of acres to cultivation, and no part of Egypt will benefit more than the Fayum. The whole of the district is a curious natural depression, much beneath the level of the Mediterranean, which of course simplifies the supplying of water once it is conducted from the Nile. The water entering at the lowest irrigation-level rushes from the sluices with great force. It is utilised to drive undershot water-wheels as it passes to the low-lying lands. These wheels elevate the water, by means of pottery buckets, to the highest-level conduits, some thirty feet above. The waste water supplies the middle levels. Nor is this all. The force of the lowermost stream is utilised to drive a number of grain mills along the watercourse. The whole apparatus is automatic, and is at work night and day perpetually. This is the ancient system, and, like others peculiar to the province, has been found incapable of improvement. All that now remains of the ancient Lake Moeris is known as the Lake Qurun, about thirty miles in length and eight or ten wide. This is west of the Fayum province, away in the Libyan desert. The lake must have been vastly larger in ancient times, for its former coastline is marked miles off in the desert by ruins of towns, former ports, with quays and piers for commerce. These quays are now actually 150 feet above the level of the lake. As they are Graeco-Roman towns they show the level of the ancient lake in those days. The waters of the existing Lake Qurun are remarkably salt, and contain inexhaustible supplies of extraordinary fish of various species. One variety resembling roach is found, which often exceeds five feet in length and thirty inches in depth, with eyes four inches round and scales to correspond. A sort of eel resembling a dogfish exceeds six feet in length, and is like a man's leg for girth. Many other varieties of aquatic monsters of brilliant hues and extraordinary shapes were lying on the bank when I was there. A great take had just been brought to bank. They seemed all alive, and the snapping of their great mouths was unpleasantly suggestive of bites. They are caught on iron hooks nearly a foot long, fastened to stout beams imbedded in the shallow waters. These are baited overnight, and the great fish are lifted off by several men in the early morning and hauled in with ropes. A tax is levied on these fisheries, which brings in upwards of £3,000 a year to the Government, and one day's haul will frequently require a train of trucks to convey the fish to Cairo, where it finds a ready sale. The fishermen are not much removed from naked savages. With unkempt locks and scantily clothed in skins, they seem a fierce lot. I had a voyage on the lake in one of their rude craft, which floated quite high out of the water owing to its briny saltness. When a short way from the land, on our return, these wild wretches refused to put me ashore without an enormous " baksheesh." My Arab servant agreed diplomatically, and, when we landed after some delay, left the money in the hands of a police officer, who threatened to imprison them for their extortion, gave them a small gratuity, and returned my money.

Herodotus describes the wonders of the Labyrinth, which was in this province; also statues and pyramids which he visited and which were perfect in his day. For many years these were not believed to have existed, but recently Dr. Petrie discovered where the Labyrinth, of which Herodotus told such wondrous tales, had been situated, but it was completely effaced. The country around was covered for miles with chippings of its beautiful white stone, different from anything in the district. A town had been built there 2,000

years ago, as proved by inscriptions on coffins and tombstones in Greek, Latin, and Demotic. For more than a century a colony of stonecutters had sawed up and sold the huge blocks of white limestone, using the great temple as a quarry to build distant Alexandria, until not one morsel of it remained larger than mere chippings.

FAYUM: CAMELS LADEN WITH CLOVER.

E 2

Herodotus also described
certain pyramids with great colossi of the kings who had
made them.   He supposed the
colossi were erected on the
pyramids.   This is explained
ingeniously by Dr. Petrie, who
says Herodotus possibly visited
them ·when the Nile was in
flood, when the statues, on

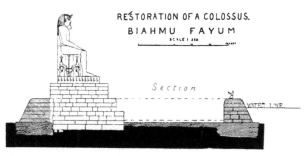

RESTORATION OF A COLOSSUS.
BIAHMU FAYUM

Section

WATER LINE.

DR. PETRIE'S RESTORATION OF ONE OF THE COLOSSI.

their pedestals with slanting sides, might appear to rise out of the water.   As
to there being either pyramids or colossi, the stories of Herodotus were doubted
for 2,000 years.   It remained for Petrie to discover their site and their ruins,
and to re-establish the credit of the Father of History.   Wanton violence had
destroyed these great effigies of the king who developed a poor marshy oasis
into a fruitful province, or who may have discovered that there was an extraordinary depression in the desert, to which it was possible to convey the surplus
waters of the Nile by gravitation.   Herodotus distinctly tells us that in his
time, and for thousands of years before, the Lake Moeris had been used to
receive water in time of the inundation, and to give it back to the cultivable
land during low Nile.   This cannot be done now, but doubtless it was done
in ancient days, when the great river ran at a different level.   However, in
remoter times than Amenemhat and Usertesen, no doubt the Fayum was
used as a reservoir.   The king who seems to have achieved the greatest works

was Amenemhat III., who lived about
2600 B.C.   He occupied himself in re-
claiming a large district from the then

ANCIENT RUINS OF THE COLOSSI PEDESTALS, BIAHMU.

great Lake Moeris. He put an immense tract of this new land under rich cultivation, colonized it with agriculturists, built a town and quays and piers for the commerce of what remained of the lake. This town he called "Shed," meaning that it had been "cut off,"—gained from the lake. He was so proud of his work that he erected two great stone platforms (the "pyramids" of Herodotus), to be used as quays, possibly, and on each he placed a colossal statue of himself. The pedestals of each, or their remains,

CYLINDER OF USERTESEN II. AND AMENEMHAT III.
(Dynasty XII.)
(In the Author's Collection.)

are still to be seen. They enclosed a court or terrace, and a quay seems to have stood alongside; this was then on the margin of the lake.

Dr. Petrie detected, among the pulverised granite fragments which lie about

PORTRAIT OF AMENEMHAT III.
(The original is at St. Petersburg.)

the yellow stone pedestals, the nose of one and some other parts of another colossus, and various little fragments, from which he had no difficulty in restoring (in imagination) the statues complete. The huge feature and other fragments are now preserved in the Ashmolean Museum, Oxford. The statues were of different shades of red granite, which enabled Petrie to prove that the fragments belonged to two statues. They both exceeded forty feet in height, and were monoliths brought from far Assouan.

Amenemhat III. and Usertesen II., the two great monarchs who made the Lake Moeris and the fortune of the province, were so devoted to the Fayum that they built their funerary temples and tombs at the entrance of the canal which gave the land its life. One of these is the pyramid of Illahun, in which Petrie found the remains of King Usertesen II., and the other is that of Hawara, in which were the bones of Amenemhat III. I bought from a native a notable cylinder with the names of these two kings clearly told in hieroglyphics; and by Dr. Petrie's kindness I am enabled to supply a portrait of the greatest of these kings, taken from his *History*

GOLD COIN OF ARSINOË PHILADELPHUS.
(Found in the Fayum.)

lies down to sleep on the sand, with a watchfire burning near to keep off the hyena or other unfriendly nocturnal visitor. Ordinary mortals, however, can reach the Fayum by railway from Cairo to the station of Medinet-el-Fayum at a small expense in a day's journey. Once there, it is well worth a fortnight's stay. A clean inn is to be found at Medinet-el-Fayum, the only town. It does not boast many comforts, and certainly is not encumbered with furniture, but, as in the East the more furniture the more insects, it is better to dispense with a superabundance of both. After the desert it is a pleasant contrast to find one's self in a land of running waters, amid the noise of streams, the plash of rapid brooks of clear crystal, and the music of countless water-wheels. Herds of many animals—camels, buffaloes, horses, sheep, well-bred kine, and goats,— testify to the growing riches of the fellaheen under the British management of this prosperous province. There are no banks, and their savings are invested in this kind of moveable stock. The town has a branch of an ancient canal running through it, and is situated in a forest of palms and other trees, surrounded by meadows and cultivated fields, all permeated with rivulets of sweet water brought from the distant Nile by the oldest canal in the world. This is the Bahr Yusuf, the famed *Water of Joseph*, said to have been the work of the great Hebrew when his people were a power in the land, and the persecuted son of the Patriarch Jacob had risen to be Grand Vizier of the Land of Egypt. No doubt Joseph found the great irrigation canal in need of repair, and did so much for it that it henceforth bore his name, for recent discoveries have proved that it was planned and doing its beneficent work long before the time of Joseph. When Herodotus visited Egypt (430 B.C.) he found the irrigation works of Lake Moeris in full operation, and has left us a clear and intelligent account of what he saw and heard of the wonderful buildings in the neighbourhood. He tells us they had existed for 2,000 years before his time. Great engineers they must have had, at least as clever surveyors as ourselves.

BRICK PYRAMID OF ILLAHUN: ENTRANCE OF THE FAYUM,
In which Dr. Petrie discovered the tomb of Usertesen II. (Twelfth Dynasty, 660 B.C.).

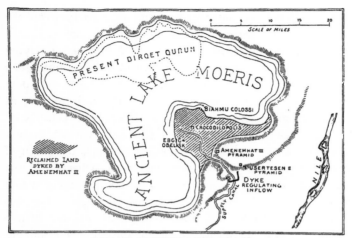

MAP OF ANCIENT LAKE MOERIS.
The shaded part shows the land reclaimed from the Lake by Amenemhat III.
(From Petrie's "History of Egypt.")

of Egypt, vol. i. The cylinder was doubtless a royal sign manual given to the officer who was entrusted with command of the irrigation works of the province, which was, in these remote days, the richest in Egypt, as it soon will be again. The two pyramids are now mere heaps of sunbaked bricks. All their casing of white polished stone has been stolen long ago. But in his excavations round the rubbish at the bases of both of the Fayum pyramids Dr. Petrie found the lower courses of Tourah stone still remaining *in situ.*

In later days the people who inhabited the Græco-Roman towns of the Fayum made mummies of their dead, and painted outside their coffins the portraits of their dear ones. Hundreds of such were dug up, and the portraits, done in oil or wax, brought away. Several of them are in our National Gallery, in the British Museum, and the Cairo Museum. These are by far the oldest oil portraits in the world. When I visited this district I sheltered from the sun in a large house, owned by a wealthy agriculturist, which possessed a small steam engine. The boiler was fed by wooden coffins 2,000 years

CAMPING SCENE IN THE FAYUM.

GRÆCO-ROMAN PORTRAIT FROM
HAWARA NECROPOLIS.
(*From a Coffin.*)

GRÆCO-ROMAN PORTRAIT FROM
HAWARA NECROPOLIS.
(*From a Coffin.*)

old, each one of which had the fragments of the portraits still adhering. The yard was full of the coffins and remains of the mummies, which, being preserved in pitch or bitumen, formed good stoking material. Some of the coffins, Dr. Petrie found, were made of " cartonnage," or papier mâché, of old documents. These proved to be ancient papyri pasted together into a sort of cardboard, and among them, when carefully separated, were found many Greek manuscripts, and especially one treasure, the earliest manuscript of Plato yet known to exist. But recently more wonderful documents turned up. It was in the Fayum neighbourhood (at the old Greek town of Oxyrhynchus) that Messrs. Grenfell and Hunt, agents for the Egypt Exploration Fund, recently discovered an immense mass of papyrus documents (filling sixty or seventy boxes), among which fragments of the lost works of classic poets were discovered two years ago. These manuscripts were found in the rubbish heaps of the forgotten town. The dry, sandy desert had buried the place but preserved the documents, as is only possible in a rainless country. They are now mostly in England, but will take several years to arrange and translate. Two pages of " Sayings of Christ," possibly part of a gospel not yet fully identified, were found. Upwards of 1,500 papyri have been discovered, and the few examined already have yielded remarkable results—a page of St. Matthew's Gospel earlier by 200 years than any other MS. of the New Testament, a poem of Sappho, fragments of Homer, Herodotus, Xenophon, Sophocles, Thucydides, Demosthenes, Plato, Aristotle, Euclid, Virgil, and others. It is the most wonderful collection of ancient MSS. ever found in modern times. Many of them have already helped to explain existing texts, and others give entirely new readings. A volume of fac-similes and translations has just been issued by the Egypt Exploration Fund, but it is impossible to tell what literary treasures may yet remain to be discovered as the work of decipherment proceeds. Anyone subscribing about £1 a year can obtain these publications from the Fund.

PRESENT STATE OF THE BEGIG OBELISK.

In later days the town "Shed" became "Crocodilopolis," and the priests made the crocodile a sacred animal. It is conjectured that, as the irrigation of this province was important, the necessity of providing numbers of tanks of fresh water was essential. Now the waters of the Lake Moeris, having no outlet, were salt. As crocodiles can only live in fresh water, the priests made the hideous creatures an object of worship. In the Cairo Museum there is a painting of a young mother offering her infant to a crocodile, giving her dearest in sacrifice to the deity she was taught by her faith to appease by this act of devotion. In Ptolemaic times the name of the town was changed again. The province was then given as a dowry to Queen Arsinoë, and the town was called after this celebrated princess. In still later times, the last Egyptian Queen, the lovely and unfortunate Cleopatra, drew the revenues of the Fayum to purchase cosmetics, it is said; most probably for her privy purse. She gave banquets at Alexandria, where the couches of the guests were adorned with garlands of roses, from the Fayum. At intervals, showers of them were allowed to fall in the apartments, and in her progresses through the streets the course was bedded with sweet-smelling roses. Then, and before this time, the province was known as "The Oasis of Roses." In later days the district was neglected, the ancient city shrunk to a mere country town or village, which the name "Medineh" signifies. There are huge mounds of grey rubbish, with much broken pottery, which mark the extent of the various ancient towns that existed near where "Medinet el-Fayum" now stands, and possibly many buried records of the past may some day be discovered in them. I possess a very beautiful gold coin of Arsinoë, with a fine portrait of this great princess. It was discovered by an Arab among some ancient buildings in the town, probably the ruins of Arsinoë's palace. It was possibly buried under the foundation-

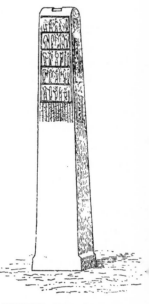

OBELISK OF USERTESEN I.
AT BEGIG.
(Restored by Mariette.)

stone when the pal-
ace was built, and
is as fresh and
sharp as when it
left the mint 2,200
years ago. Future
visitors may or may
not pick up similar
treasures.

The Fayum
seems to have been
first developed by a

THE FAYUM: VIEW ON LAKE QURUN,
With its rude boats, and rough planks which are used as oars.

still earlier king of the wonderful Twelfth Dynasty, Usertesen I. About 2750 B.C.
this great builder erected many obelisks at Heliopolis, of which one yet remains.
Some have supposed that obelisks were typical of sunrise, or the origin of life,
while pyramids were emblems of sunset, or death. But a text at Edfou states
that they were intended as lightning conductors!

When we come, however, to examine the Fayum granite monolith, it is not
a real obelisk in form, but a stele—a standing stone recording the great works
done or to be done in this remote oasis. I subjoin a restored outline of its
original form; it is now broken up, and lies ignominiously in a field near a
village called Begig, and is often covered with water. Major Brown tells me
that he recently excavated the ground from about it, and discovered the granite
base or plinth on which the obelisk had stood. The change in the level of
the water had buried it several feet underground.

I have alluded to the enormous fish still caught in Lake Qurun. I append a
copy of a drawing of such monsters, which was found in the tomb of an ancient
gentleman who was officially employed in this province 5,000 years ago. This
was copied by the ubiquitous Dr. Petrie in the Medum cemetery, and his
volume contains many coloured illustrations
of the life in this province about 5,000
years ago.

A thick fog lay over the lake when I
visited it, with threatening of a sand storm,
so I was unable to reach the opposite
bank. But I am enabled to give some
illustrations of the strange cities whose
ruins mark out the ancient limits of the
Lake Moeris of Roman times.

ANCIENT PAINTING FROM MEDUM.
(Representing the fish of Lake Moeris.)

ANCIENT RUINS OF A TOWN OR SEAPORT
In the Western Desert beyond Lake Qurun.

My son made an interesting tent expedition this year to the Fayum, and brought home some photographs of the ancient buildings and highways, and the piers and quays, now found 150 feet above the present level of the lake, and also some interesting views of this delightful province. The western side of the lake is now a howling wilderness, but the richly cultivated land on the eastern side is full of running streams. It is still as it was in old times—full of wild flowers. There are now many more canals in progress preparing for the coming increase of Nile water. Major Hanbury Brown hopes to not only restore its ancient fertility, but to make it, for all future time, what it was in the past, the most advanced agricultural province of Egypt. One cannot but be struck, in travelling over this interesting district, with the enormous accumulations of Nile mud—forty feet high in some places. With irrigation abundantly applied, all these reserves of rich soil would become useful as fertile land, after having lain barren for several thousand years. The cultivation improves every day, and a company has been formed to lay down light railways all over the province. The Fayum's ancient prosperity will soon return, and, doubtless, be exceeded. The light railways will be a great advantage; at present there are no roads, only tracks through the fields. All the officials were natives; there was not a European in the province save

ANCIENT ROMAN CITY, ROAD, AND QUAY
In the Western Desert beyond Lake Qurun.

SCENE ON THE BORDERS OF THE DESERT: EVENING.

THE FAYUM.
Flocks and herds returning home at evening along one of the ancient dykes.

the Greek shop-keepers, who are found all over Egypt; but they could not speak English. When I was there it was necessary to have introductions to some native dignitaries, who showed me much kindness. They supplied me with donkey, camel, horse, dogcart, etc., as the roads or tracks permitted. But all this will soon be changed by the light-railway system, part of which is already at work, and the travelling public will soon be able to visit the Fayum without such formalities. The first thing to be done to popularise this interesting and little-known province would be to build a hotel, and put it under efficient management, so that a residence of a week might be made. All the excursions can be made from Medinet with facility, being a good central point.

LAKE QURUN: DISTANT VIEW OF THE LIBYAN DESERT.

CHAPTER VI.

THE ANCIENT CITY OF ANNU, OR ON.

THE KING OF UPPER AND LOWER EGYPT CARRIED ON THE SHOULDERS OF
HIS BODY-GUARD.

He is attended by the royal fan-bearers. The soldiers have their helmets decorated with ostrich feathers.

HELIOPOLIS—THE VIRGIN'S TREE—THE OSTRICH FARM—
THE MAKING OF SOLDIERS FOR THE SOUDAN CAMPAIGNS IN ANCIENT
AND MODERN TIMES.

CHAPTER VI.

HELIOPOLIS—THE VIRGIN'S WELL—THE MAKING OF PEASANTS INTO SOLDIERS.

THE OBELISK, HELIO-
POLIS.
Erected by Usertesen I.

ONE of the most interesting short excursions in the vicinity of Cairo is the drive to the site of the ancient city of Annu, or On, which the Greeks called Heliopolis. It was sacred to the sun-god Ra, and the Greek name is merely a translation of its ancient title—the City of the Sun. It was well known to the Hebrews and is frequently mentioned in the Bible. In Genesis xli. 45 it is called On, but in Jeremiah xliii. 13, the name is translated literally, " House of the Sun." The holy temple was perhaps the most ancient in Egypt, and its priests were long celebrated for their learning. It had a famous university, which was possibly the place where Moses studied "all the wisdom of the Egyptians." When Joseph sought to raise himself by matrimonial alliance he espoused the daughter of the high priest of On, very possibly a distinguished professor of the great university. Being in or very near to the "Land of Goshen" of the Bible, " On " seems to have had a large population of Jews, and as it was a rich and flourishing Egyptian city at a very early date, doubtless its inhabitants were those from whom the Israelites unscrupulously borrowed the gold and jewels, which was afterwards known as the "Spoiling of the Egyptians." It was on the ancient road from the East to the Nile, and Alexander the Great halted here on his journey from Pelusium to Memphis. But long before his time, Cambyses, with his hordes of Persians, destroyed and conquered it. It was even then on the wane, and doubtless they despoiled the rich treasury of the ancient city. It never seems to have been as great after the Persian invasion. But although they ruined the city (about 525 B.C.), they seemed to have spared the temple and university, for we find them existing in the time of Herodotus, who visited the place about 430 B.C. Plato, in his search for knowledge, went to study there, and resided thirteen years, it is said ; his

(79)

PORTRAIT OF USERTESEN I.
From Abydos.
(From Dr. Petrie's " History of Egypt.")

house was pointed out to Strabo, who describes his own visit (40 A.D.) to the decaying site of ancient learning. But the renown of Heliopolis was much reduced in the time of the Ptolemies, and, instead of rebuilding or repairing the sacred buildings here, as they did in other Egyptian cities, they despoiled the temple, carrying off many of its obelisks to beautify Alexandria. In this way the one obelisk we possess—that on the Thames Embankment—was removed from Heliopolis, possibly with many others, 250 years B.C. Fortunately, one obelisk still remains on the original site, and it now stands the only remnant of the ancient City of the Sun. There was a second great obelisk here, but it was destroyed by the Arabs a few centuries ago. This is the oldest of all obelisks, fully 1,000 years older than the one on the Thames Embankment. Its vast age is undoubted, and the object in erecting it is fully recorded, four times over, on its sides in hieroglyphic characters, with the king's name, Usertesen I., who erected it, clearly given. It is a monolith of Assouan granite, nearly 70 feet high. The soil has been recently excavated so as to expose the foundation and the entire inscription. Till lately ten feet of the monument was under ground, and at high Nile under water, owing to the change of the level of the inundation since it was erected 4,300 years ago. This sublime monument is the only sculptured relic left of the great city of Heliopolis. It is difficult to account for the entire disappearance of the city and a great temple. But it was long used as a quarry, and many of the houses of modern Cairo, in Ismail's time, were built with stone of Heliopolis, from a temple of Nectanebo.

Obelisks were the emblem of the Creator, and of the Sun, as His greatest representative. They were already venerated in the time of the Ancient Egyptian Empire, and this, the most ancient seat of religion and learning, seems to have had quite a number of them. They were worshipped as the personification, so to speak, of the great God of heaven and earth. Long before Usertesen's time, Shepses-kaf, a king of the Fourth Dynasty (3740 B.C.), is recorded to have erected and dedicated three obelisks to Ra (the Sun), and to have endowed a priesthood especially for the religious services connected with them. Pepi I. (VI. Dynasty,

3500 B.C.) set up an obelisk at " Annu " (Heliopolis). Tombs of priests have been found, on the other side of the Nile, who were specially appointed to conduct the religious services in connection with these monuments. There were many obelisks erected in the flourishing times of the great Eighteenth Dynasty, but those at Luxor and Karnak were all imitations of the much more ancient obelisks of Heliopolis. There are many obelisks in Rome, Constantinople, and other European cities. Most of them were brought from Alexandria, but it is believed the greater number originally came from Heliopolis. So it is very interesting in this home of those

wonderful monuments, all of which were brought 600 miles down the Nile—from the granite quarries of Assouan—that at least one is left to us on the spot where its pious founder placed it so many thousand years ago.

At Thebes an interesting record of an obelisk has been discovered in the tomb of an overseer connected with the erection and construction of one, who was so proud of his skill that he had a picture of his work engraved to show the gods the great labours of his life, lest they might be overlooked in a future state.

At Assouan a similar granite obelisk is to be seen, partly cut out of the living rock, but abandoned because of some flaw in the stone. We may imagine what the Temple of Heliopolis may have been like from remains of a building erected by Usertesen at Koptos, not far from Denderah. There Dr.

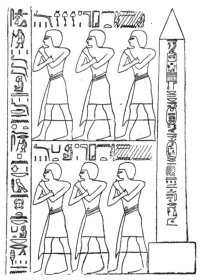

THE OVERSEERS AND OFFICERS CONNECTED WITH THE ERECTION AND CONSTRUCTION OF AN OBELISK.
(From a Tomb at Thebes.)

Petrie found a slab, of which we give a photograph, which shows Usertesen performing a religious dance before a deity and gives us some notion of what excellent work the old temple here must have possessed. The original can be seen in the Museum of University College, London. Usertesen is here represented as engaged in some act of worship before the great deity Min. He here wears the crown of Lower Egypt, and is possibly returning thanks for some victory. This portrait of him is very expressive. In the other portrait of the king (page 80) he is seen wearing the crown of Upper Egypt only. There may, perhaps, be remains of the great temple of On underground, as no exhaustive excavations have been made, and ten to fifteen feet of Nile mud would entomb much of the ancient structures. Mounds of rubbish and broken

F

pottery form a parallelo-
gram of about 4,000 feet
square, which mark the
ancient temple
enclosure ; but
the city must
have extended
much farther
than this. The
obelisk now
stands almost
as perfect as
when erected.
Instead of be-
ing in the cen-
tre of a popu-
lous city it is

USERTESEN I. DANCING BEFORE MIN.
Carving from the Temple of Koptos
discovered by Dr. Petrie.
(*Original in University College, London.*)

now found among corn and clover fields and in the midst of a fertile plain.
The Nile surrounds it like a sea during the inundation,
only the great mounds (showing the girdle walls of
the old seat of learning, and beyond them the heaps
that mark the ancient town) being above the
water. Its necropolis has not been scientifically searched, if it, indeed, has been found
at all.   The few tombs discovered cannot
be the burial places of the millions
that once lived in a city that had
possibly much more than 5,000
years of healthy existence.
What a splendid effect its
great temple and obelisks must
have had, standing as they did,
high up out of the desert, on
a raised terrace ! As late as
1200 A.D. the obelisks retained
their bronze-gilt cappings, and
an Arabian traveller of that
date describes their splendour
and what he saw of the ruins

UNFINISHED
OBELISK
In the Granite
Quarries of
Assouan.

of the ancient city. Recently a leather roll has been found in a tomb, describing how King Usertesen I., in the third year of his reign, "stretched the cord and laid the line of the foundations" of his great temple here, but it evidently refers to its being the restoration of a much earlier structure.

As I have said above, Heliopolis was situated on the ancient road from Egypt to Syria. The obelisks and their golden cappings must have proved a landmark from afar across the perfectly level country and distant desert. Of all the great buildings of this seat of learning of almost pre-historic times, this one majestic shaft alone remains. There it was, an ancient monument, when Abraham passed by on his way to Egypt, and when Moses was being educated at its foot, and when Joseph went to woo his Egyptian bride. There it stood, as now, when another Joseph took his wife and the Holy Child to Egypt for refuge from Herod's persecution. For the ancient place was on the highway from Palestine to the Nile, and not far off we find the Virgin's well, sheltered by the sacred tree of Mary, under which the holy family rested by the way. The well is undoubtedly of extreme antiquity, and is the only one of pure fresh water in the neighbourhood, the others being brackish. The tree is several centuries old, and is doubtless an offshoot of the original sycamore which has been pointed out as Mary's tree for 1,600 years. When the Empress Eugénie visited Egypt to open the Suez Canal, Ismail Pasha bought this spring and the garden adjoining from the Christian family who had possessed it for centuries, and presented it to the Empress, whose private property it still is. When I

OBELISK.
The only existing remains of the City of Heliopolis.

THE SACRED TREE, WHERE THE VIRGIN AND HOLY CHILD
RESTED DURING THE FLIGHT INTO EGYPT.
The Well is hidden behind the foliage on the left.

saw it first it was a most beautiful place; the sakiya was constantly at work
supplying refreshing water to the adjoining orange gardens. The whole was
surrounded with hedges of roses, and rich verdure abounded everywhere. When
I visited the place this year an ugly high wall had been built round the
little property—the whole beauty of the place was gone. This was done,
I was informed, to "improve the place" for the expected visit of the Emperor
of Germany! The guardians of the sacred place offered me sprigs of the tree
for sale. From these "signs of the times" I fear that the tree, as well as
the beauty of the ancient shrine, is doomed to extinction. As I saw it some
years ago it was one of the most interesting sights in Egypt. The bullocks,
driven by an old picturesque Arab, patiently labouring at the wheel, the
musical cadence of the rude mechanism, the bright stream of pure crystal
water issuing from the chain of brown earthen pots; then the rivulets refreshing the surrounding gardens and giving health all around—the scene was one
of idyllic beauty.

When driving in this district (the whole excursion only occupies three or four
hours) the Ostrich Farm which Ismail founded some thirty years ago is worth
a visit. It is now owned by a Frenchman, who finds that the production

of ostrich feathers can be made a profitable industry. There are nearly a thousand of these queer birds, and they are penned into twenty or more enclosures, according to age. Quaint, downy-yellow creatures are seen just escaping from the shells; then birds of three, six, or twelve months and onwards, progressing up to eight years, when they begin to produce marketable feathers. The male birds are rather dangerous at times, and their wild, fierce eyes can look very mischievously over the enclosing walls of ten feet or so. One of our party entered one of the parks and essayed to photograph an interesting group of parents and their quaint young flock. The attendant said in his presence there would be no danger, but hardly had the snap-shot been fired than the irate father charged ferociously at the camera and its manipulator, causing a hasty retreat.

SCENE IN THE OSTRICH FARM.
Male and female parents and birds of two months.

The birds produce plenty of eggs, but decline to hatch them unaided. A large house is provided, where the hatching is done by artificial incubation. When the young bird chips the shell, the eggs are slipped under one of the laying hens, and the mothers then do their duty of rearing the young birds. Both parents take their share of tending and feeding their offspring with jealous care. The very large birds can overleap the walls, and as the whole colony is situated on the edge of a wide sandy desert constant outlook has to be kept from a platform in the centre of the establishment.

The "farm" itself is a polygonal structure, and the sentinel can see from his elevated position into all the "parks" radiating around him, and thus is general watchman of the whole colony. No decoration is more generally appreciated by the ladies of all countries than the beautiful feathers of these queer, uncouth birds, and seeing that the creature's body is almost destitute of clothing, and that each

one possesses only a few feathers fit for commercial purposes, it is marvellous whence the
world's supplies can come. This is the only
place in North Africa where the animals are
now domesticated and reared for their feathers;
but on a tomb at Thebes there is a repre-
sentation of an ostrich establishment which
must be four or five thousand years old. A
pair of ostriches and their brood are really an

ANCIENT OSTRICH FARM.

interesting subject for study, and the rich black or brown plumes of a well
developed bird are not devoid of beauty; but the ungainly creature seems a
strange object for such decoration, and is one of Nature's whimsical arrangements. Yet the little ones are very pretty, downy and fluffy beings in their
early stages. The young of almost every animal is beautiful.

These strange birds of the African desert seem to have some grotesque
affinity to the camel. They are both used for desert travel in various parts of
Africa. The "Ship of the Desert," that quaint quadruped, so weird and ungainly,
so superciliously viewing mankind, whom he seems to regard as an inferior creation, can yet look lovingly down on its young offspring. And a young camel
trotting beside its mother is one of the prettiest sights imaginable. Its warm,
downy coat, its playful gambols, its soft, gentle eye looking upward to its huge

SCENE IN THE OSTRICH FARM.
Birds of one year.

gaunt parent, the
one so round and
soft, the other so
angular and shag-
gy, is one of the
greatest possible
of contrasts. Does
the young camel
suddenly put on
antiquity? Does
it change in a
night, in a twink-
ling of an eye?
The gradations
of transition are
never seen; it is
one of Nature's
mysteries.

On our way back to Cairo we passed the great barracks where the Soudanese and Fellaheen troops are drilled who did so much towards conquering the Soudan. It was interesting to watch the process going on. Raw recruits, tall, gaunt, wiry creatures, just arrived from the far South, as black as jet, were getting their first experience of the goose-step. They were all so keen and anxious to learn that it seemed an easier task to teach them than to convert white recruits into war material. Then a squad would be seen who had learnt their preliminary drill and marched

SCENE IN THE OSTRICH FARM.
Birds of six months.

already like soldiers. Others, further advanced, were being taught musket practice and how to form squares, to change front, to fire and stand fire, and how to use the bayonet. Such keen pupils were never seen before in barrack yard. When their drill was over, these earnest recruits would assemble in little groups and go all over their lessons again, voluntarily, and so pass their time under the blazing Egyptian sun.

In another part of the barrack square a number of yellow men—"fellaheen" or Egyptian peasants—were being drilled. They did very well, but had not the enthusiasm of their dusky neighbours. What an admirable duty is ours, to be the means of making out of such material a patriotic army to defend its country's borders, its hearths and homes, from the miseries of slavery and the rapacity of the slave-raider—the fiendish cruelty of the Dervish robber-horde and the destroyers of civilisation ! Africa helped to the blessings of peace by its own sons being trained to protect their native land, and taught to wage honest warfare against brutal ignorance and fanatical cruelty ! I saw these native soldiers under and after drill in 1896—of course being drilled by patient British officers.

This year (1899) it was my good fortune to meet on the Nile the black fellows' gallant commander, Colonel Hector Macdonald, who led them to victory at Omdurman. I was charmed by this great soldier's simple, unostentatious manner. When I said that I had seen these fine fellows under drill, in process of being made into soldiers from very raw material; indeed that I could well understand how, under his command, they had made their wonderful change of front in face of the Dervish attack of fanatical ferocity, Macdonald replied : " They are fine fellows, and deserve all the credit. I could lead them like lambs wherever I wanted them to go. I feel towards them as if they were my own fellow-country-men from my native hills of Inverness; I could do anything with them, they are born soldiers. I was proud to have such men and to have helped to train them. But it was the steady work of other British officers before my time that laid the foundation of the making of these Soudanese troops." I would have liked to get snap-shots of these ardent recruits, but could not, as the light was bad.

But in modern Egypt, when anything wants explanation, it is well to refer to the ancient historical documents. So I found what I sought in the Museum, and there learnt how, 5,000 years ago, another Egyptian commander had drilled out of native material two very similar sets of soldiers. Models, exquisitely carved in wood, are shown of two companies—one carrying bows and arrows and another the long Dervish spears and shields still in use in the Soudan. The weapons of the Egyptian soldiers are tipped with bronze, those of the Soudanese with flint. The general who enlisted these savages and made them into soldiers for his country's defence was so proud of his work that he had models made and placed in his tomb, hoping that at the judgment-day the deities would give him eternal life, or at least fair treatment in a future state, for his great work. This remarkable example of the saying " History repeats itself" was found recently by Arab tomb-robbers at Assiout, and by them sold to the Gizeh Museum.

It was with great pleasure that I made the same day the acquaintance of another celebrated military genius of a different type, one who had much to do in bringing about the crushing of the Mahdi's and Khalifa's tyrannical rule. This was Sir F. R. Wingate, the chief of the Intelligence Department. By his skill, his wonderful knowledge of the Soudan, his acquaintance with the languages, customs, and caravan routes, he organised and carried out the escape of Slatin Pasha from the clutches of the Khalifa. The whole story is simply told in Slatin's book " Fire and Sword in the Soudan," which was edited and largely inspired by Major Wingate, as he was then called. Slatin's reports of the strong and weak points of the Dervishes gave the Intelligence Department all it needed to know. Feeling that he owed his liberty and his life to Wingate,

Slatin attached himself to his liberator and became one of the greatest factors in the success of the campaign against the Dervishes.

Sir Reginald Wingate is one of the most popular of soldiers and is beloved by the natives. He lives unostentatiously (and such is everything about him) in Cairo, and a visit to his house is an especial treat. To be taken by himself through his collection of war trophies, of each of which a story has to be told, is indeed an interesting experience. The pulpit from which the Mahdi preached is there, an erection of deal boards, not much the worse for wear; the armour and the saddle of Abdullah, the best of the Dervish generals, on which

TWO COMPANIES OF SOLDIERS RAISED BY A GENERAL OF FIVE THOUSAND YEARS
AGO FOR SOUDANESE WARFARE.
One is of black men, the other of yellow fellaheen.
(*From a Tomb of the Old Empire at Mêr, near Assiout. Now in Cairo Museum.*)

he was sitting when killed; swords and spears, arrows and lances, guns, pistols, ancient and modern, ammunition made by the Dervishes, British cartridges, gathered up on the field and recharged over and over again, suits of chain armour from the days of the Crusaders; Turkish scimitars of the time of Saladin, and European swords as old as Richard Cœur de Lion; saddle and trappings presented to Wingate by Menelek, of Abyssinia; arrows, bows, and quivers used by the Pigmy natives of the Equatorial regions—all the arrows are poisoned, and need cautious handling. The mention of foreign armour turning up in Egypt recalls one of Slatin's anecdotes of his experiences. When he entered the service of Egypt in 1878, at the request of General Gordon, he had with him his sword, of Austrian make, on which he had engraved his name in Arabic characters. When he became the Mahdi's prisoner, in 1883, he was of course deprived of his sword. After his escape from the Khalifa's clutches, when he visited London in 1895, he was presented with *his own sword*, on which he had inscribed his name, by Mr. John M. Cook, who had purchased it from an Arab dealer in Luxor, being attracted by the inscription. Sir F. R. Wingate was shown it, and at once found that it was his friend Slatin's weapon. It had possibly been picked up on the battlefield of Toski, when Sir Francis Grenfell drove back the Dervishes—the first victory won by native Egyptian troops. Lord Kitchener is now organising an expedition of Egyptian and Soudanese to finally rout and capture the Khalifa, and Sir F. R. Wingate, as chief of the Intelligence Department is with him. They have no doubt but that this time the remnant of the Dervish rebellion will be finally crushed. If they catch the Khalifa himself, I hope there may be no false pity for his fate. He should be hanged or shot. He has been proved to be a blood-thirsty, sensual wretch, without one redeeming feature in his character. He is a false prophet, and is regarded with distrust and disgust by all true Mahometans. When Arabi broke his oath to his sovereign, and corrupted all the colonels and the army under them, he should have been shot as a traitor. His rebellion was crushed at a cost, with its disastrous consequences, of several millions sterling. Yet he was carefully spared and given a fine estate in Ceylon, where his establishment costs Egypt several thousands a year. Let us make no similar mistake when the Khalifa is caught, and the Dervishes shown who are their true friends.

Upper Egypt.   Lower Egypt.   Upper and Lower Egypt.

ROYAL CROWNS OF THE VARIOUS TYPES OF EGYPTIAN SOVEREIGNTY.

CHAPTER VII.

A REFORMER OF ANCIENT DAYS.

BAKED CLAY TABLET FROM TEL-EL-AMARNA.
(Now in the British Museum.)

This is a "letter" from one of the Egyptian colonies of Syria addressed to Amenhotep IV. (Akhenaten). It is written in cuneiform characters impressed on the clay when soft. The date of this correspondence is about 100 years before the time of Moses. This tablet was part of the royal library or record office discovered in 1887.

A SAIL IN A PASHA'S DAHABEAH.

MINIEH—BENI HASAN—ANTINOE—EL BERSHEH—TEL-EL-AMARNA—

AKHENATEN, HIS PALACE AND HIS TOMB.

THE ROCK TOMBS OF BENI HASAN.

Those represented are all of the Twelfth and Thirteenth Dynasties. The columns supporting the façade, and also the internal chambers, are the earliest known types of architecture bearing an extraordinary resemblance to the so-called Doric architecture of the Greeks of a thousand years later.

CHAPTER VII.

MINIEH—BENI HASAN—ANTINOE—TEL-EL-AMARNA— THE STORY OF AKHENATEN (AMENHOTEP IV.).

WE speak of " The Reformation " as a well-known historical period, forgetting that the world has seen other reformations and many attempts at reform that were unsuccessful. The one of which I propose to write occurred 3,200 years ago. The efforts of an honest, earnest man, far in advance of his time, may be worth describing. This ancient reformer, instead of merely objecting to novelties in religious ritual, desired to simplify and purify the sacred creed. He wanted to prevent the addition of deities to the divine Pantheon, and to lead his country back to the worship of one God alone. The priests had been adding deity after deity, and building temples to them all. Each temple had its priesthood, with revenues and estates all over Egypt. The country must have been in much the same state as Henry VIII. found England, when seven-eighths of the land was owned by the Church. We do not know if Amenhotep IV. contemplated the forcible seizure of the Church lands; possibly, had his project of religious reform been successful, things might have come to that. But he seems to have been a good man and a just, anxious for the redemption of his people from a rapacious priesthood, who had bound even royalty with

COLUMNS WITH EIGHT SIDES (ROCK-CUT): TOMBS OF BENI HASAN.
This tomb has beautiful paintings, and is now protected by the Government.

burdens that could not be borne. They had conventionalised literature, art, and architecture and had stifled and strangled originality through every branch of the wonderful civilisation of ancient Egypt. Amenhotep IV. at an early age succeeded to a great empire, inherited from his father, the great Amenhotep III., of whom we shall hear more when we visit Thebes.

Doubtless our young monarch tried to curb the power of the proud priests during his six years' residence at the ancient capital; but, as he early announced himself as the worshipper of one God, he had small chance of success. Despairing of reforming them or bringing them round to his view, he left the city of his fathers, and sought, lower down the Nile, about 200 miles from Thebes, a site for a new city, to be the centre of his reformation—a reformation of religion, art, architecture, and a model of good government, free from the dominance of an arrogant and bigoted priesthood. He was no sun-worshipper; but he took the sun's disc as the emblem of his one god, the grandest and most evident of the Creator's works and the emblem of the source and origin of life. He seems to have attracted round his court literary men, poets, and artists of no mean ability. Several religious poems have been found, either composed by the king, like another David, or at least by the poetic talent attached to his court.

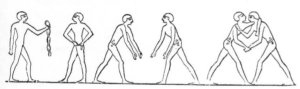

ATHLETIC AND OTHER SCENES.
(*From the Tombs of Beni Hasan*)

The morality expressed in these hymns and epics is of the highest tone, almost on a level with Christianity. It was even to be a domestic reform, for he seems to have had no "harem" establishment, and only one wife, the beautiful

Queen Nefertiti, a princess of high rank, a native of Mesopotamia. His mother, Queen Tyi, whom Amenhotep III. seems to have associated with himself in governing Egypt, had been a remarkable woman. In her lifetime she was accorded much honour, and no doubt her son's talent and originality were inherited from her. The young king was much devoted to his mother. Domestic affection was held up as his ideal of perfection in life, his queen and children being shown, in all the sculptures, along with him; he is never seen alone. In art his aim was to cast aside conventionality and study Nature herself. The animals are shown in motion, and natural treatment is given to plant forms, analogous to modern Japanese decorative art. Dr. Petrie gives some illustrations from this reformer's hymns to the deity.

COLUMN WITH SIXTEEN SIDES: TOMBS OF BENI HA'SAN.

Here is a morsel :—

> " Thou makest the seasons of the year to create all thy works,
> The winter making them cool, the summer giving warmth ;
> Thou makest the far-off heaven that thou mayest rise in it,
> That thou mayest see all that thou madest when thou wast alone."
> *　　　*　　　*　　　*　　　*　　　*
> " Thou art very beautiful, brilliant, and exalted,
> Thy beams encompass all lands thou hast made.
> . . . How excellent are thy ways ! O Lord of eternity."

Not bad verse this for a royal poet of about 1380 B.C., long before the time of King David, " the sweet psalmist of Israel."

Amenhotep IV. reigned in Thebes, as has been said, for six years, we may suppose vainly endeavouring to carry out his great reforms. Then, feeling his task hopeless, he sought and found a new site for his capital, and moved his court down stream. He spent his life in rearing and embellishing

Very possibly this represents soldiers being trained. The scenes are executed in the simplest manner in fresco painting.
(*From the Tombs of Beni Hasan.*)

BENI HASAN: |ROCK-CUT TOMB OF KHNUM-HOTEP II.,
Showing the cornice afterwards copied by the Greeks.

his new city. He did not neglect his kingdom, however, for remains of his works have been found north and south, indeed all over Egypt. But his main interest was centred in the new capital. Its site has been discovered at Tel-el-Amarna,* some distance south of Minieh. When the founder of the new city quitted Thebes, he changed his name from Amenhotep to Akhenaten, and to this he added the title Ankh-em-Maat (Living in Truth). He discarded all the old deities, reverting to the ancient worship of one God, his only guide being Truth. But, though he built a fine city to be the metropolis of his simple faith and chose an admirable site, his efforts for a permanent reformation failed. He had no son, daughters only were born to him, and he died at a comparatively early age, after reigning less than twenty years. His two successors came to the throne through marriage with his daughters. They endeavoured to continue the pure, simple faith introduced by the reforming king, but their struggles against the priests were unavailing, and the worship of Amen was restored, with all its attendant mythology. The seat of government was moved back to Thebes; the city of the reformer was destroyed, swept off the face of the earth, or at least his enemies worked hard to this end. The violent hatred shown by the hierarchy was evidenced by their destroying every monument and smashing into fragments everything, small and great, that bore the hated name of Aten, the typical sun disc that was the symbol of the new faith.

---

* Dr. Petrie has published a fine volume about Tel-el-Amarna, but, unfortunately, it is out of print. The story is told in short in his *History of Egypt*, vol. ii. (Methuen & Co.). I am indebted to these works for several illustrations. The site of the city and temple was first discovered by Lepsius. Professor Sayce tells me that when he first saw the place, in 1878, the houses and streets of the city were still discernible.

In 1891 Dr. Petrie visited the site, and made a careful survey of the mounds and lines of ancient foundations. He set to work with gangs of Arab labourers, and soon made the most wonderful of all his discoveries, for he unearthed the floors and foundations of Akhenaten's own palace. The destroyers of the city had demolished the public buildings and carried off all the stone. They had levelled all the city walls and thus allowed the sand to drift over the whole. site to the depth of several feet. Then the sandstorms came, and buried all in one desert of destruction, covering many square miles.

I had heard Dr. Petrie tell of his wonderful discovery, and I longed to see the place with my own eyes. But how to get there? I was on one of Cook's steamers going down the river, but there is no landing-place, and the Nile is full of shifting sandbanks at this part. Even if dropped on a firm bank I should have a mile to walk, and no village exists to afford shelter, or where any food could be obtained. So I was forced to abandon for the moment my adventurous project. Next day we were off Minieh, a populous town with a depôt of resident British irrigation-engineers. I got Cook's steamer to drop me on a sandbank, the water now being very low, and signalled for help. A procession of eight Arabs came to my relief and soon was threading its way to the bank. Each man carried one of my packages on his head, and, when we neared the edge, a stalwart native ducked his head between my legs, and astride of his shoulders I was carried across a branch of the Nile, and found myself at Minieh. This is an Arab town, but I knew enough to tell the party of natives to take me to the Irrigation Office. I found it about a mile off, a fine building in a lovely garden, a former palace of Ismail's. Here a tall Nubian opened the gate and volubly saluted me in an unknown tongue. When he found I did not know a word of his lingo he suddenly exclaimed " Telephone ! " and I followed him into an inner room, where he began to ring the bell violently and shout into the instrument. Presently I heard some very forcible English sentences come out of the telephone, whereupon I took up the tube and poured my wants into it, giving my name and the name of a friend in Cairo, a great man in the Public Works Department. The effect was magical. The Nubian

ATHLETIC AND OTHER SCENES.
(From Beni Hasan Tombs.)

was told in his own shibboleth to bring me along, and " blessed " greatly for not having done so at once. Then I was led through a rose garden, which my friend's wife, when stationed there some years before, had laid out with much skill. Everything was enriched by

SCENE AT RODAH.
The steamer's station opposite Antinoë.

plentiful irrigation, and shaded by tall date palms overhead. Thus I was brought by rills of running water coursing among luxuriant flower-beds to the harem buildings. Here, unfortunately, none of the former occupants are now to be found, but three honest British engineers occupy the splendid apartments and the great deserted halls. It was Easter time, and the engineers had a week's holiday, and were just hungering, they said, for some society from the civilized world.

I was regaled on tea and muffins, given a bedroom about the size of an ordinary drawing-room, with windows opening into the lovely garden, and made to stay the night. They would have put me up for a month, but I was in haste to visit Tel-el-Amarna, so I said I must sail up stream on the following morning. When I told my wants to mine host he said the Government steam launch was away inspecting or I should have had it; and that there was nothing to be had but a dahabeah. A rich pasha, a friend of his, would gladly lend me one, and we would call on him after dinner. The engineers were charming hosts, and we dined in good style; then I was taken into the town and to visit the pasha, who greatly admires the British and was the owner of several private dahabeahs. We had to go through salaams to our "highnesses" and various elaborate introductions when we came into the great man's presence. He was a little round fat man, and sate on a yellow silk pillow with his legs tucked under him. He kissed my hand, made me sit near him, and put my friend the engineer officer beside him on the divan. Coffee was ordered in, then sherbet and sweetmeats. I had just had a hearty meal, but my host thought, because I did not partake of everything, that I did not like the good things, and ordered tea to be brought. Still he was disappointed at my want of appetite, and he said to my friend, "You know, I am a good Mussulman, and have no drinks in my house, but I will borrow some from a neighbour, a Greek," and then an array of bottles—whisky, brandy, and several sorts of wine—was produced and pipes lit and handed round. Of course, all the conversation was in Arabic. I ventured to whisper to my friend that I was utterly unable to do justice to such hospitable treatment, but he only said, " Swallow all you can ; we will soon have your dahabeah." I did as I was bid, and then a tall, solemn-looking man was introduced, kissed hands, and sat down. This was the captain of the vessel, and all was arranged to be ready for me to start at once, early in the morning. We had a warm leavetaking from the kind old pasha, who said it was the pleasure of his life to do a service to any English gentleman. I started next day. The dahabeah was a fine sailer, and spread her wings like a bird before a north wind. The boat had accommodation for six, and was

ANTINOUS.
(*British Museum.*)

beautifully furnished, being that reserved for the pasha's ladies. A young Copt, a clerk in the Government service, wanted a holiday and came with me as interpreter. He knew English, French, Arabic, and other tongues, and was a nice, modest young fellow. I thought so much of him that I made him take his meals with me, a proceeding which the engineers did not approve, but I was only a visitor and no harm came of it. We took several days to get to our destination, as we had to sail against the stream. On the way I visited each spot of interest.

Beni Hasan, with its rock-cut tombs, attracted me greatly. It is doubtless the cemetery of a forgotten town of great antiquity. The cliffs on the eastern side of the river, about a mile from the bank, are here nearly vertical, and have been hollowed out into chambers with columns left to support the roof. Some of these pillars are square, others have eight or sixteen sides and are almost as symmetrical as those of the Grecian Doric style. They undoubtedly are the origin of that order of architecture, although vastly more ancient, being of Dynasty XII. (about 2600 B.C.), while the earliest Greek columns are more than 1,500 years later. The gradual development of the fluted

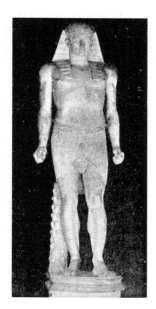

FULL-LENGTH FIGURE OF ANTINOUS.
(*From the Vatican, Rome.*)

column—four sides, eight, sixteen—is very clearly seen. The
capitals, architrave, dentals, and cornices are gradually evolved,
all cut out of solid rock, and evidently copied in their incep-
tion from still more ancient wooden structures. The inside
of these tombs was covered with well-preserved hiero-

QUEEN TYI,
Mother of Akhenaten. and
Wife of Amenhotep III.

glyphic inscriptions and scenes
of industry, training of athletes,
male and female dancers and
gymnasts, and military and
pastoral scenes. These were
quite perfect fifty years ago.
Unfortunately of late years the
inscriptions have been greatly

AKHENATEN.
His original title, Amenhotep IV.
(From the Louvre.)

mutilated before the monuments were taken in
charge by the Government, and the present
guardians are far from trustworthy. But the inscriptions are most interesting, and their records
extend over 2,000 years. The Egypt Exploration
Fund has published several vol-

umes of them, and subscribers can still obtain them all at
very moderate rates. The representations of games, agricultural
scenes, etc., painted on the walls are among the most ancient
in Egypt. There is no doubt that Queen Hatasu took the
idea of the fluted columns and arcades of her temple at Thebes
from these tombs, which were already ancient when she designed her beautiful work. Good donkeys can be obtained
for the excursion, which occupies two or three hours and

QUEEN NEFERTETI,
Wife of Akhenaten.

is mainly a pleasant
ride through cultivated fields, followed by
a stiffish climb to the rocky terrace.

Opposite the modern town of Rodah
are the ruins of Antinoë, where Antinous
put an end to his miserable existence, and
Hadrian erected the city to his favourite's
memory, about 130 A.D. But it must have
been an ancient town long before his day,
for I came upon the ruins of a beautiful painted temple of fair Egyptian art,
built by Ramses II., still preserving its

THE KING'S DAUGHTERS WITH THEIR
NURSES.

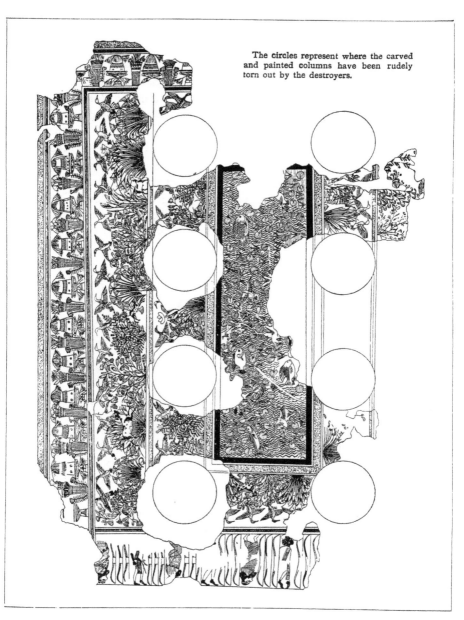

The circles represent where the carved and painted columns have been rudely torn out by the destroyers.

TEL-EL-AMARNA:

WEST HALF OF THE PAINTED PAVEMENT, AKHENATEN'S PALACE.

DETAIL OF PAINTED FLOOR
(Tel-el-Amarna).

coloured decoration, among the mounds of the Roman city. The site is now utterly desolate, and the greater part of the stones of many Egyptian and Roman temples have been utilised to build a steam sugar mill on the opposite bank, one of the practical undertakings of Ismail's time and still worked for the Government.

At El-Bersheh, not far off, there is a valley of tombs, one of which contains an instructive painting of the transport of a colossus on a sledge. The occupant of the tomb was an officer of Usertesen (2400 B.C.), who was so proud of his skill that he painted the scene on the walls of his tomb to call the attention of the gods in the future life to his great labours here below. The scene is most spirited. All is done by manual labour. Crowds of slaves draw the great ropes, men stand by with whips, a ganger standing on the statue beats time with his hands. The great figure, forty feet high, is trussed and strapped on its carriage, and moves along securely. It is a wonderful scene of activity, and the picture tells its story admirably.

DETAIL OF PAINTED FLOOR
(Tel-el-Amarna).

We came to anchor at Hadji Kandeel, on the edge of the great plain which the reforming king had chosen for his building site. A broad belt of palms lined the river, with some cultivated fields, now dry and destitute of crops, as the Nile was low. The wretched village was opposite us, we hired donkeys from the natives, and soon had crossed the sandy plain, noticing lines of hillocks and pieces of broken sandstone strewn about, by

DETAIL OF PAINTED FLOOR
(Tel-el-Amarna).

which the ancient highways and buildings could be detected. The women and children offered bits of pottery, fragments of blue porcelain rings, and bits of sculptured stone, with hieroglyphics. I bought everything I could get, and afterwards found that all were interesting and many had valuable cartouches and inscriptions, all of Akhenaten's time. I got some bearing his own and his wife Nefertiti's names, and a fine bit of blue pottery with his mother's name, the Queen of Amenhotep III. (Tyi), thereon. But the pleasure was to come.

We came to Petrie's excavation on the site of the Royal Palace. Here was laid bare the floor of the king's chamber, made of concrete, exquisitely adorned with coloured hunting scenes, painted in fresco in natural style more resembling Japanese art than anything else. It is quite different from Egyptian, Greek, or Roman decoration. Wild cattle break into the reeds and disturb a flock of wild fowl. A fishpond is

DETAIL OF PAINTED FLOOR
(Tel-el-Amarna).

represented in the centre. A beautiful foliaged scroll border surrounds the design, which has aquatic birds and game of every kind, drawn with great spirit and in delicate colouring. It is the only instance of fresco painting applied to a floor, and is quite a new idea of decoration, albeit upwards of 3,000 years old. Dr. Petrie has figured part of this beautiful floor in his work on Tel-el-Amarna, but still it is necessary to see the decoration itself to understand and appreciate its beauty and originality. Fortunately it is well cared for and protected from violence and from the elements. The Society for the Protection of Egyptian Monuments erected a house with a good roof over it. (This had been carried out under the direction of my kind host at Minieh when he was young in the Government service. He had not seen it for four years and was greatly pleased, on my return to Minieh, with

DETAIL OF PAINTED FLOOR
(Tel-el-Amarna).

my praise of his excellent erection.) There is abundance of light, and planked ways are bridged across and above the painted floor so that no damage can be done. It is well guarded by several careful custodians chosen by the village sheikh and all paid by the Government. The columns which supported the roof were all broken up or carried off at the time of its destruction, but many fragments were found under the ruins and remain to show the scheme of ornament. They were all covered with exquisite tendrils of creeping plants and flowers in low relief and painted in quiet tints.

We rode across the desert to the cliffs, where the tombs of the officers of state and some of the royal family are still to be seen. They are full of carvings and paintings on the walls, representing their intended occupants in adoration of the One god—as represented by the solar disc. The sun's rays,

DETAIL OF PAINTED FLOOR
(Tel-el-Amarna).

extending downward, terminate in minute hands, dis-
tributing gifts and blessings
to the worshippers under-
neath.   Akhenaten and his
wife and six daughters are all
shown in attitudes of deep
devotion, and the inscriptions
are full of the praise of truth
and many noble principles
advocated by Christianity.   I wished to visit the tomb of the poor king himself.
It is far away, hidden among the barren mountain gorges.   We took another
day for this, and this time my captain and all my crew turned out, armed as my
escort, for the villagers said rough characters might be met with.   But nothing
happened to us.   We found the tomb; it had only been lately re-discovered, but
had been rifled and destroyed thousands of years ago.   I descended deep down
a hewn tunnel into the mountain side.   I saw where the coffin had lain.   It had
been a handsome red granite sarcophagus.   I picked up many little fragments,
each showing remains of the polished surface and some with traces of carving.
I also found many pieces of alabaster showing remains of hieroglyphs and traces
of colour.   A wilder and more desolate spot could not have been chosen for a
sepulchre.   Barren rocks everywhere; not a green leaf, not a drop of water;
narrow chasms with vertical sides of limestone rock, hard as flint.   Above, the
burning sunshine and deep blue sky.   The overhanging cliffs cast purple shadows
athwart the narrow
valleys.   Not a living
thing was to be seen,
save a vulture or an
eagle soaring high
aloft, or a great hawk
sailing majestically a-
cross the blue.   We
rested in an unfinished
tomb and lunched un-
romantically.   We had
a long ride of about
fifteen miles under a
burning sun, and rested
for some time in the

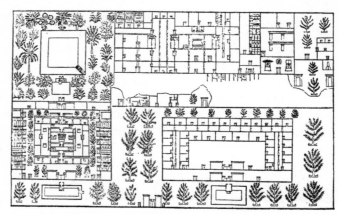

THE ADJOINING BUILDINGS OF THE TEMPLE OF THE
SUN-DISK.
(From the tomb of Merye', at Tel-el-Amarna.)

delicious shady recesses of the rock-hewn sepulchre. Before we started again, I brewed tea with my Etna lamp, and when the sun got lower we mounted our donkeys and threaded our way back through the narrow gorges of rock to the plain of the lost city, the scene of the unsuccessful effort of an old-world reformer.

A very wonderful discovery was made here a few years before my visit. The record office of Akhenaten had been close to the palace, and in 1887 its ruins were discovered by the fellaheen. The bricks composing the building were each stamped with the words, " The Record Office of Aten-Ra." All the

AKHENATEN, HIS WIFE, AND SIX DAUGHTERS WORSHIPPING THE SOLAR DISC AS THE REPRESENTATIVE OF THE ONE GOD.

"documents" found here, and nearly three hundred were preserved, were written in the old cuneiform script of the lands bordering the Euphrates. They are now in the museums of Cairo, London, and Berlin. They are small plaques of terracotta, something in form and colour like Scotch bannocks. They are all covered with minute inscriptions, and were, in fact, letters from foreign kings and Egyptian officials, some of them appealing to the home government for help against neighbouring provinces which had joined the Hittites and other tribes against Egypt. When Akhenaten was absorbed in the building of his new city he neglected his Syrian subjects, and they were lost to Egypt shortly after. Nearly all these "documents" have been translated by Winckler, Delattre, and Prof. Sayce. A very interesting article on these tablets will be found in Mr. Ball's *Light from the East*, and I have to thank Messrs. Eyre and Spottiswoode for lending me an engraving of one of these curious records of antiquity. Dr. Petrie makes much use of them in his *History of Egypt*. Prof. Sayce,

CYLINDER OF ANKH-SEN-AMEN, DAUGHTER OF AKHENATEN (Wife of King Tut-ankh-amen).

in his *Higher Criticism and the Monuments,* has been enabled to elucidate many obscure passages of the Bible and unknown localities by translations of these letters. Many of them are quite touching in their appeals for help from Egypt. The colonies were overrun by invading tribes from the north

and west, and were unable to protect themselves.   In consequence of the
reformer's attention being solely directed to religious matters, sacred rites and
ceremonies at home, his foreign affairs and duties were forgotten, and Egypt did
not recover from this neglect, which brought about the downfall of the great
Eighteenth Dynasty, as his feeble successors, although they restored the worship
of Amen, were unable to keep the kingdom together, and only prepared the
way for the advent of the military despotism of the Nineteenth Dynasty of
the Ramessides.

Sailing rapidly down stream, we reached Minieh in due time.   I found that
the services of my crew and all the expenses of the voyage had been defrayed
by the kind old gentleman who owned the dahabeah.   So all I could do was
to buy a fat sheep for the crew, on which they made merry, sitting up all night
to enjoy the good things provided for their revelry.   I spent the evening with
my kind friends at the Irrigation Department, related all my adventures, and,
parting from them with mutual regrets, made my way to Cairo.

"PROGRESS" ON THE NILE.
The smoke of a sugar factory poisoning the lovely air.

CHAPTER VIII.

THE TABLET OF ABYDOS.

STATUE OF RAMSES THE GREAT, FROM ABYDOS.
(British Museum.)

BALIANEH—ABYDOS—THE TABLET OF ANCESTORS—
THE TEMPLE OF SETI I. AND RAMSES II.—TOMB OF MENA AT NEGADA—
TALES OF MODERN EGYPT.

HÛ, ON THE NILE.
(From a Water-Colour Drawing by the late Edward Lear. Lent by Miss Griffith.)

CHAPTER VIII.

THE TABLET OF ABYDOS.

It is a long, dusty ride from the modern town of Balianeh on the Nile to the temples and mounds of the ancient city of Abtu, called by the Greeks Abydos. It is one of the oldest places in Egypt, far older than Thebes, perhaps older than Memphis, for it was the birthplace of Mena, who was the founder of Memphis, and the first king who ruled over all Egypt. When King Mena died (about 4800 B.C.) he was buried, not in the great city called after him, but in the neighbourhood of Thebes. Here his tomb was discovered by M. de Morgan. Nobody ever expected that the burial-place of Mena would be found. Even Dr. Petrie wrote in the first edition of his history that Mena must be regarded as a mythological personage. Now this has to be altered, for Mena's very tomb has been discovered, a huge edifice of brick, with an elaborate plan of many chambers. It had been burnt, whether as a funeral pyre or by the malice of enemies afterwards, it is impossible to tell. In it, among the ashes, was found an ivory tablet giving the king's name, titles, and qualities in excellent hieroglyphics, showing that the Egyptians had a complete written language about 4800 B.C., using the same characters as are found on the Rosetta Stone of 250 B.C. There was also found in the tomb a number of wine jars sealed with Mena's cartouche. All these are now to be seen in the Cairo Museum.

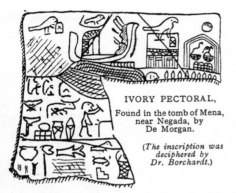

IVORY PECTORAL,

Found in the tomb of Mena, near Negada, by De Morgan.

(The inscription was deciphered by Dr. Borchardt.)

There are vast mounds at Abydos and in its neighbourhood, the ruins of ancient cities, as yet unexplored. Mariette unearthed the temples of Seti and Ramses, which though not as old as Mena's time, yet can show a very respectable antiquity (1370 B.C.), and have the most beautiful sculptures to be found in Egypt, and the most wonderful genealogical record in the world—the Tablet of Abydos. The first time I visited it we had glorious weather and a delightful ride from the Nile bank through richly cultivated fields, among flocks and herds of fine cattle. Many villages were passed, with tall, fruitful date palms, and crowds of comfortable-looking peasants. A busy fair had been held that morning, and everyone seemed happy and contented with their sales or purchases. No "baksheesh" was demanded of us, showing how well off the people were. This district is infested with multitudes of small birds which prey upon the crops, and many towers are erected through the fields, on which boys are perched with slings to frighten off the marauders. These slings we were importuned to buy; they were made of palm fibre, and seemed effective weapons for the purpose in the hands of those who knew how to use them. No doubt the youthful David killed Goliath with an exactly similar sling.

During another visit we experienced a sandstorm on the way. The dry, black, dusty earth was caught up by the fierce wind, and blotted out the land-scape. Our donkeys could scarcely proceed, and vainly sought shelter against any wall or projecting structure. The black dust seemed to penetrate eyes, ears, and nostrils, and we were breathing the land of Egypt into our throats and lungs, while our faces were so grimed with dirt that we were like mummies as to complexion. Fortunately we had only half-an-hour of it, but I suppose we rode through the sandstorm, for the sky cleared, and we saw the black clouds roll away towards the river. In a rainless land there are other atmospheric disturbances worse than a good wetting of the temperate zone. The natives squat down and throw their draperies over their heads on the approach of a sandstorm.

SETI OFFERING TO THE GODDESS OF TRUTH.
(Temple of Abydos.)

Even the donkeys and camels know how to protect themselves, and turn away their heads from the blast and huddle together, crouched as low as possible; but Europeans, no matter how they try to shirk it, always suffer much in a blinding dust squall, and several ladies of our party came out of this one with faces more thickly powdered than would be consistent with good style.

The great temple of Abydos was begun by Seti, but the design of the sculpture is so good and all that artist-king's work so perfectly executed, that one does not wonder at its being unfinished at his death. His son, Ramses the Great, completed it, but his work is inferior to that of the father. Seti is shown standing beside the young Ramses and pointing to the celebrated tablet

of ancestors, as an encouragement to one, ruling an empire with such a history, to fill the throne creditably. There are seventy-six royal cartouches, with the names and titles of each king from Mena to Seti. No kingdom the world ever saw could show such a genealogy of real kings. This wonderful document was lost to the world for 2,000 years. Two Christian apologists, Julius

SETI'S TEMPLE: TABLET OF ANCESTORS.
Seti directing his son's attention to it.

Africanus and Eusebius, gave a long list of Egyptian kings (copied from Manetho, a historian whose other works have been lost). But modern historians scouted this list as apocryphal, and no one believed in the supposed antiquity of Egypt as a kingdom. When Mariette discovered this tablet twenty-five years since, it was at once accepted as a proof of the genuineness of Manetho's list, as it agreed with it. Strange to say, the papyrus from which Seti may have arranged his wonderful tablet has been discovered. It is now at Turin, and though much mutilated, has cleared up some discrepancies found in this and other lists of kings. It is, of course, much older than the time of Seti.

Year by year the tomb of some of the ancient royal personages is discovered, and it is quite possible that every one of the whole seventy-six will be thus accounted for. The tablet comes to light to affirm the truth of the list given by

ABYDOS: TABLET OF ANCESTORS (SECOND PORTION).

Manetho, and discoveries of the tombs, the coffins, and the mummies prove it. The whole chronological picture is carved in low relief on a beautiful white limestone. It was painted originally, but the colour has disappeared. When Mariette unearthed the temple a dirty Arab village had long existed above it, and all the sculptured halls had been filled with filth and rubbish or converted into cellars for the houses above. In addition to completing Seti's temple, Ramses built another great temple for himself, at some little distance off. But it is now in a more ruinous state than that of Seti, and much of the stone has been carried off to make roads and bridges or to burn for lime. But, fortunately for us, Seti's temple is perfect in many chambers. There are seven chapels or sanctuaries, each dedicated to a different divine attribute, and carved with sculpture of a very high order of artistic merit. The roof of each is domed, but with joggle-jointed large beams of stone, not being arched. The Egyptians did not trust the arch for stone buildings, though they knew all about it, and used it for inferior brick work.

Before our party came to Abydos, as well as on the way, some scarabs with royal cartouches had been collected from the Arabs. It was interesting to compare these with the hieroglyphics on the wall and to use old Seti's document as a dictionary to prove and explain the inscriptions on the scarabs. But the cool columned-halls of the temples were put to a baser use. We were hungry and the sandstorm had made us very thirsty. Fortunately supplies had been provided, two camels being laden with all sorts of provisions and refreshments, and sent on from the steamer early in the day. So when we reached the welcome shelter from the hot desert air, after the sandstorm, we found a well-spread board being arranged in the hall of columns. Most of us went round the shrines and the pictures, and the scientists of the little party had a good look at the famous tablet before sitting down to "the square meal" provided for us. Luncheon ended, some of us rode several miles farther to visit a Coptic convent away in the rocky desert. It was rudely and strongly built, and in the old days doubtless had to stand many a siege. It was very interesting to see even such a fragment of early Christianity left in the land. All Egypt was Christian until conquered by the Moslems, and the wonder is that any trace of the faith survived the relentless persecutions which followed. Its long isolation from the Christianity of Europe is evident in the present aspect of this forlorn little monastery. The few monks seemed steeped in poverty, were barely clean, and from their way of showing their rude manuscripts (as they held some of them upside down) we thought it likely that they were quite unable to read them. They seem to worship the pictures of their saints, and these and their paintings of the crucifixion and Biblical scenes are of the most primitive character, utterly

vulgar, gaudy, and tawdry in the extreme. Some of us felt that we would rather not have seen such ignorant specimens of a debased Christian worship. But there are young educated priests coming forward at their seminaries in Cairo, and the old priests are dying off. The Copts are intelligent, and now that they are free from persecution

ABYDOS: PAINTED WALL FROM SETI'S TEMPLE.

their religion will gradually become fit for a great civilizing work. In this remote place the Copts have not benefited as have their fellows in the larger towns along the Nile. At all the principal places on the river where Cook's steamers call—such as Minieh, Assiout, Luxor, Esneh, Edfou, Assouan—the traveller is surprised to find intelligent, clean, neatly-dressed Coptic lads, who can speak English, who demand no "baksheesh," but politely offer to show the way and ask visitors to inspect the "American school." If offered money, they say, "No; only give me an English book, I can read it." The Copts are the descendants of the ancient Egyptian people; the Arabs and Bedouin are all interlopers. You ask these boys where they learnt English. The universal reply is "At the American school." All these lads were Copts and Christians. This response was so often made to me that I visited several of these schools. I found them full of pupils, male and female, fair, yellow-skinned folk, all tidy, well-behaved, intelligent-

H

looking children, taught by Coptic teachers. I asked how these schools were supported. " Mainly self-supporting, all the children pay fees; when necessary, Mr. Alexander, the head of the American College at Assiout, gives help." So I visited Assiout and the college there. I found Mr. Alexander a most courteous gentleman, an American clergyman, who had lived in Egypt for twenty years, devoting his life to this good work. The college was a fine, modern building, in the best portion of the town. There is a model school for boys and another for girls. Copts, Mahometans, Jews, and some Arabs attended the schools, which were all crowded. No question was ever asked as to their religion. No doctrine was taught in the schools. The Christians said the Lord's Prayer at a certain time ; the Mahometans or Jews were not asked to say any prayer unless they liked. They were all being well educated. All could read and write Arabic and English. Many of them acted as monitors, and were, if they wished, trained for teachers. Small fees were charged to all. Cleanliness was insisted upon, and punctual and regular attendance, and the discipline produced good results.

Strange to say, of late quite a number of the respectable Mahometans had sent their girls to the female school (a wonderful event), and they were found clever, attentive, and quick to learn. Mr. Alexander also told me that the College had never asked, and certainly never got, one dollar from any of the numerous American tourists who visit Egypt, as all it required came from one small American Presbyterian Association in the Far West. Some thirty years ago, Mr. Alexander told me, a clergyman of this religious body happened to visit Egypt, and returned much interested in the poor, ignorant remnant of ancient Christianity that he found there. He urged on his congregations to give all they possibly could to help the Copts to a modern, enlightened Christianity. They nobly carried out the good man's advice. The Coptic schools of the American Mission are the result ; they are flourishing all over Egypt. Now, also, Mahometans and the Jews send not only their boys, but their girls to the American Mission schools, and the good they have done, and are doing, is enormous. The merchants find the pupils clean, well-educated, trusted assistants. The clerks in the Government offices and post-office are Copts and others who have been educated in the American schools. But the educating of the girls— Coptic, Jewish, and Mahometan—will be productive of still higher and of far-reaching benefits from a domestic point of view. All honour to the little American town in the Far West that originated and carries out such a truly Christian mission ! The ignorant, lonely Coptic monastery has led me into a long digression, but I wanted to show what Coptic Christianity might become under good guidance. When we reflect that the Copts are undoubtedly the remnant of the ancient inhabitants of a land that was once entirely Christian, this good work must command our sympathy.

CAIRO: THE TOMBS OF THE CALIPHS.

From the great mounds of the old city. The pyramids in the distance (after sunset,

(From a Painting by John Varley.)

H 2

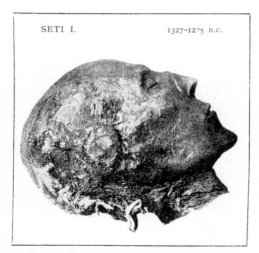

SETI I.   1327-1275 B.C.

The king's mummy was discovered at Thebes in 1881, and is now in the Cairo Museum. It is the only one of the royalties which is pleasing to look upon. He seems in a calm sleep. The king's fine intellectual head and handsome profile is wonderfully preserved, and it will be noticed that the likeness to the sculptured portrait (p. 110) is remarkable. His superb tomb we shall visit in Chapter XI.

On the way a gentleman who had voyaged much on the Nile gave us his experiences of the natives, when some were inclined to call them a set of cringing, fawning creatures, who never smiled but to gain "baksheesh." They were as good and faithful as any in the world, this gentleman said, and he had reason to know. He was once sailing up the Nile in a small dahabeah with a few companions. They stopped where they pleased, and, as they could speak Arabic, went much among the people, seeking antiquities, scarabs, etc. Every Englishman is supposed to be a doctor. My friend especially was regarded by the natives as the "hakeem" (doctor) of the party, and as such was asked to see a poor woman who was very ill. He gave, to please them, some simple remedies. Some days after my friend felt inflammation in his eyes and his sight growing dim; he had contracted small-pox! He told his companions to alight at the nearest village, and he would remain where he was—in fact, he was too ill to move or to be moved, and his Arab servant and a boy would remain to attend to him. They were far up the Nile and remote from any town. He gave his servant some simple directions—to moisten his lips with milk and water, and now and then make him swallow some, and to send the boy to the village morning and evening for fresh milk. If he became violent to hold him down, and get the boy to help him. To cover his face to keep the flies off him. He closed his eyes, and one day he awoke. "Are you there, Hassan?" "Yes, sir, I am here." "How long since I spoke to you, Hassan?" "Ten days, sir. Now, sir, take some milk. You are quite cool. You will soon be well. Go to sleep." And my friend did as he was told. Next day or so he was convalescent, and his sight returned. He found that Hassan had never left his side, and when he would snatch a little sleep himself had the boy to keep watch for him. My friend soon made a rapid recovery, but his handsome face was for a long time completely ruined by the marks of the small-pox. His life had been saved by the faithful Arab. I know this man, and employ him when I can obtain his services. He is now one of the most trusted dragomans in Egypt, and deservedly a prosperous man. At the time of my friend's illness he was only a poor donkey-boy. He has told me that my friend became very violent and completely delirious, and tried to throw himself into the river. It took all his strength, and the boy's too, to hold him down in the bottom of the boat, and he had to keep awake always after that till his master recovered. Then another tale was told of native character of a different sort.

An old Nile traveller was one day standing on the post-boat, which was about to draw up at the landing-stage of a village. There is always a crowd of men, women, and children on the arrival of the mail steamer, and on this occasion a little girl stepped forward, offering something for sale to one of the passengers. Perhaps he misunderstood her, but this man pushed her off rudely, and the poor child fell into the river. She emerged dripping and crying, more at the insult before her people than for any real hurt. But when the gentleman saw that the man never apologised, but only said something rude, he took the fellow by the collar of the coat and dropped him into the Nile! The man crawled out as best he could, and was no more seen—hid himself somewhere. But the poor child came up to my friend, and in her own tongue blessed and gave him her thanks, and then the steamer moved off on her voyage up the river. Three years afterwards my friend was again going up the Nile on the post-boat. This time he had his wife and daughter with him. At the landing-place they noticed among the little crowd of villagers a tall, handsome girl, who seemed to be on the look-out for some one. When my friend landed she came up to him, knelt and kissed his hand, crying with joy at meeting him again.

It was the child he had seen at the same place some years ago, whose wrongs he had avenged. He raised the girl up and spoke kindly to her. "You don't forget me, I see. Why, I hoped you would be married long ago, and I never thought you would remember me." "I will never marry anyone but you, sir, and I have come here to every mail boat since

ABYDOS: TEMPLE OF SETI (LIST OF NOMES).

the day I saw you last to look for you and tell you so." "It is quite true what she says," said an elderly woman coming forward. "I am her mother. We had a good man for her, but she would have no husband but you, sir." "But I am married, and here are my wife and daughter." "No matter, marry me. I will be the lady's slave, and I will follow her, and work for her, and never leave you; only I can never marry anyone but you, my gentleman." And then the poor girl went up to my friend's wife and repeated her offer with many tears. But the lady, who could speak her language, said, "My husband is a priest, and in our country the law allows but one wife." They bade her good-bye, tenderly as possible, but the poor lassie went away sorrowfully, and the post-boat started again on her voyage.

I have already alluded to the difficulties formerly thrown in the way of British explorers by the French authorities in the Cairo Museum, who claimed, without any reason or right, control over the whole antiquities of Egypt. The abuses of the last few years, when Frenchmen were licensed to dig (and carry off what they found), while honest English scientists were refused, caused Sir Wm. Garstin to interfere. He is now president of a Committee of the Ministry of Public Works, who receive and decide all applications to search for antiquities. This Committee has just granted Dr. Petrie permission to dig (for the Egypt Exploration Fund) at Abydos and twenty-five miles round! So subscribers to this admirable Society's fund may soon expect a rich reward, and Egyptian studies a vast impetus.

Abydos was the cradle of a great dynasty, and there are, doubtless, many remains of it, and also of the later rulers, yet to be discovered. Seti located his greatest

achievement here, and it was accounted the holiest district of Egypt for several thousand years. So we may hope for good results, especially under the guidance of the greatest Egyptian digger of modern times.

SUHAG.

CHAPTER IX.

THE LAST EGYPTIAN PRINCESS.

EGYPTIAN PORTRAIT OF CLEOPATRA AS ISIS,
DENDERAH.

DENDERAH AND ITS FAMOUS TEMPLE—CLEOPATRA—JULIUS CÆSAR—
CÆSARION—MARK ANTONY—AUGUSTUS.

FOUR-TIER SHADOOFS AT
WORK, LOW NILE.

*(From a Picture by Lear;
the property of Miss Griffith.)*

CHAPTER IX.

DENDERAH—THE LAST EGYPTIAN PRINCESS.

MY reminiscences of Egypt seem to need, for those who would visit the banks of the Nile, some account of Denderah, with its temple in various ways differing from all the others, as it connects the old and the new and shows how Europe gradually began to influence Africa. The temple of Denderah, although not covering as much ground as that of Edfou, is in several respects more wonderful. It also, as we now find it, is a Ptolemaic building, but a careful and costly reproduction of a previous structure of hoary antiquity, going back to the days of the ancient empire. Cheops (called Khufu by the Egyptians), the builder of the Great Pyramid, had founded a temple on this site. Dr. Petrie in his recent diggings in the adjoining cemetery found tombs of the Third Dynasty (4000 B.C.), before the days of Khufu, and proved that the place was still a populous one when the native rule came to an end.* Thebes was better placed for a metropolis, and ancient Abydos was not far off. This prevented Denderah from ever rivalling these neighbours, but still it was a seat of learning; mainly (perhaps) astronomical science was cultivated, for two representations of the zodiac were found in the great temple there, and many astronomical inscriptions, showing what accurate sidereal knowledge was possessed in early times. This ancient abode of learning had evidently become neglected during the long dark period of decadence of the later native Egyptian rulers. The Greek kings of Egypt (during what

---

* It is to be hoped that Dr. Petrie will soon be able to publish the results of his two seasons' discoveries in this neighbourhood.

DENDERAH: FAÇADE OF TEMPLE OF HATHOR.

is known as the Ptolemaic period—from Alexander's death till the Christian era)
undertook the complete rebuilding of the temples.   The restoration went on
long after the time of the last Egyptian princess, Cleopatra VI., renowned for
her beauty, her accomplishments, and her efforts to graft a Roman stock on the
enfeebled Egyptian genealogical tree.   During the troubled reign of this gifted
princess the external decorations were added on the sculptured walls of the
superb structure, which had been several centuries in building, of which we shall
speak further on.   The Greek rulers had rebuilt and the Romans protected and
endowed the great Egyptian temple, which seems to have flourished down to
the time of Constantine the Great.   Dr. Petrie discovered, in 1898, in the cemetery
outside the ancient town, some of the temple furniture, which had been hidden
away possibly by the last of the priests left when all the land became nominally
Christian.   The famous decree of Theodosius had been promulgated abolishing
in the Roman provinces everywhere all religions save Christianity.   Egypt was
thenceforward, until Mahometan days, a Christian country, and all Pagan temples
were of course allowed to fall into ruin, and were devastated by iconoclastic
zealots.   Denderah was a town of no importance after this, and gradually
dwindled into a mere Arab village.   The poor folks grovelled in the magnificent
halls, which they gradually filled up with refuse till at last the buildings were
almost hidden from view.   Having obliterated the temple, then the miserable
inhabitants built their hovels on the top of the great platform of the roof.   In

this state it was "discovered" in the present century by French explorers, the most notable being Mariette, who completely extricated the splendid building from the mounds of rubbish which had eclipsed it.

AUGUSTUS ADORING ISIS.
Sculpture in the Temple, Denderah.

The great temple is entered through a grand hall of columns, twelve at each side. Each pillar has the head of the goddess Hathor represented on each of the four sides of the capital. Hathor was the Egyptian "Venus," which may account for the beautiful Cleopatra's fancy for the place. The temple was richly decorated with carving and painting. Much of the colouring remains, and the sculpture. though rather rudely executed, is bold and effective. Every portion of column, roof, and wall is carved with hieroglyphs and pictorial decoration relating to the great goddess Hathor, to whom the building was dedicated. The cartouches of the earliest founders of the ancient temple are depicted, as well as those of the Ptolemies, who rebuilt it, and of the Roman emperors who succeeded—down to Tiberius (who completed it about A.D. 35).

DENDERAH: THE PRONAOS, TEMPLE OF HATHOR.

But Roman rulers had their portraits added to the walls long after this. The Greek and Latin names and titles are rendered in Egyptian hieroglyphs, and the Imperial names are contained in cartouches just as was done in ancient times with the Egyptian rulers' royal names.

A court is then entered, with more massive columns and six chapels behind them. Then again a vast apartment, with the "holy of holies" within it. The whole building must have been

DENDERAH BAS-RELIEF OF AUGUSTUS.
Interior of the Hypostyle Hall.

very dark, though there is now no doubt, from Sir Norman Lockyer's discoveries, that on certain days and nights in the year the light of the sun (and stars heralding its approach) shone in through the open portal, illuminating the shrine within the "holy of holies." Inscriptions on the temple describe this phenomenon, and Lockyer's discoveries have elucidated their meaning.* Still, even in the sunny clime of Egypt, the temple in its recesses must have been a gloomy place. But this is characteristic of all ancient Egyptian temples. The priests doubtless had artificial light of some kind, for it is only when illuminated by magnesium wire that the beautiful painted walls and ceilings are visible at all. By this means the magnificent astronomical paintings on the roof can be seen distinctly. The goddess Nut (or Night) is impersonated by a female figure bent over the earth, painted with stars on a blue ground, while the various constellations are represented, and the planets sail in boats across the azure sky. There are twelve constellations shown, and these can all be identified with our present similar divisions of the zodiac. Every corner, every surface of stone above and below, is sculptured and painted and carved with texts and literary matter which must have been intended to be read.

---

* "The Dawn of Astronomy," by Sir Norman Lockyer. (Cassell & Co.)

There are in this temple, more than in others, however, many slanting apertures, which were doubtless intended to admit the sunlight, as they are angled so as

to catch it. These may have been assisted by powerful mirrors reflecting the light from without, and carrying the rays by prismatic reflectors into remote recesses. But still it is a mystery even to our scientists to tell how the carvers and artists of old carried on their minute and beautifully executed work in the dark, where no reflected light could reach. There are crypts under the building, to which in ancient days there must have been an entrance from outside. If so, it is not now available, and we have to crawl through a forced passage to reach the staircase

DENDERAH: CALIGULA
OFFERING TO ISIS.

which descends to the vaults. The whole of this subterranean passage is completely covered on roof and sides with exquisite carving, and storied with hieroglyphic inscriptions. Now it is pitch dark, and, without candles, lanterns, or magnesium wire, all the decorations are invisible. How did the ancient artists do this work? For it has all been done after the walls were built; the stones were laid with rough faces, polished and engraved afterwards. Innumerable bats hang from the ceilings of these passages. When disturbed they dash about, extinguish the candles, and, flying in our faces, make the ladies scream. This and the close air of the place cause us to shorten our visit to these weird caverns of antiquity. It is thought that this portion of the building may be part of the former temple of the ancient empire of five thousand years ago, as many of the earlier founders' names and cartouches are found, and none of those of the restorers. Doubtless there are

DENDERAH: THE WONDERFUL LITTLE TEMPLE
ON THE ROOF.

JULIUS CÆSAR.
(From the British Museum.)

many more vaulted passages underneath and below the vast mounds of rubbish that still surround the temple on three sides.

Let us now ascend to the roof by the easy staircase cut in the thickness of the walls. Here we find a great platform of several levels connected by flights of easy steps. A lovely little temple in one corner, at right angles to the great one which carries it, was dedicated to Osiris, and is a perfect gem of architecture. This building had a wonderful astronomical decoration on its roof representing the passage of the sun through the twelve constellations of the zodiac. This was carried off to Paris, and is now one of the greatest treasures of the Louvre. It shows a most advanced state of astronomical knowledge as well as mathematical science. It is worthy of note, however, that the Egyptians of those days represented the constellation "Cancer" by a scarabeus (or beetle) instead of a crab! The scarab was their sacred emblem, and they preferred its use. Another small building was the "Manmisi," or sacred chamber of the birth of the deity, who was worshipped in the adjoining temple some way akin to the adoration of the sacred mother and babe of the Church of the Nativity at Bethlehem. The view from the roof of the great temple is very fine. The Nile is seen for many miles, wandering among its narrow bright green banks fringed with dark date palms. This district now suffers much from deficient irrigation, and a great canal is being made to supply its wants all the way from Thebes. When I was last at Denderah, we could see with our glasses Dr. Petrie's digging encampment far away on the slopes of the hills to the west. This enterprising little exploring party of eight ladies and gentlemen spent four months there, and made great discoveries for the Egypt Exploration Fund. Many very early tombs, of the Third to the Seventh Dynasties, glass mosaics and decorations of Greek and Roman age, and

MARK ANTONY.
(From the Louvre.)

sacred implements and utensils used for the temple worship in the last days of pagan worship were found there. When the establishment of the Christian faith rendered these last useless, the priests seem to have hidden away the emblems that had thus become obsolete! Dr. Petrie discovered chalices and altar emblems and decorations thus religiously interred, and has hopes of finding many more interesting antiquities in the same localities. Any spot where this talented digger desires to work is very likely to prove a wise selection. He has been thus hunting in Egyptian rubbish heaps for over a dozen years, and most seasons discovers something wonderful. The collections at the Cairo Museum, the British Museum, the Ashmolean at Oxford, and the rich store of Egyptian relics at the museum of University College, London, over which he himself presides as Professor of Egyptology, are a proof of this.

In ancient times the crocodile was worshipped at Kom Ombo, where the hideous beast seems to have been typical of the Evil One. Men strove there to "give the devil his due," and worshipped him to propitiate his terrors, for they supposed they perchance might have to face his satanic majesty in the future purgatorial courts of the under-world. The good people of Denderah, however, regarded the crocodile differently. They held the abominable batrachian in abhorrence; as the most odious (says Strabo, who visited this neighbourhood about A.D. 40) of all animals. The crocodile-lovers and the crocodile-haters often came to blows. There were frequent struggles between the disciples of the opposite

AUGUSTUS.
(*From the British Museum.*)

faiths or factions—something like an Orange and Green riot of the present day. In the time of the Romans, visitors used to go to Denderah to witness these exhibitions of intolerance, much as if a party of tourists nowadays went to Ireland to see the Twelfth of July celebrations! Juvenal tells of such an exhibition of rival "religionists" which it was his good fortune to witness. In this case the larger crocodile attacked and swallowed up the smaller sacred beast. But we are left to guess which of the animals represented the sacred powers of darkness! Doubtless each party claimed the victory. However, from Juvenal's satirical remarks, it is evident that in his day the religious part of the exhibition had died out, and that visitors went to Denderah, as they would now go to a circus entertainment, merely for the fun of it. The rival crocodile factions came eventually to Rome with their tamed monsters, where they were exhibited as a spectacle in the arena.   There is a strange lesson taught us of the Roman policy towards the faiths of conquered nations by the sculptures of the Temple of Denderah.   We find Augustus, Tiberius, Caligula, Claudius, Nero, and other noble Romans pourtrayed bearing gifts to the great patron deities Hathor or Isis, their names and title, " Kaisaros," spelt in elegant Egyptian hieroglyphs, and their cartouches made to imitate the style of several thousand years earlier than Roman times.   The Romans seem to have contributed largely to the vast cost of the buildings, and to have aided the endowments; and all express themselves as devout believers in the Egyptian faith, and they in their turn are assured of the love and protection of Ptah, Hathor, Isis, and all the gods.   In some places, however, the priestly superintendents have been ignorant of which emperor or ruler they were under, and have left

the title, or rather the name, blank, to be filled up when the succession was known and established! They were not quite sure, for instance, in Cleopatra's time, whether young Cæsar would live to be ruler, or whether another might take his place.   So they transliterated the Greek word "Autokrator" into Egyptian hieroglyphics, and left the name to be filled up afterwards according to circumstances!   The Romans must have been a power in the land when this temple was nearing completion.   A great pylon stands at some distance with the names of Trajan and Domitian on it.   Another pylon

DENDERAH: NERO
OFFERING GIFTS.

bears the name of Antoninus Pius, who built the " Roman wall" in Britain between the Clyde and the Firth of Forth.   Although so much restoration work was done by the Romans, no Latin inscription is found on the building.   The texts recording the Romans' restoration and dedication of the temple are not in hieroglyphics, or in Latin, but are done in excellent Greek, the characters being beautifully cut.   The decorations and inscriptions in the crypts in some cases seem to go back to King Pepi, of the Sixth Dynasty (3230 B.C.), but are mainly those of the Ptolemies.   The principal buildings of the temple itself have at least been completed (or sculptured after building in the rough) by the Romans, while most of the fine sculptured history of the great external walls of the main building was done by the last of the Egyptian princesses, Cleopatra.

As remarked above, this gifted and beautiful woman may have selected Denderah and its temple sacred to Venus (Hathor) as the most fitting place to record the great desire of her eventful life, that her son by Julius Cæsar might be regarded as her successor on the most ancient throne in the world.

TEMPLE OF DENDERAH: INTERIOR OF THE HYPOSTYLE COURT.

She had been unfortunate in her previous marriage to her young half-brother, which was merely an affair of State. She had to publicly marry him, for the ancient law compelled the Egyptian princesses to marry a Royal kinsman. When freed from him, Julius Cæsar came to Egypt, saw her, and was conquered! He espoused her, much to the disgust no doubt of his childless, elderly, but excellent, wife, Calpurnia, who was at home in Rome. But we cannot judge marital matters of those times by the strict and wise laws that we live under. The lovely Egyptian queen was attracted by the stern soldier, and when her son Cæsarion was born she announced him as the heir to the Throne of the Pharaohs, and

CLEOPATRA AND HER SON, CÆSARION.
(From the west wall of the Temple, Denderah.)

it was on the walls of the great temple of Denderah that the proclamation was made, and there it stands to this day, boldly and skilfully sculptured on the outer wall of the temple. And, as if to proclaim it to the West, towards Imperial Rome, it is on that side of the temple that the proclamation is pictorially displayed — and done twice over. Her cartouche labels her the "Great Egyptian Princess — Royal wife, Royal mother," and beside her own tall, handsome figure her young son Cæsarion stands, her hand on his shoulder, presenting him to Hathor, Isis, and the other protecting deities. Cæsar took Cleopatra and her son to Rome. They lived in Cæsar's house, and the boy was regarded as the heir to his father's name and titles. It is, however, very unjust to the great Cæsar's memory that he should be supposed to have spent all his time in dalliance in this talented woman's society. He took much pains to learn the lore of old Egypt. The Roman Calendar up to this time had never been revised. It was most confused, and its astronomical principles utterly inaccurate. So Julius Cæsar, when resident in the country, saw the advantages of a fixed year of twelve months, which had obtained here for ages, adopted the Egyptian system, and introduced it into the Roman Empire. The Julian Calendar thus came to us from Egyptian learning, as their written language ages before originated the alphabet. The alphabet reached us from the Greeks, through the Romans. Therefore, as the Greeks derived their architecture, their astronomy, their letters, and their art from Egypt, and the Romans their calendar from the same source, it follows that we owe much of our present intellectual advancement, through a lengthened chain of inheritance, to the wonderful knowledge of natural phenomena possessed by the Egyptians. All their astronomy was developed by the learning of the colleges attached to the temples. It was used to calculate the correct date of the rising of the Nile, which thus the priests were able to predict.

On Cæsar's death Cleopatra and the boy Cæsarion went back to Egypt. Had Julius Cæsar

GYASSAS OR CARGO BOATS LADEN WITH MERCHANDISE.

not been murdered the fate of the lad might have been different. He was allowed by the Romans, however (in 42 B.C.), to take the title of King of Egypt, and in 34 B.C. Antony gave him the title of "King of Kings." Antony at the time had espoused Cleopatra, and was kindly disposed to his stepson. But under Augustus the poor boy was put to death (30 B.C.), when he was but seventeen. If the portraits of the lad be correct, he resembles his lovely mother, and is a fair, tall young fellow, reaching up to her shoulder. That Cleopatra

THE NILE: SAILING BEFORE THE SOUTH WIND.
The eastern hills, near Denderah.

had a strong belief in the importance of alliances with the Romans is proved by her union with Antony after Cæsar's death. Antony, too, had a good wife at home, but Cleopatra caused him to forget her. She bore a daughter to Antony, whom she took with her to Rome on her second

VIEW ON THE NILE NEAR ABU FEDA.

visit and made a ward of the Roman State, with the understanding that the young princess should be wedded to a prince of noble blood, as became the daughter of the queen of the oldest empire of the world. After Cleopatra's death Augustus had this daughter married to Juba, Prince of Numidia (Morocco)—not exactly the alliance her mother would have sought. However, Juba was not a "nigger," as some have thought. I have coins of his and of his son by Cleopatra (for so she was called also), and they show the Numidian royal family to have been handsome folk, of Greek or Roman type of features.

Shakspere, in his wonderful play, gives full credit to Cleopatra's beauty and powers of fascination, but his version of her life is not quite correct. There is little doubt but her desires for Roman alliances did not terminate with the death of Antony. She aspired, we are told, to the hand of the handsome Augustus himself, and he was so fearful of falling a slave to her charms that he was actually afraid to meet her. He, however, determined to have her brought a prisoner to Rome. Finding she could make no impression on the stony heart of Augustus, and was about to be imprisoned, or made a part of his triumphal entry into Rome, she is said to have poisoned herself. Of course she may have been made away with, as her son was "removed" shortly before her death. She had sent this boy away for safety in the care of his tutor, who traitorously delivered him up to the Romans, when Octavian had him put to death. She was thirty-nine when she died, and yet is said to have been at the prime of brilliant beauty. Cleopatra was the most accomplished princess of her time, as well as the most beautiful.

ABUTIG, NEAR ASSIOUT.

She knew many foreign languages, and was accomplished in classical lore, and practised all the Arts. Plutarch says for actual beauty none could compare with her, and the contact of her presence was irresistible. Her conversation was bewitching. Her voice was like the sound of an instrument of many strings, and she could pass from one language to another, so that few barbarian envoys needed an interpreter. This may not all have been flattery. But the portraits on her coins show more of intellect than personal beauty. Still we can see reasons for her captivation of the greatest and sternest of Roman leaders. There is something touching in the sad fate of this gifted woman. Her race had run out. She was the very last Egyptian princess. The Romans became allies of Egypt, and their armies fought her battles. No wonder she looked to this power to rehabilitate her exhausted kingdom. The Romans embraced Greek civilisation, of which Cleopatra's capital, Alexandria, was the head and centre. She was last of the race that founded the great Alexandrian Library, where all the classic literature of the world was stored. No wonder she wished to save her native Egypt as a nation. Cleopatra used all her intellect, her arts, her charms, to accomplish this end of cementing Egypt with Rome. She failed, and with her death the Romans abandoned all the sham of "protection," and Egypt was declared a Roman province. The great Augustus perhaps might have saved her life, but she was evidently, although thirty-nine years old, thought too beautiful, too dangerous, to live. It is strange that no authentic portrait of the most lovely of women exists. I have a coin of hers, but it shows her in late life and is itself of poor execution. It is the head of a refined woman rather than that of the captivating siren which her jealous enemies represent her to have been.

SHADOOF WORKERS AT KÛS, BEYOND DENDERAH.

With the death of Cleopatra, its last Princess, the ancient history of Egypt came to an end. It never again was an independent kingdom. Rome ceased to rule it,

PORTRAIT OF CLEOPATRA, STRUCK
SHORTLY BEFORE HER DEATH.

and it was transferred to the sway of the still more corrupt Byzantium. In after ages Egypt was an easy prey for the Arab conquerors, and was utterly crushed, never attempting even to revolt. The time for her regeneration has come at last. Under British training the poor fellaheen of the Nile banks and the black men of Nubia have been made into good soldiers, and taught to patriotically defend their native land and repel the brutal hordes of slave-raiding dervishes. Egypt has at last got her chance of winning back the semblance of an independent nation. Its modern history begins from 1882–3, when, by the withdrawal of the French, the Dual Control came to an end, and Britain, remaining true to her engagements, became the paramount power to save the old country from utter ruin. Events have moved rapidly since then, and the culminating success of British guidance was only achieved in 1898, when Egyptian soldiers, under English officers, drove back the enemy and reconquered the Soudan. Egypt now begins a new career, this time guided and protected by an empire of far greater extent than that of ancient Rome.

Sailing south, after quitting Denderah, we pass the site of ancient Koptos, an important place in ancient times, whence there was a caravan route to the Red Sea. Then we pass Kûs, where many shadoofs are seen for irrigating the fertile soil, here found at a considerable elevation above the river. There are frequently three, or even four, tiers of shadoofs at work, giving employment to many stalwart men, whose wages are two piastres (5d.) per day ! The pictures in the tombs show us that the same method of raising water was practised 4,000 years ago.

SHADOOFS OF 4,COO YEARS AGO.
(From a Tomb at Thebes.)

CHAPTER X.

THE CITY OF THE LIVING.

KARNAK: COLOSSAL STATUE OF RAMSES THE GREAT.
The Temple of Ramses III. is seen beyond.

THEBES: EAST BANK—LUXOR—OBELISK AND TEMPLE—
TEMPLES OF KARNAK—QUEEN HATASU'S OBELISKS—MEDAMUT

THEBES: THE EASTERN HILLS, LOOKING ACROSS THE NILE.
The ruin in the foreground is the brick pyramid of a king, as yet unexplored.
(*From a Water-Colour Drawing by the Author.*)

CHAPTER X.

THEBES: EAST BANK—THE CITY OF THE LIVING.

THEBES is by no means the most ancient city of Egypt; Memphis was far older, but it has disappeared from our sight. The ruins of Thebes remain, still stupendous even in decay, and old enough to excite our wonder and admiration. Thebes was in its greatest glory long before Homer's time, and yet it was the Greek poet that gave the western world the earliest tidings of the ancient city. The date of the composition of his poems is supposed to have been about a thousand years before the Christian era. Thebes, perhaps, may have been heard of through the Syrian provinces of Egypt, which flourished 1500 years B.C., for no tidings could come from Egypt direct. It was a closed land to the outer world. No foreigners were allowed to ascend the Nile in those days, and any knowledge of old Egypt can only have been hearsay. When the Iliad tells us of the vast extent and enormous wealth of Thebes, its hundred brazen gates, and twenty score of armed men guarding each portal, the author did not draw on his imagination. Its ruins bear out the truth of his statements, even though a poet's licence be allowed. After the Persian invasion (about 525 B.C.), the veil was lifted, and Egypt in the time of

(137)

Herodotus was but a province of "the great King." The Egyptians, now a conquered race, had lost their soldierly qualities. They were ruled by Persian satraps, and their martial spirit was broken, never to return. To hold her own against invaders, mercenaries had to be employed, and, among others, warlike Greeks were enlisted to defend the north-eastern frontier. Foreign settlers were now permitted to settle in the cities at the mouths of the Nile, and gradually the land that had been closed to the outer world for thousands of years, became accessible to adventurous Greeks. In this way Herodotus, about 430 B.C., was a welcome visitor to Lower Egypt. He tells us what he was told, but he never actually *saw* Thebes. Though the decadence of the ancient State was

LUXOR FROM THE RIVER.
The columns in the centre are of the Temple of Ramses II., those to the right are of Amenhotep III.

complete, and the line of Egyptian rulers had become extinct, a powerful priesthood still held sway, the old faith flourished, and seems to have been protected by the Persian conquerors. Herodotus tells us he learned much from the priests, but they did not teach him their sacred writing. He says their buildings were covered with "pictures." These pictorial writings he evidently could not decipher, but it was reserved for us to reveal their mysterious meaning. By aid of the Rosetta Stone we can now translate the language of the hieroglyphics lost to the world for several thousand years. The true story of ancient Egypt comes to us from the inscriptions on the monuments, such as Herodotus saw but could not read. At the same time, now that we can read them, they serve to prove the general truth of the history told him by the priests. After the first Persian conquest there was a return of native rulers, the Nectanebos, who did much temple building, showing that there was art still among the

TEMPLE OF AMENHOTEP, LUXOR.
The pylons of Ramses's Temple with the Obelisk in the distance.

people. But after the second Persian invasion the royal line became extinct, and no king of Egyptian race ever ruled over Egypt again. Alexander wiped out the Persian empire. The Macedonian Greeks replaced the Persian rule, and prepared the way for the legions of Rome. Then in Christian times all Egypt adopted the new faith and accepted the rule of Constantinople. The faith of the Cross was held from Alexandria to Abyssinia.

Christianity was crushed in Egypt when the conquering hordes of Mahomet overran the land, led by Omar, in 640 A.D. The blighting rule of the Moslem has lasted ever since. Under all the destroying influences of 2,500 years the wonder is that so much remains to prove the ancient glories of this extraordinary land. Thebes bears some traces of Roman rule, and many of the temples that the Persians destroyed were rebuilt and redecorated by the Greek rulers, successors of Alexander. But Thebes, which was under construction for 2,000 years, has been a decaying city for a similar period. For 2,000 years the kings of succeeding dynasties employed their wealth to erect and beautify the temples, each telling his own story, and adding his name and cartouche to show his devotion to the deities. Many Pharaohs mentioned in the Bible contributed their share to embellish it. The Pharaoh of the Oppression, Ramses II., and Merenptah, the Pharaoh whose host perished in the Red Sea, also Shishak, who besieged Jerusalem, record their titles and their conquests on the walls of Karnak. The later Pharaoh (Tirhakah, 700 B.C.) who attacked the host of Sennacherib in the days of Hezekiah, as related in 2 Kings, did much work of restoration. I found his name on the temples, and in the records of the Nile's height on the quays. Here I obtained a wonderful scarab with his and his ancestor's cartouches.   What Thebes must have been in its glory, when even to-day its ruins are among the most stupendous of their kind in the world !   There is a railway from Cairo to Thebes, but it is a mistake to use it, although there are now well-appointed sleeping cars for those who have not time to

THE OBELISK AT LUXOR.
Its twin obelisk is at Paris.

travel by the river. The landing-place of the steamers is Luxor, where comfortable hotels are to be found. A dirty Arab village grovels over and around the hoary temple, but fortunately the hotels are well situated.   Pagnon's Hotel, possessing a lovely garden, with shady walks, tropical plants and flowers flourishing among rills of irrigating Nile-water, is a refreshing bowery paradise. Electric lights in abundance, in the hotel itself and in the various *dépendances* scattered through the garden, make it brilliant after sunset. A pretty little English church is in its precincts. An English doctor lives in a substantial dwelling close at hand.   Many invalids visit this part of Egypt in winter, and for their care a special wing of the great hotel is set apart, with competent nurses and a lady matron.   In December and January the climate of Luxor is at its healthiest point, and the delicious, dry, warm air has brought about recoveries when such seemed hopeless. Luxor and Karnak are the only vestiges of ancient Thebes remaining on the eastern bank of the Nile.

A visitor to Thebes in search of pleasure more than the restoration of health, should choose his time during full moon. The first sight of the temples of Luxor and of Karnak then will fully repay all the trouble and cost of reaching them.   Arriving at Luxor by dahabeah or by steamer, the solemn grey lotus columns of Amenhotep's temple (1500 B.C.) seem to rise suddenly out of the Nile. As a matter of fact, their floor is now beneath the river, which is but poorly kept out by a solid quay wall of Roman times. One must be struck with the elegance of these early pillars. Beyond them we come to the huge ungainly columns of Ramses II., which are much inferior in taste. Then we reach his pylons with their row of colossal statues and one of his obelisks. The other was carried off to Paris by the French. There is a mosque here, built on the level of the populous village that once covered the entire temple. Some day the mosque must come down, too, and the excavation of the temple be completed ;

HOTEL GARDENS AT LUXOR.

THE TWIN OBELISK FROM
THE LUXOR TEMPLE.
(Now at Paris.)

meanwhile it prevents us from seeing the full extent of the great structure, although its minarets are rather picturesque.   The bed of the river rises several inches every century, and in 3,000 years and more many ancient structures have perished, or been covered up, in this change of level.   Thebes, being on higher ground, has been more fortunate than Memphis, which has disappeared beneath the Nile and its devouring annual deposit of mud.   It is only at the time of highest Nile that the river reaches the level of the temple floors of Karnak.   In ancient times the possibility of this was prevented by huge dykes round every temple enclosure, and no doubt the Egyptian engineers of those days knew how to exclude the high Nile, and were able to pump their cellars dry.   Much good has been done by the British irrigation officers, and the land round old Thebes is fast recovering its ancient fertility.   The water which percolates into the temples is collected in tanks and pumped out. This good work was begun by the Society for the Preservation of Egyptian Monuments, originated by Sir Edward Poynter, P.R.A.   Its labours resulted in the saving from extinction of the great Temple of Karnak, the Nile water (or rather the earth charged with its salts) having the effect of corroding the columns at the bases, causing them to topple over.   Now the Nile overflow does not injure them, the Egyptian Government has taken over the pumping as part of the irrigation work, and the temples' preservation is almost assured.

We will assume that the tourist has landed at the Roman quay at Luxor and installed himself at Pagnon's Hotel.   After an excellent dinner we enjoy a rest under the date palms.   Then donkeys are provided, and the time is chosen to allow of the full, round moon being above the horizon on the arrival at Karnak, a pleasant ride of about two miles from Luxor.   We journey through fields of rye and wheat in full ear, and crops of peas and beans with their pleasant-scented blossoms.   Passing by the Arab town of Luxor we skirt the British cemetery, through groves of tall date palms, then a fringe of sandy desert, and looming in the distance rises up the great pro-pylon of the Temple of Khonsu.

The road from Luxor in ancient days was marked out by an avenue, or dromos, of sphinxes, and many of these still remain, about twenty feet apart, half buried in the sand.   Each temple had its own dromos, some with lion-, ram , and human-headed sphinxes. We pass the ruins of temple after temple right and left. The builder of each is known, for the whole walls bear hiero-glyphic inscriptions telling the deity to which they were dedicated and the cartouche of the sovereign who had them built. When we see great ruin and inferior sculpture, proceeding from indifferent workmanship, we may safely conclude it is "late work"—that is to say, from Ramses III. to the Ptolemies. When we see good workmanship, beautiful carvings, and solid walls of enormous blocks, strong as when erected, we may conclude the work to be of the great men of the Twelfth Dynasty or the even more elegant work of Seti's time (1360 B.C.), of Thothmes or Queen Hatasu (1600 B.C.). In Egypt the older the work, the better is the architecture, and the taste more refined.

THE SACRED LAKE OF KARNAK.
The Great Temple in the centre, Queen Hatasu's obelisk at the right.

The Karnak temples face all points of the compass. It needs several visits to understand their apparently conflicting angles, and at first one temple seems placed to impede the view of the other. But this confusion of plan is only apparent. Mariette thirty years ago solved the limits and plan of each temple, but it was reserved for an Englishman, Sir Norman Lockyer, to unveil the mystery of the "orientation," as it is termed, of these buildings especially. Each temple had a deity, and each deity its heavenly representative in a particular star. The rising of the star on one day in the year was at the point of sunrise. This point the temple was made to face. The sun at sunrise illumined through the open door, penetrating its horizontal rays through openings in the columned halls, to the central cell. This was the holy of holies, and the sun, shining directly into the

HYPOSTYLE HALL, TEMPLE OF RAMSES THE GREAT.
Columns recently re-erected by M. Legrain.

shrine, its light was caught by mirrors and flashed all over the darkened interior. By night the star of the protecting deity of the temple shone into the same holy of holies, and was at the moment of appearance caught and mirrored in the same way. The fine air and starry sky of Egypt rendered these phenomena successful. The constellations of the zodiac played their parts in other temples, and they were under their protection. Many constellations which were circumpolar 4,000 years ago (that is to say, were always visible by night) now dip beneath the horizon. There is known to be a gradual change going on in the position of the pole star and in the precession of the equinoxes, and Sir Norman Lockyer has been able by this discovery not only to tell the particular star to which each temple was oriented, but actually to fix the date of the foundation of the temple itself. The ancient Egyptians were great astronomers, but it is pleasant to find that we have among us to-day men who can read the riddles of their lost astronomical knowledge.

We ride on past the ruins of temple after temple, with a pond—remains of the sacred lake—attached to each. Then the ruins thicken, and seem a mere desert of stones surrounding a fallen obelisk of granite, with one perfect one, ninety-eight feet in height, standing beside it. These both were erected by the great Queen Regent, Hatasu (of whom I will have much to relate when I cross to her temple on the other side of the Nile). The great fallen obelisk is smashed into huge blocks, tumbled about everywhere around. It is said to have been overthrown by an earthquake, but it is more likely that some Roman contractor employed to convey obelisks to Constantinople or to Rome, went about his work clumsily and occasioned the fall and its destruction. (The Romans carried off twenty or thirty of the finest obelisks, and, imitating them, the French stole theirs from Luxor, and we our "Cleopatra's Needle" from Alexandria. The latter had originally been purloined from Heliopolis.) On one hand are the remains of the lovely lotus columns and papyrus capitals of Usertesen (2400 B.C.), on the other the excellent work of Thothmes (1600 B.C.). Within these was the treasury, which the Persians had destroyed. It was restored in the name of Alexander the Great. Other works were rebuilt by the Ptolemies, with the cartouches (in good Egyptian) of the Greek kings—Philip, the brother, and Alexander Ægus, the unhappy son of Alexander.

The moon, we hope, is now high and brilliant. We descend from our donkeys, and pass two other erect obelisks, to penetrate through the ruins of Seti's temple to the Temple of Amen, with its vast hall of Ramses the Great, the most impressive of all Egyptian temples. The columns are nearly seventy feet high—there are many of them standing and as many gone.* The lintel stones were forty feet long; all were richly carved and painted. Part of the attic storey still remains, together with the bars of the windows. The moonlight gilds the sculptured halls into their ancient splendour; the shadows lend mystery to depths of shade; the utter stillness and weird

QUEEN HATASU'S OBELISKS, KARNAK.
The whole of this part shows great damage by fire.

* It is most satisfactory to see the successful labours of M. Georges Legrain in raising fallen columns and straightening falling ones. He has thereby added much to the beauty of the Hall of Columns, but has also prevented the possible falling of the whole edifice, like a house of cards. The labours of this talented engineer deserve all praise.

K

GRANITE LOTUS AND PAPYRUS
PILLARS OF THOTHMES III.,
KARNAK.
Representing Upper and Lower Egypt.

loneliness of this ancient place of solemn worship are most impressive, and the most frivolous party of visitors is hushed into reverence for a faith that could build such stupendous monuments to the glory of religion and morality, which put to shame our modern sacred edifices. These ancient people show us indeed their faith by their works.

Outside, engraved on the great temple walls, Seti, the enlightened patron of the arts in his day, the restorer of monuments, the builder of temples (whose handsome, intellectual face we can see in the Museum at Cairo, where his body is preserved), tells us the story of his conquests to consolidate his kingdom before he settled down to peaceful arts. He fits out a great army to cross the N.E. desert to punish the Syrians and others who had revolted. He is shown at the head of his troops, mounted on his favourite horse, whose name, "Victory in Thebes," is written underneath. In another place the victorious king is shown coming home by way of the Red Sea Canal, of which a clear plan is given, and it is marked by its name, "The Cutting." Commissariat barracks are built along it. Crocodiles swim in the canal, showing that it was a fresh-water channel conducting from the Nile. Bridges crossed the canal at intervals.* Part of the war was in Palestine, and "Canaan," "Lebanon," and other Biblical names are frequent. But these events occurred long before the arrival of the Jews in the Promised Land. On the southern walls of the great temple are inscribed the wars of Shishak against the Jews, and weird portraits are given of Israelitish captives of unmistakable Semitic likeness; but these events occurred much later (930 B.C.) than the wars of Seti described above.

It is well worth the trouble to climb to the summit of the northern pylon of the great temple when the moon is still brightly shining. From this height the beauty of the site of the great city is manifest. The mountains

COLOSSAL GRANITE HEAD
OF THOTHMES III.
(British Museum.)

---

* We give an engraving of this ancient canal on page 5, Chapter I.

recede from the Nile east and west, leaving a basin of cultivable land, with the river, bordered with palms, winding its serpentine course, here dividing in two great branches. To the west the river stretches far towards the desert, bounded by the ruddy hills which hold the tombs of the kings hidden away in their recesses, many of them as yet undiscovered. The eastern horizon is enclosed by a beautiful serrated range of mountains, their ruddy tint even discernible in the moonlight, contrasting with the brilliant green of the cultivated ground, fringed with dark date palms. It is a wonder-

GREAT TEMPLE, KARNAK.
Lattice window lighting the clerestory.

ful scene, never to be forgotten. Then we descend from our lofty point of view and ride back to Luxor by the banks of the Nile. As we traverse the Arab town the white domes of the mosques and their tall minarets gleam like silver in the moonlight. The village is lit up by its Greek dealers' shops and the gaudy lanterns of the *cafés*. In some we hear the drone of Arab music, and a "Fantaseea" is being held preluding or concluding the entertainments at a native wedding. Then a bend of the road brings us back to the river and past the half-buried pylons of Ramses' temple at Luxor. His statues sit before the gate—monoliths of granite buried waist deep in rubbish. Only one of his granite obelisks is left, the other one is in the Place de la Concorde in Paris. We descend from our patient beasts, and, dismissing them and the donkey-boys, we walk through the halls of Ramses into and through the more elegant aisles

DROMOS OF RAM-HEADED SPHINXES, KARNAK.
Leading from the Great Temple to the Nile.

of Amenhotep III. to our hotel. Its pretty garden is lit up by many lamps, and the building by electric light. The air is balmy, dry, and not too cold to let us sit out of doors and enjoy our coffee and cigarettes. To bed betimes, for we must make an early start if we want to cross the Nile and the western desert before the sun is high; and if we are to visit the Tombs of the Kings on the morrow we have a long day's work before us.

A splendid avenue of sphinxes with rams' heads has recently been excavated. It leads from the great temple of Karnak to a quay on the ancient bank of the Nile. On this quay-wall the heights of the Nile, mentioned before, are marked with the name of the king in whose reign the record was made.

Before quitting eastern Thebes, I would advise my friends some day, when the sun is not too strong, to devote a morning ride to a visit to an ancient suburb, or perhaps a holy place of pilgrimage, now known as Medamut, about seven miles off towards the north. You can proceed along the railway embankment most of the way, and then through pleasant fields full of luxuriant crops of every kind. Thus the ruins of the ancient temple and mounds of Medamut are reached. The temple must have been a beautiful structure, the lotus columns are of the best period, of the time of Seti and Ramses II., but some of them bear the cartouche of Amenhotep II. The situation, among a grove of palms, is most lovely; unfortunately the encroachments of the ever-rising Nile has ruined the buildings greatly. The mounds here probably mark the remains of a country palace of some of the old kings.

GROUP OF VILLAGERS AT MEDAMUT.

CHAPTER XI.

THE CITY OF THE DEAD.

THE COLOSSI AT THE TIME OF THE INUNDATION.

THEBES: WEST BANK—THE COLOSSI—THE TOMBS OF THE KINGS—
QUEEN HATASU'S TEMPLE—THE RAMESSEUM—
TEMPLE OF GOURNAH—MEDINET HABU.

EMBLEMS OF UPPER AND LOWER EGYPT AT THE FOOT OF QUEEN HATASU'S THRONE.
(From a Painting by Mr. Howard Carter.)

CHAPTER XI.

THEBES: WEST BANK—THE CITY OF THE DEAD.

WE have visited the vast remains of eastern Thebes, the abode of the living, whose dwellings clustered round the great temple enclosures in ancient days. We must now devote ourselves to visit the dwellings of their dead, which were always placed, when possible, on the western bank of the river. The sun was supposed to die in the west each evening, to rise again, a daily resurrection, on the eastern horizon. So the west became the locality for the departed ones, awaiting their return to an eternal life after the final judgment. The Nile, the River of Life, flowed between the living and the dead. It was a beautiful allegory, and the Egyptian religion is full of such poetic symbolism. Not a trace remains of any ancient domestic habitation, the houses of the citizens have utterly disappeared. But the abodes of the dead exist on the western side by thousands. The cliffs are honeycombed with tombs, and the remains of great funerary temples hewn in the rock and built on the terraces out of reach of the Nile floods, extend over several miles. The city of the living has vanished—the dwellings of the dead remain to-day.

We have ordered our donkeys overnight, and they and their Arab attendants have been ferried across the river, and stand waiting on the opposite bank. We are rapidly borne across in the morning breeze, which makes our trim felucca expand her wings to good effect. My donkey answered to the name of Ramses, the other steeds were called after the Sirdar and Washington, and we also had Telephone and Telegraph. The donkeys' names show the progress of the Arabs of to-day. Riding over a mile of sand and hardened mud, which was the river bed a month ago, we disturb industrious agriculturists, busily engaged in planting water melons in little dirt pies about a yard apart, arranged tidily in rows. Our donkeys pick their steps daintily, never touching the seeds, and carefully avoiding the labourers. These mud pies will nourish grown plants in another month, and in twice that time will bear their luxurious crop of delicious fruit. The fellaheen do not grow this profitable crop for nothing, however. Early in the spring, as the Nile falls, they arrange among themselves the "plots" to be planted, marking out the limits for each cultivator with stakes. When the bottom becomes dry land they begin to plant the seeds. A tax is paid to the Government on the ripe fruit, the head man of each village being responsible for an honest account being rendered. All the revenue from other crops is collected in the same way. If irrigation is required there is a special rate for it, but it is not paid till the crop is realised. There is no rent for the land itself—no crop, no pay. This is under British rule. In former days the tax for crop had to be paid in advance whether it grew or not. If water was needed it was charged for in advance, and perhaps the pasha took it all, and the poor farmer got none.

THE COLOSSI, TWIN STATUES OF AMENHOTEP III.
His great temple formerly stood behind them.

Now each gets it in turn, whether peasant or pasha, all alike. No wonder that the fellaheen become richer every year, and the cattle multiply exceedingly, twenty fine animals being seen for one of ten years ago. This is the "stock" in which the Egyptian farmer invests his savings.

To return to our excursion—we cross a great canal, the restoration of an ancient one that had fallen into decay. It is now empty; we ride down one steep bank and up another—requiring good donkeyship. In the bottom of the now dry canal industrious fellaheen are planting certain crops that speedily mature, and herds of shaggy goats are grazing on the banks, tended by little Arab boys and girls. When the Nile is high enough this canal will convey supplies to Denderah and thirty miles away. Now it is closed off, and its bottom and sides available for cultivation, or the mud of last year can be dug out to spread over the land. Wherever Nile mud goes rich vegetation follows; no manure is ever used in Egypt for this purpose; it is dried and used for fuel. Then a stretch of sandy desert intervenes. By and by when the great reservoirs are made, the Nile flood will be husbanded, and will supply this desert with its fertilising waters.

Next we gallop through richly-cultivated fields for a mile or so, and far away we perceive the two colossal figures of Amenhotep III. rising out of the cultivated ground. One of these, known as the statue of Memnon by the Greeks and Romans, was said to utter musical sounds at sunrise and sunset. The music has not been heard for 1,700 years, and after its overthrow by an earthquake in the reign of Tiberius it was restored by the Romans in the reign of Severus, but it was a poor piece of patchwork of the old fragments. No wonder the ancient musician declined to perform the gentle airs of his monolithic days. However, although there are two statues, only one king is commemorated. Amenhotep was such a great monarch that he had to be made not only the greatest figure the world had seen, but done *twice over !* and these were merely the guardians of his temple which stood behind them, but has now disappeared. The foundations remain, and Mariette said there was a third colossus buried in the Nile mud which entombs the foundations of the great temple. There is a likeness of Amenhotep III. in his tomb, not far off, and also a portrait of his renowned wife, Queen Tyi. In life this royal pair seem to have been models of conjugal bliss. The finest portrait of this great monarch is now in the British Museum, and from it we can judge what manner of a man was represented by these much-mutilated colossi.

The cartouches of Queen Tyi and Amenhotep are found side by side on scarabs of their time. I got one from an Arab, who doubtless found it here, but one still more curious came into my possession. It is the largest scarab I have seen, and has the story of how Amenhotep, before his married days, was a mighty hunter, and slew " of lions fierce " 102. But, when Tyi took him in charge, he gave up this dangerous amusement. Her cartouche, and the king's also, appear on this "document." A remarkable thing happened about this scarab. The one I got first was broken in two places. Several weeks after I got, from another Arab, another of the same, also imperfect. But, on examination, I found that what was missing on one was perfect on the other, and so I was able, by Mr. Griffith's kind help, to obtain a full translation of the famous story of the lion-hunting king's exploits.

The statue that remains entire is still a very impressive figure, a splendid seated giant, cut in one block of sandstone over sixty feet high. The king's name and titles, and those of his great queen Tyi, are still graven on his throne; his daughter stands at his knee. Two stalwart men are carved on each

GRANITE HEAD OF
AMENHOTEP III.
(*British Museum.*)

side, represented binding the Nile with strong ropes—significant of the kingly power of controlling the mighty river—the life-giver of Egypt. The Nile is represented by lotus and papyrus plants; the action of these figures is very fine. I have chosen a copy of it for the cover of my book. Looking towards the encircling range of rocky cliffs the effect of these solitary seated giants is impressive. They seem to be the guardians of the tombs. These pierce the vertical rocks in long rows of square openings, tier over tier, in parallel lines. At the left the huge mass of the temple of Medinet Habu, on the right the gigantic ruins of the Ramesseum, balance one another in the picture. In the distance rise up the cliffs which contain the Tombs of the Kings, while the sculptured Terrace Temple of Queen Hatasu fills up the centre. We are now at the limit of the cultivated land ; the Nile can rise no farther, and vegetation ceases, deserts of sand taking its place.

When the colossi were put there—(how were they brought, for they are not the stone of the country, but from near Assouan, though they are not of granite but of a hard conglomerate rock ?)—they were well above water ; now the poor giants have their bases covered at high Nile, and their feet bathed by the flood. When thus surrounded by water, the scene is very grand in its desolate deluge, and in moonlight is one of the most impressive sights in Egypt. The figures seem to rise out of the waste of waters, mounting higher as we gaze upon their impassive countenances, the ghosts of the departed glory of 3,000 years.

We strike off to the right by a pathway through the fields, among fragrant crops full of flowers, disturbing dense flocks of quail and innumerable other varieties of birds, many pretty hoopoes being among them. We pass a picturesque sakiya, with two handsome oxen hard at work in their dizzy circle, or at least what would be dizzy work were not the cattle blindfolded. A happy-looking Arab boy drives them from morn to night for a piastre (2½d.) a day. The crystal rivulet runs out, enriching the florescent clover with its refreshing rills, poured out by chains of earthen pots from thirty feet below. Before us are the vast ruins of the Ramesseum, the only one standing of a group of six magnificent temples, whose foundations were unearthed by Dr. Petrie in 1896. They were all side by side, and in one was discovered the great stele of Merenptah, the Pharaoh of the Exodus, whose army perished in the Red Sea. On this stone was found the first mention in any Egyptian inscription, of what was, to them, the hated name of Israelites.

Around the Ramesseum Dr. Petrie excavated the huge wine cellars belonging to the religious body attached to this great establishment for the worship of the Ramses. The cellars, arched with brick, were in perfect preservation, and many of the wine-jars entire—their corks undrawn, sealed with the king's seal, and the name and date of the vintage rudely written on the outside. But, unfortunately, they were all hollow mockeries. In the 3,300 years the liquor had all been "absorbed." I was fortunate enough to be at the place when the stele and the wine-jars were discovered. Dr. Petrie and his assistants were living in the emptied wine cellars. They were cool apartments, being built with thick walls arched with sun-dried bricks. One was the dining-room of the exploring party ; another vault was the gentlemen's room, and two pleasant wine cellars were reserved for the ladies. But

SETI'S MORTUARY TEMPLE OF GOURNAH,
At the entrance to the road to the Tombs of the Kings.

on windy days the ladies' apartments (open at both ends) were rather draughty, so I employed myself in looking about (for the ladies' comfort) for a comfort-able rock-hewn tomb with several apartments. Dr. Petrie has often said that there is no more healthful and delightful dwelling (for the living) than an Egyptian rock-hewn tomb! When he was engaged on the survey of the pyramids he lived in "a dry, comfortable tomb" for several months.

The pylons of the Ramesseum have been overthrown by the water of the Nile in flood, which rises some 20 feet higher than in ancient days. They are now heaps of ruins. Inside this temple stood the great granite colossus of Ramses II., which was 70 feet high. It must have been shattered by lightning, and is now a heap of broken blocks (page 164).

We now took the road to the right leading past the temple of Seti, where this good man was worshipped by pilgrims to his tomb in the cliffs above the Tombs of the Kings. Here is a poor Arab village, where there is a good well of icy-cold water. Several little girls followed us, each with her small jar of water on her head. The climb up the ravine that led to the royal tombs is steep and stony, and no water is obtainable by the way. So we each engaged a little maiden to attend to our wants. They were sweet children, good-looking, and one named Amina was a little beauty. They all ran after the donkeys, prattling their English words with innocent familiarity and amusing terms of affection for their employers. Some of them had necklaces of beads—gaudy modern things, brass bangles, and earrings or nose jewels. Amina had none; her mother was too poor and her father was dead, she said. One of the bigger girls, called Fatima, was well supplied with decorations and said, "Amina have no bangles, no necklace, not anything. Fatima will sell some of hers. Buy for Amina. She have no father. She is too poor." So we purchased a selection for a few piastres for Amina. This transaction made her look so happy that she became more attentive than ever, and her terms of affection stronger still. She proposed to marry the

GIRL WATER CARRIERS AT GOURNAH.

purchaser of the beads if he would come back for her when she would be fourteen and allowed to wed the "nice gentleman" she so much loved. The little convoy kept with us for the greater part of the day, their pretty figures in their single long robe of dark-blue cotton, their heads tied up in yellow and red kerchiefs, giving a picturesque element to our party. When they came to the topmost ridge of the hills all turned back by the way they came; they would not leave their own valley. Their water-bottles were empty, and each carried back the well-earned baksheesh. It was pleasant to see the little girls' happy faces, and hear their laughing voices.

Toiling up the steep, rough way, covered with sharp flints, our donkeys made slow progress, and we got off to walk. The barefooted natives never seem to feel the cutting flint flakes, though they made sad havoc of our boots. Then the rocks closed, and we found ourselves in a narrow gully, about 500 feet above the Nile. It seemed to be the dry bed of a stream, rounded pebbles and old water-courses everywhere. But it is a rainless land. Once in thirty years or so a heavy shower may come to fill the "wadi," as these dry river beds are called. One of these a few years ago came in such volume that it burst into several of the royal tombs, doing much damage to the painted rocky walls. As they had remained fresh and perfectly dry for 3,500 years, it shows how rare the rain must be. The path descended into a deeper and wider valley, and we mounted our beasts again, and after a mile's

DEIR-EL-BAHARI: QUEEN HATASU'S TEMPLE—SHRINE OF ANUBIS.
Showing the fluted columns—origin of the Doric style.

ride halted where some square-mouthed caves were seen here and there on each side. The donkey-boys now began to act as guides. "Here the tomb of Ramses, sir. Ramses the Great. You know him? Here the tomb of the small Ramses. Ever so many Ramses. But here is the best tomb of all, the tomb of Seti, sir."

There are many tombs of kings, a very avenue of them, but we thought one would do on this occasion. We said we would go down into Seti's, and were about to do so, but a tall Arab barred our way; a dignified looking man in a white garment and yellow turban wound round his tarboosh. Then he said politely, "Your tickets for the tombs, sir." Then we saw that the slanting passage, running steeply downwards to the tomb from the path, was closed by an iron gate. These tickets are sold to every tourist by Cook and Son, acting for the Government, cost £1 each, and without them none of the "protected" monuments are visible. This regulation was made none too soon, for enterprising Arabs were found who were making traffic of the wall-paintings, selling them to agents in France and America. Fortunately we were all provided with the talismanic tickets, and the gate was opened. Down, down into the bowels of the mountain we penetrated, sometimes by steps, sometimes by sharply-inclined planes, till we reached several chambers, about 100 yards beyond the entrance. The passage was lofty and wide, and daylight finds its way for a while, then total darkness. The custodian lit his candles, and when a finer chamber than usual was reached flashed the flame of ignited magnesium wire that we had provided. Chamber after chamber, passage after passage, all beautifully painted, exquisite drawing, and in many places as fresh as when done 3,500 years ago! The ceilings are blue, with golden stars thereon, the whole walls being painted with coloured hieroglyphic texts from the ancient Egyptian Bible, the "Book of the Dead."

Scenes from the past life of the great art-loving king—scenes of his future life beyond the grave—he appears before the gods and justifies himself by showing his well-spent life, and enumerating the evil deeds he did not do—a negative kind of virtuous self-justification. The soul of the dead man is weighed, and found true; he is deemed ready for future bliss! Volumes would be needed to enumerate every column of literature from Seti's tomb. Some illustrations and translations have been published, but to decipher all would be over much.

In the days of Herodotus, who gave the outer world the earliest tales of Egypt, the Tombs of the Kings, as far as known, were empty. Their entrances were closed, though the priests could enter them by secret passages only known to themselves. In later days many were violently broken open and robbed, but the *locale* of the tomb of Seti seems to have been lost, unknown even to the Arabs of the neighbourhood. Belzoni discovered the entrance to Seti's tomb in 1817, and in the uttermost splendid domed chamber there lay the empty coffin, its lid broken in fragments. It was of purest Egyptian alabaster, nine feet by five, completely covered with hieroglyphics within and without, beautifully engraved and filled in with blue enamel paint. In the bottom the angel of death spreads out her arms and wings to receive the body of the dead king. It is the most impressive and most beautiful sarcophagus in the world! Sir John Soane, the architect of the Bank of England, bought it from Belzoni, and it is now deposited in the Soane Museum, in Lincoln's Inn Fields. Anyone who has not visited this beautiful record of the past should do so without delay.

But a more wonderful thing still was the discovery of the actual body of this great and good monarch. In 1850, or thereabouts, some Arabs on the other side of these mountains discovered a deep shaft leading to a tunnel in the rock. This was found to contain fifty or more mummies of the lost kings of Egypt, which had lain in their place of concealment since a thousand years before the Christian era. In time of war or invasion the guardian priests had removed hastily every king's mummy from their tombs, and hidden them here for safety.

QUEEN HATASU'S TEMPLE,
As seen from the overhanging rocks, when returning from visiting the Tombs of the Kings.

Every mummy was labelled and separately rolled up, so that they could be easily restored. But this had never been done, and they are all now on view in the museum at Cairo. Seti's body has been well preserved, and his fine handsome head exposed.* He looks the great and enlightened man his works prove him to have been. He must have died about 1320 B.C. It is the only royal mummy that is not repulsive. His beautiful clear brow, his handsome symmetrical countenance, are really as if in a calm sleep; his arms folded across his chest. The whole is really impressively dignified. His son's body (Ramses the Great) is also to be seen in the museum, and his tomb is in

---

* An engraving of Seti's head will be found at page 116.

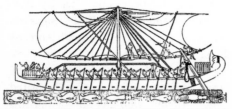

ONE OF THE SHIPS BRINGING TREASURES
FROM THE LAND OF PUNT.

this valley also. Ramses left more temples and gigantic statues than his father, and he also greatly extended the boundaries of Egypt. He reigned for sixty-seven years, and left 115 children. (Some records make him the father of 170!) His name is found on nearly every monument in Egypt, and records of his victories in Asia Minor, Syria, and Nubia. His features show a strong will, and he possessed a vigorous frame too, but he was a mighty tyrant, while his father was an intellectual, refined, and worthy sovereign. Seti's reign was perhaps the golden age of ancient Egypt. He restored and built everything in excellent taste. Petrie calls him the "Grand old Archæologist."

We emerged from the cool, deep-tunnelled tomb of Seti, and found ourselves in the burning sunshine, with dazzled eyesight. It was too hot to proceed, so we sheltered in the empty tomb of a later King Ramses, and had our luncheon-baskets opened. We rested a while, and then mounted the narrow path leading up the cliff, winding round giddy precipices to a height of about 800 feet. Looking down deep into the ravine we had just quitted we saw beyond its vertical sides another valley, and in it some figures working about a crevice in the rock. We soon ascertained by our glasses that they were a posse of Government officials, and found afterwards that they had been specially sent from Cairo, and had opened the tomb of Amenhotep II. It contained the sarcophagus and the body intact, and had never been touched since his entombment, about 1550 B.C. The coffin was unopened, and was covered with wreaths of olives, and flowers strewn on the floor and on the coffin were still perfect. The jewels and wrappings of the king's mummy were as when buried with him. When this unique "find" is shown it will be interesting indeed. On the floor of the tomb a strange spectacle presented itself, three naked corpses, their throats cut and their breasts gashed, lay across the entrance. They had not been mummified, but the dry air of the vault had perfectly preserved them. It was conjectured that these had not been killed on the spot, but were possibly the corpses of malefactors thus mutilated and placed there to terrify any violators of the tomb; and this gruesome group at the very door may really have saved the burial-place from the desecration which befell the other kings' tombs, every one of which has been robbed in ancient times. It seems wicked even now to violate such a monument, but the Arabs would despoil everything of the kind if left unprotected. A gate will be put at the entrance, and a guardian to look after it, and as much as possible of its contents will be left as it was

QUEEN HATASU.
The only portrait left undestroyed in her Temple.
(Egypt Exploration Fund's Volume.)

found. Sir William Garstin interfered in this case, and made the Cairo Museum authorities leave the mummy and its belongings in the tomb, so that at least one of the poor old kings will be left unmolested in his long rest. Of course, any golden ornaments or jewels will be removed for safety to the Museum at Cairo.

A short time before this the tomb of Thothmes III. was discovered also in the same locality. Contrary to what we might expect of such a great conqueror, it is a poor tomb. An Arab named Abderasool, who made this latest discovery, living in a village on the other side of the hills, was also the finder of the other lost mummies of the kings, about twenty years ago. He and his tribe had been working the treasure as a mine for several years. The Government sent down a hundred soldiers, and when he would not tell his secret, bastinadoed him and threw him into prison. This was before the British Occupation. Abderasool had been donkey-boy in the suite of the Prince of Wales, and someone wrote to the Prince about the affair, with the result that interference from such high quarters was obtained. He was released, paid, it is said, £200 for

his discovery, and the mummies taken to Cairo. This gentleman is a friend of mine, and I have been a visitor at his house. He offered me his bread and salt, but I much preferred his coffee. In 1894 he offered to show me the tomb, since proved to be that of Amenhotep II., and begged me, like another Belzoni, to undertake the opening of it. I mentioned it to Dr. Petrie, but he could not do so without official leave. Now, however, the Department of Antiquities has rewarded the discoverer, and the Government has properly taken possession of the monument and its contents.

PRINCESS NEFRURA,
Daughter of Queen Hatasu.
(Egypt Exploration Fund's Volume.)

L

PRINCESS KHEBT-
NEFERU,
Queen Hatasu's sister, who
died in infancy.

We now began to descend the opposite side, and by a zigzag rather dangerous path cut in the face of the rock reached Deir-el-Bahari, the terrace temple of Queen Hatasu, vertically beneath us. We could actually drop a stone upon it. This wonderful woman, daughter of Thothmes I., was half-sister and wife of Thothmes II., and regent during the minority of Thothmes III. She was by birth a " Royal Princess," and conferred honour on her husband as " Royal wife." Her mother bore the proud name of Aahmes, being directly descended from the great deliverer of the Egyptian people, who bore the same name. This was the author of the expulsion of the Hyksos, who had held the country in 500 years of bondage. Queen Aahmes had no sons. Thothmes II. and III. were children by another wife not of royal blood. Besides, Hatasu was much older, and her father had associated her with him in the government in his old age. As to her ward, Thothmes III., she did what she could for him, and married her daughter to him to secure his royal claim to the throne. Yet he seems to have done all he could to obliterate Hatasu's name from memory when he came into the kingdom. She erected this temple to the glory of her father, mother, and herself. They are frequently pourtrayed, and represented as very handsome people. Perhaps she took too much glory to herself, for when the ungrateful Thothmes became king he erased Hatasu's name everywhere, substituting his own. But this was so hurriedly and roughly done that the deposed queen's name can be still read. He even chiselled out her features, but in the upper parts of the work a perfect likeness of her still remains. Perhaps he made away with her, for her tomb has not been found in later days, although her throne and other things likely to be interred with her have been in the British Museum for some years.

The masculine-minded queen is frequently represented in the sculptures as a man with a beard. This is, of course, only a symbolical allusion to her strong character and intellectual ability. When

QUEEN AAHMES,
Mother of Queen Hatasu.
(*Egypt Exploration Fund's Volume.*)

she ruled the land, which she practically did for twenty years and more, it was in a state of peaceful prosperity. She had large armies, but there were no battles or need of foreign conquest under her reign. She devoted all her great abilities to peaceful commerce and geographical expeditions to distant lands. She seems to have perfected Egyptian architecture in inventing the rock temple and the columnar arcades and cornices which long afterwards developed into the graceful buildings of the Greeks. Yet Hatasu's temple is earlier by nearly 1,000 years than the oldest Greek temple. The pure Doric style had its origin here. Wonderful to relate, the name of the architect of the building (if such a temple, in most part rock-hewn, can be so called) is well known. The queen allowed him to build himself a tomb, overlooking his masterpiece. His name was Senmut, and the story of his life and his works is fully told in the inscriptions on his monument, which is in the Museum at Berlin.

The beautiful white temple lay at the foot of the vertical cliff. The view from this point was lovely; the desert alternating with green plains directly

COLONNADE,
QUEEN HATASU'S TEMPLE,
DEIR-EL-BAHARI.

beneath us, the Nile shining like burnished gold beyond. Arrived at the end of the steep path we entered the temple of the great queen, which rises in three terraces, cut out of and against the perpendicular limestone cliffs which we have just descended. Colonnades of fluted pillars, pure in style as a Doric temple, are cut out of the rock, or built so as to veil the flat walls. Others are covered with pictorial representations, beautifully sculptured in low relief, and coloured with exquisite taste. In some cases the pigments are gone, and here and there they are as fresh as when executed. They tell the story of this great queen's scientific and commercial expeditions to the Land of Punt. We see the ships being fitted out for some long voyage. Then the explorers arrive at foreign ports; they fight their way with some, and make treaties with

L 2

others.   The barbarians live in houses built on piles.   The ladders are drawn up
and wait alongside the dwellings.   A treaty is shown as being concluded with
the queen of this foreign country.   She is represented as a very large person,
enormously stout, and it was evidently meant to be a portrait.   Her subjects are
dark in colour, much darker than the Egyptians, but they are not negroes, nor
have they woolly hair.   Some of the aborigines came home with the Egyptian
fleet as "samples."   The whole expedition savours of Captain Cook's voyages, or
of Darwin's exploration in the present century.   Verily there is nothing new under
the sun!   All sorts of foreign animals, strange plants, flowers, and trees are
brought away.   Tribute of rings of gold and copper is weighed out and checked.
It was evidently a paying expedition wherever it was, possibly in Somali-land or
Sokotra.   The rare birds, animals, and fish are all correctly depicted.   Trees are
shown, their roots packed carefully in boxes, being carried to the queen's vessels.
Among these are incense and ebony trees, which did not grow in Egypt.   At
the rear of the temple are several chapels cut into the rock, all beautifully
decorated.   Some of these chapels or cells seem to have been beautifully carved
and painted and their doorways built up.   They were not done for show; they
were meant for the deities only.   Like the Greek sculptors, who made the back
of their statues of equal finish to the front, even though it could not be seen
by mortal eyes, so the Egyptian queen with her temple.

> " In the elder days of Art
> Builders wrought with greatest care
> Each minute and unseen part,
> For the gods see everywhere ! "

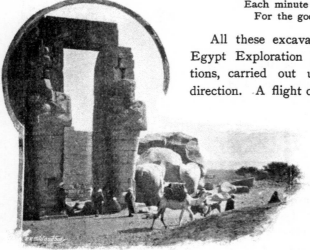

THE RAMESSEUM, WITH THE GREAT FALLEN COLOSSUS
OF RAMSES THE GREAT (see page 155).

All these excavations have been done by the
Egypt Exploration Fund by voluntary contribu-
tions, carried out under Dr. Edouard Naville's
direction. A flight of easy steps descends towards
the plain.   From this an
avenue of sphinxes, three
miles long, in ancient days
conducted to the river, opposite a similar avenue at
Karnak on the eastern bank.
Dr. Naville found in the
inscriptions allusion to the
rare trees growing before
the temples. This made him
uncover all the platform to

see how this could be. He found pits twelve feet square filled with Nile earth, and in the centre of several the stumps and roots of trees, which must have been supplied with water at this height above the river by some hydraulic apparatus. These trees must have ceased growing about 1600 B.C.

Naville also disco-

WINE CELLARS OF RAMSES THE GREAT, RAMESSEUM.
Used as a dwelling by Dr. Petrie's digging party (see page 155).

vered the ancient ebony door of one of the shrines, which seems to have been made to contain the sacred images. It is now in the Museum at Cairo, and is covered with carving and inscriptions evidently done in Hatasu's time, 3,500 years ago. It is the only thing of the kind known of this date; but the same queen's ebony chair is in the British Museum, and several of her chessmen, one with a lion's head, and her board for playing the game, are also preserved. I possess several of her scarabs or seals. Everything belonging to her was beautiful.

The work of drawing and copying the sculptures of her temple has been in progress for several years, and will form three or four handsome volumes which will be given to the subscribers of £1 per annum to the Egypt Exploration Fund. A house has been built for the gentlemen in charge of the work. We were shown over all the temple by Mr. Carter, the chief artist of the Exploration Fund, who entertained us afterwards in his cool drawing office when the sun became too hot to be borne, and brewed for us refreshing tea, which we needed after a hot day's work. When the sun got low we saddled our donkeys and rode back towards Luxor. It needed care to avoid the yawning shafts leading downwards to innumerable tombs. The ground is covered with them, and riding among them is not without danger. The Arabs are constantly burrowing among them, searching for mummies to strip of their decorations, and never think of filling up the pits. There are

MERENPTAH,
The Pharaoh of the Exodus.
(*From Dr. Petrie's History.*)

many richly-painted tombs in the cliffs belonging to private citizens of ancient Thebes. These are closed by iron gates, and under careful custodians chosen from the respectable villagers. The sun was sinking low in the heavens, and we had now to hasten back to Luxor, devoting another day to examine some of the interesting records of the past belonging to humbler individuals than kings and queens.

It is well to devote some time to visit a few of the many interesting tombs in this wonderful necropolis. The tomb of Rekhmara (No. 35) is especially interesting, for he was Grand Vizier of Amenhotep II. He gives the orders he received from "my lord the king," and altogether seems to have been a very powerful man, occupying much the same position as Lord Cromer does to-day. He submits the valuation of each "nome" under his rule, and shows how the taxes were levied, and how much he paid in for each district under his charge. He collected revenues from foreign places under his control, from Syria, East Africa, Nubia, and also from the Ægean, and beautiful Greek vases are shown which were brought to him as tribute from the Archipelago.

There are many tombs in this neighbourhood which were opened and pourtrayed by Champollion and by Wilkinson and others forty years ago ; but to show how unexhausted is the supply of ancient historic monuments, I will describe several that have been found this year (1899) by Mr. Percy Newberry and Dr. Spiegelberg, working in concert with the Marquis of Northampton. They have explored several most interesting tombs of the Eighteenth Dynasty. All these had been robbed in ancient times, but the carvings and paintings on the walls were still as fresh in many places as when executed 3,500 years ago. One of them had been the last resting-place of a state physician. He recounts his qualifications for the post, states that he was the son of a doctor equally learned, and both father and son had enjoyed the royal favour and emoluments of practice at court. Another tomb was that of an artist in bronze, a sort of Cellini of his day, who made the bronze doors for Queen Hatasu's temple, near at hand, and also the bronze cappings of the great queen's obelisks at Karnak. His tomb shows him to have been a man of taste and great artistic ability. He gives sketches of the obelisks he adorned.

But the best of Mr. Newberry's discoveries was the tomb of a more humble individual, and was found in better preservation than the others, and, strange to say, underneath the house where Mr. Newberry's party was living. When they took a native cottage for their dwelling on the edge of the desert they little thought that underneath it were buried the records of the life and work of a grand old gardener of 1500 B.C. This ancient florist was named Nekht, and was Head Gardener of the temple of Karnak, on the opposite side of the Nile. Floral decoration of the sacred buildings seems to have been considered very important, the quantity of festoons, wreaths, and bouquets of lovely flowers required for temples covering many acres must have been enormous. The official who supplied them must have been a small capitalist in his way. But his family tomb is of small extent, though very beautifully decorated with emblems of his craft. The principal apartment is about twenty feet by ten. It is shaped like a bower, its domed roof being hollowed out of the living rock, and is decorated with a trellis-work of cane or bamboo, in squares, each containing a bunch of purple grapes or a ripe vine leaf hanging downwards from the tendrils of the vine, which seems to overshade the whole. Round the corner of the apartments, lotus-flowers, pendulous, are painted as a decorative frieze. Underneath the lotus cornice the gardener and his family weave garlands and arrange bouquets of lovely flowers of varying hues and offer them to the effigies of the gods and goddesses of the Karnak temples.

REKHMARA,
Grand Vizier of Egypt.

Below, a plan of the actual garden is shown, with its flower-beds and water-tanks to give them life. The labourers are at their work of planting, pruning, and irrigation. A picture of the gardener's house is given, showing his practical dwelling in the centre of his horticultural establishment. On another wall the gardener and his wife are painted sitting side by side, the lady, a fair-skinned, buxom dame, with her rounded arm resting on her husband's shoulders lovingly, and both are regarding their son approvingly, a tall youth of eighteen or so, who weaves garlands of flowers and offers them to his parents, to gain their approbation of his skill in the mysteries of his craft. On another wall is seen the portrait of the great King Amenhotep I., the consolidator of the so-called new empire of Egypt, who reigned about 1700 B.C. His wife sits beside him. She was a celebrated princess, and gave royal rank to her husband, who was of meaner birth, though a great conqueror. These sovereigns have left us many records of their time, and 1 am fortunate enough to possess scarabs with their " cartouches," or royal seals, which were possibly used by themselves in their day.

MEDINET HABU, THE PAVILION OF RAMSES III.
The building to the right is where the royal chambers still remain.

The tomb of Amenhotep I. has not yet been found. Mr. Newberry hopes to discover it next year, and has good reason to know that it is not far off his present "diggings." His body is preserved at the Gizeh Museum, where it can be seen in its original coffin. It was removed for safety, about 1,000 years before Christ, to the cave in which so many royal mummies were found in 1884. The body of Amenhotep is still enveloped in wreaths of flowers, which have never been disturbed. These floral emblems of grief and love were possibly culled and woven by the Royal Gardener of the time. This lends additional interest to the tomb of the other gardener and his family, which I have described above.

The most perfect temple in this locality is, however, the great pile of buildings about a mile south of the colossi, that of Medinet Habu, where two distinct structures of different epochs stand side by side. They have different angles, the apparent position of the sun in the heavens having changed so much during 1,000 years that a new temple had to be built to suit the worship of the sun-god, and admit the rays into the holy of holies at the moment of sunrise on a certain day. There is here a unique building—remains of the palace of Ramses III., which that monarch probably occupied when he came once a year in state to worship at the temple, and there are some very curious domestic scenes depicted on the walls of the upper chambers. The architecture of the temple of Ramses III. (1200 B.C.) is massive and majestic, but when compared with the earlier work of the smaller structure beside it the latter shows much more elegance. Queen Hatasu shows more taste in the portion built by her, and refined old Seti is seen as a restorer with the good work that always bears his *marque de fabrique*.

The perfect state of this wonderful pile of ancient buildings is owing to a populous Arab village having been built over the whole place, and at an early date it had been inhabited by a thriving community of Christians, who had built a fine Coptic church within the temple courts. The Government authorities recently expelled the Arabs, giving them quarters elsewhere, and the whole ruins have been excavated from the 100 feet of rubbish that had hidden and preserved them for 2,000 years. The French, under whom the work was carried on, have

MEDINET HABU: PTOLEMAIC GATE OF THE TEMPLE.
The buildings of Queen Hatasu and Thothmes III. seen beyond it.

INTERIOR COURT OF THE TEMPLE OF MEDINET HABU,
Erected by Ramses III.

removed the Coptic church, which was a most picturesque object, and did no harm whatever. Tirhakah, an Ethiopian king (who made himself master of Egypt in her later degenerate days and adopted her religion and language), records on the outside of the front that he repaired it. This was the king who came to relieve Hezekiah from Sennacherib (700 B.C.).   I fortunately got a scarab of Tirhakah which was found there, probably a foundation deposit of his time.

Archæologists consider the pavilion at the entrance to the great temple of Ramses III. to be built in imitation of a Mesopotamian palace.   It is the only royal dwelling ever found in Egypt.   The walls of this great temple are occupied by pictures of this monarch's wars in Syria and beyond it.   The Asiatic provinces of Egypt had been first lost through the unwarlike reign of the pious Akhenaten, and, although Ramses the Great may have re-conquered and held them for a time, his weak successors were unable to hold them.   But Ramses III., the first of the Twentieth Dynasty (c. 1200 B.C.), made successful war in Asia, and, returning with enormous plunder, seems to have built this temple with the riches he amassed and as a record of his victories.   The sculptures cover almost every wall, inside and outside the great building.   Many of these have been copied, translated, and published.   The names of the cities and peoples conquered have been read, and have added much to our knowledge of the history of the countries he conquered.   One of these scenes is a naval battle, carried on with a Mediterranean nation, possibly from the Adriatic or the Archipelago.   In one of the scenes the Egyptian soldiers are shown trying to save some of the drowning men of one of the enemy's vessels that had come to grief.   This is the first case of kindness to conquered enemies that has been found in such records in Egypt.   The architecture of this temple is fine, but the sculpture is coarse and shows a decline in art.   On the upper floors of the pavilion of Ramses III. some curious domestic scenes are represented, the king, in his hours of ease, is shown amusing himself with the ladies of his family, playing chess with some, and various games with the younger members of his household.

RAMSES III. PLAYING CHESS AND OTHER GAMES WITH HIS FAMILY.

CHAPTER XII.

A VOYAGE ON THE NILE IN A FELUCCA.

THE INNER PORCH OF THE GREAT TEMPLE, EDFOU.
The granite monolith-shrine is seen in the distance.

ASSOUAN—DERAWI—KOM OMBO—SILSILEH—EL KAB—
KOM-EL-AHMAR—EDFOU—ESNEH—LUXOR.

SUNSET SCENE ON THE NILE.
(From a Picture by E. Lear; the property of Miss Griffith.)

CHAPTER XII.

A SAIL ON THE NILE IN A FELUCCA—KOM OMBO—EDFOU.

MESSRS. COOK AND SON'S steamers for a preliminary voyage on the Nile are indispensable, and without the aid of this enterprising firm Egypt and all its wonders would still be unvisited by tourists. I had made use of their steamers and their post-boats for many voyages up and down the Nile, and always found the vessels comfortable, and everyone in the great firm's service polite, kind, intelligent, and in all matters, small and great, reliable. The very name of Cook becomes in Egypt a magic talisman, securing all who trust in it immunity from fraud and protection from rudeness, incivility, and petty annoyances of any kind, such as are frequently the experience of travellers in many parts of Europe. Messrs. Cook take an ignorant Arab or an ebon-tinted Nubian from his native village, put him through some mysterious training, known only to themselves, and in a short time he is fit for use, is labelled "Cook" in large letters, and lo! he at once becomes a patient, efficient, and trustworthy servant of all bearers of their tickets. The change is wonderful, and, as Mr. Cook's servitors are found everywhere from the Mediterranean to the frontier, it follows that these pioneers of civilisation are a great power, and have done, and are doing, much to make Egypt one of the safest countries for travel.

A trip on the Nile is now one of the most enjoyable experiences, whether for scientific purposes or an outing for mere pleasure. For those in search of health, to whom blue sky and warm sun in winter time are essential, it may almost seem to promise a renewal of existence. With all these benefits offered and conferred by Messrs. Cook is associated the civility and experience of a staff of British gentlemen, under whose intelligent control at their offices

TAME LION OF THE PHARAOH.
(Temple of Kom Ombo.)

at Cairo and branches at the large towns these natives have been licked into shape. Their engineers are British; every ship carries a British doctor. Messrs. Cook transact your postal arrangements, forwarding your letters free of charge, and are the bankers of every nationality in the world, with clerks of polyglot education. Yet with all these facilities the time will come, if a man visits Egypt many times, when he will seek to find some places where even Cook is unknown. In this frame of mind I felt that I would try to sail upon the Nile alone, master of my own ship, stopping when and where I chose, avoiding timebills and tours mapped out beforehand, and personally conducted only by myself. Accordingly I made arrangements for hiring a felucca, and for dropping down the river from Assouan northwards.

I had often visited my friend Professor Sayce in his floating home on the Nile. He spends every winter and spring upon the river, going where he will, and anchoring where seems unto him good. I think his wandering life, his accounts of visits to places where tourist steamers never stop, filled me with the notion of copying his mode of travel in a very miniature form. Mr. Sayce possesses the best and most comfortable dahabeah on the Nile. All that I promised myself, however, was at best but a feeble imitation of the Istar, the great ship (with a yard 132 feet in length) owned by my friend. Mr. George H. Morgan, one of the Government engineers at Assouan, found me a felucca about 30 feet long and half decked. It had one big sail, was the swiftest sailer on the river, and had been used with satisfaction by his department. On this we got built a canvas house to shelter from the sun and to act as a cabin. My friend also selected the crew and helped kindly with my outfit. I had a smart young captain, four sailors, and my own stalwart Nubian servant. There was also a small boy, who was needed to climb the bending mast like a monkey, and make himself generally useless! I paid several visits to the bazaar at Assouan and laid in supplies.

I had made the acquaintance of a delightful native gentleman, Mustafa Shakir, the Mamour, or Chief Magistrate, of Assouan, and he undertook to inform all the heads of police stations along my route of my intended journey and to afford me protection in case of need. The Egyptian police are a fine body of men, resembling, and indeed modelled from, the Irish constabulary. They are all natives, and under their care Egypt is as safe to travel in as Ireland. The Mamour came to inspect my little vessel and its outfit, and when he found that my sleeping arrangements were somewhat primitive he sent me down his own exquisite bedding—new blankets, spotless linen, coverlet of yellow quilted silk, and a luxurious mattress, in which all were rolled up out of sight by day. These were somewhat out of keeping with my other travelling gear, but it was useless to decline the help of such a powerful friend.

SUNSET AT KOM OMBO, WITH A FELUCCA IN FRONT.
(From a Water-colour Drawing by the Author.)

My captain was a handsome, gentle-looking young fellow, and, although quite black, not at all a Negro. But the four sailors, though not so black, had the aspect of cut-throats. I was glad when the Magistrate came down to see me off, and addressed a few solemn words to the ship's company. No doubt the advice of such a powerful officer made them behave well. The reis (captain) was owner of the boat. His name was Dahab (Gold), and never was a man better named; he was sterling indeed, and managed his crew with gentle words and tact. I scarcely ever heard him raise his voice. A solemn contract was drawn up and read to Dahab and sealed with his seal, for the poor fellow could neither read nor write Arabic. I was to be taken wherever I desired, and could terminate the journey at any time. No pay till the trip was finished, and baksheesh entirely dependent on my being satisfied at the end. On our first day we did not make much progress, and I had to remind Dahab of the contract and the possible loss of baksheesh. This he repeated to his men, and I had no more trouble.

Soon we left Assouan and Mount Grenfell in the distance, and anchored near a village for the night. We got an abundant supply of new milk from the fellaheen at sunrise, and started down the river with a south wind, flying along at a tremendous speed. But we wanted fresh food, and neither chickens nor eggs could be had on the previous evening, so we landed, hired donkeys, and rode some miles across the cultivated fields to the large village of Derawi. Voyagers are a rarity there, and we soon had a large escort of admirers following us through the two or three wide streets. This is the residence of a district inspector of police, who had heard of my possible visit from his chief, and received me with great kindness, my man Achmet acting as interpreter. A trial for murder was going on in the courthouse. The accused seemed quite careless of his fate, and had a peculiarly jolly expression. He was being tried before a native judge, but he also knew no language but Arabic. We got fowls, eggs, and some excellent vegetables, and good bottled German beer in the bazaar of the little town, which is sure to be an important place some day, when the railway is in full operation, for the surrounding country is populous and very fertile. Enormous prices were asked, but Achmet threatened them with police attention, and we found the real prices very moderate. We had a banquet that night on the fruits of our expedition. The cooking was of the simplest, as none of my men knew anything beyond Arab cuisine, which is rather primitive to European ideas. However, I tried to tell Achmet what to do, and we had good chicken broth, and the chicken itself afterwards ; then rice, sea-

PTOLEMY AND THE TWO CLEOPATRAS.
(From Temple of Kom Ombo.)

soned with Crosse and Blackwell's jam, and Huntley and Palmer's biscuits to our dessert. At nine Achmet cleared the floor, and rolled out my luxurious bedding, drew the canvas round, making of my deckhouse a comfortable bedroom.

The nights were very cold, and I had to pile all my wraps on the top of the Mamour's blankets : but the air was so sweetly fresh that I slept at once, till dawn, bursting in at every crevice in a flood of warm sunshine, awakened me. Then I clapped my hands and Achmet drew out the great bath (lent me by my friend the engineer) from under the half-deck, and filled from the Nile. The bedding rolled back, some

PTOLEMY AND CLEOPATRA.
(From Temple of Kom Ombo.)

boards were lifted, and I dropped into a six-inch bath of delicious river water. Then a cup of tea, made by my Etna lamp, was slipped in under the curtain at seven o'clock. At nine I had breakfast, lunch at one, a cup of refreshing tea at four, dinner at seven. The difficulty was to have variety, and many wonderful experiments were made, the mysteries of cooking being unknown. The Arabs made short work of all my leavings for their supper at dusk after coming to an anchor. My supply of plates being scanty, the small boy washed them up after each service by free use of Nile water, frequently diving under the boat and bringing them up all bright and clean on the other side. I am afraid he removed the gravy in transit, for he generally came up licking his lips, and seemed to gnaw all the fowl bones like a dog. Before retiring to rest the crew often gave me a musical entertainment. Squatting down in the "fo'castle," each produced some primitive instrument, and they led the song in turns, all hands joining in the chorus. They had fair voices for Arabs, and the airs and songs were

M

Nubian, and had some melody, which the Arab tunes of Northern Egypt do not possess. At some of the choruses they all laughed immoderately, but I could never get a true translation of what was the burthen of their song. We always anchored for the night at some distance from the shore, as they said the landsmen in these parts are expert thieves.

The rising sun disclosed the ruins of Kom Ombo, which we had seen in the distance the night before like an island rising out of the waters. The land is very flat hereabouts, and the great mounds of an ancient town rise fully a hundred feet, crowned by a fort of modern times. This town has been built of sun-dried bricks, but owing to some great conflagration, they are all converted

A FRESH BREEZE OFF KOM OMBO.

into vitrified red masses. The mounds are bright in colour, and glow like molten iron in the warm light of sunset or sunrise. The splendid ruins of several temples rise high above a sharp corner of the river, which has encroached greatly here and washed away a large part of the ancient buildings. Only half of one tall pylon remains, the huge blocks of the others lying along the bank or dimly seen in the muddy waters. M. de Morgan, when Director of Antiquities, had erected a substantial breakwater of the fallen stones, which will prevent the temple from being washed away, and he has excavated the ruins thoroughly. They had been buried for ages, and as a consequence the sculptures had never been injured or mutilated, and many of their paintings are brilliant still as when the artists produced them.

A DISTANT VIEW OF KOM OMBO—EARLY MORNING.

(From a Water-Colour Painting by John Varley.)

There are two great temples side by side ; everything is duplex. In this they are unique. Nothing of the kind exists elsewhere in the world. One temple is dedicated to Amen, the representative of God as personified in the sun ; the other is dedicated to Sebek, the evil deity, represented by the crocodile. Thus the good people of ancient Ombos endeavoured to make the best of both worlds. The ruins are mainly restorations of very ancient buildings by the Ptolemies, but there are some remains of the temples of Thothmes III. (1500 B.C.). On one of the huge blocks overthrown at the water's edge, and thus covered at high Nile, is a hieroglyphic inscription recording that this was "founded as a work to endure for ever"—a testimony to the mutability of all human labour. The architecture of the great double courts and the chapels behind them is most majestic and beautiful. The ceilings are covered with astronomical inscriptions, the sun and the stars being represented as sailing across the firmament in boats.

Here on the bank of ruins was picked up at the water's edge a scarab of King Assa, who reigned 3360 B.C., and another of Apopi, one of the Shepherd Kings (Hyksos, 2000 B.C.) in the *débris* of the temple itself. This proved to be the only Hyksos scarab found so far south. The name of Sutekh occurs on it. The scarab has been a text for many sermons and much controversy in learned volumes since it came into my hands. This Apopi was the Pharaoh under whom Joseph was vizier. Both these wonderful proofs of history are in my possession, with others that were found in the recent excavation of the ruins. They show the extreme antiquity of the place.

Rising on an elevated platform high above the river and the flat country covered by the Nile at time of flood, the site of Kom Ombo is remarkably striking, and it can be seen for many miles on the winding waters.

KOM OMBO: FACADE OF THE TEMPLE.

THE GREAT QUARRIES OF GORGE OF SILSILEH
Shrines on the Nile banks, west side.

The warm yellow colour of the buildings and the great ruddy mounds of ruins shine out and are reflected in the glistening Nile. At sunrise and at sunset the mounds become crimson, the banks change to orange, the green cultivated ground, the groves of palm on a large island opposite, all make scenery of the most picturesque character. I tried to sketch the wonderful picture many times, but would have needed the talent of a Turner to do justice to such a subject.

We continued our course down the river, and landed now and then for fresh milk, when we found herds of cows or buffaloes or where other supplies were possible. The red mountain chains that have retreated far from the river, now close in upon it, the channel becomes narrow, and for a time the rocks close in almost to meet, and we are in the gorge of Silsileh, with the vast ancient quarries, bearing the cartouches of Egyptian kings, back for several thousand years. Much of the stone for the ancient temples was worked here.

We anchored for the night in the middle of the rocky passage, under one of the shrines cut in the rock by Ramses the Great, and, after exploring that side, crossed over to the other, spending much time in examining the enormous quarries, the records of the monarchs who drew the material of their huge buildings thence up and down the great river highway. No villages were here to give supplies, so the Arabs began to fish, and drew out some huge, many-coloured, finny monsters, hard to kill. These creatures remained floundering about the boat, snapping at the boy's naked legs, much to his amusement. The Arabs cut up these queer fish, hanging them up to dry, and said they were excellent food. My own supplies, however, had not run short, so I was not reduced to partake of this coarse sort of diet; and next day we arrived in the green districts again, where milk was abundant and other products of comparative civilisation.

The next place worth mentioning is Edfou, which I had often visited, but was glad to explore once more. The temple is in almost perfect preservation, due to the superior quality of its stone, and also to the fact that it was buried

GRANITE MONOLITHIC SHRINE, TEMPLE OF EDFOU.
The only one now remaining entire in Egypt.

in sand and rubbish until excavated by Mariette. A populous Arab village and the accumulated dirt and rubbish of ages had swallowed it up. The roof was built over with huts, and the temple courts used as cellars and stables for animals. To visit the buildings of the temple we now descend thirty or forty steps, to find the entire edifice exposed to view. This temple possesses its outer enclosing walls intact; they are of great strength, ten feet thick, and entirely covered with inscriptions. The size of the principal chambers is inscribed on one of the walls, as well as the architect's name, also lists of the geographical divisions of ancient Egypt, with their names recorded. It was sacred to Horus, and the Greeks called the place Apollinopolis, thus preserving its attribution to the sun-god. The present edifice was mainly the work of the Ptolemies, who were Greeks, and testifies to the wealth of the kingdom—for its cost must have been millions sterling, and the restoration occupied 180 years. It was a faithful reproduction of a much older building, and the work of the Eighteenth Dynasty still exists within it. The monolithic shrine of the sacred hawk is in the centre, quite perfect: a chamber hollowed out of one block of Syene granite. There are six courts, narrowing as they approach the Holy of Holies, around which are arranged fifteen chapels, all sculptured and painted. The outer and inner walls of the open passage that encircles all are covered with historical and other tales, told in pictorial and hieroglyphic illustrations. Staircases lead to the roof, and from the top of the pylons a magnificent view of the Nile Valley is obtained.

PLATFORM ROOF OF THE GREAT TEMPLE OF EDFOU.

This part of the river is usually lonely, and only passed by the weekly post-boats, or by Cook's tourist steamers once a month. But at this time, the view of the river from the temple roof was a remarkable contrast to its usually deserted state, fleets of gyassas, or cargo-boats, seemed to fill the wide Nile, flying along, their great sails spread most picturesquely right and left, propelled by the north wind. Jostling one another in their hurried rush to take all advantage of this favourable northerly breeze, they flew past like enormous flocks of great birds; to watch them was quite exciting. Laden with grain, flour, and fodder for the Sirdar's army away in the far Soudan, every available vessel in Egypt seemed to be employed and guided by willing, well-paid native Arab and Nubian sailors. The boats were very deeply laden, looking quite unsafe, but in Egypt everyone can swim, and a ducking in the beloved Nile is only an enjoyment.

PYRAMID OF EL-KULEH.
The builder of this Pyramid is as yet unknown.
(*From a Sketch by the Author.*)

We experienced north winds after leaving Edfou, and, as my sailors knew not how to sail against the wind, and were entirely ignorant of tacking, we made slow progress. But the cool air was pleasant, and I landed now and then for exercise. One lone pyramid is found here, El-Kuleh. It has no history, and no inscription has been found. It is strange to find a pyramid so far south, the pyramid builders' work ceased in very early times, and pyramids are mostly located in the north.

Groups of pyramids are known to exist far away beyond Dongola, at Gebel Barkal and Meroe, but they are only small imitations of Egyptian work. The little pyramid of El Kuleh made a beautiful object as the sun went down across the desert, and a fair sketch was made of it.

I was beginning to feel lonely, but this evening a surprise awaited me. Turning a great bend in the river, we suddenly found two large dahabeahs at anchor. Professor Sayce's "Istar," with her great masts, was recognised at once, and just beyond a large and handsome vessel, with the flag of Mr. Somers Clarke fluttering in the evening breeze. My tiny felucca looked so absurd beside the great vessels, that in early morning I moved it lower down the river, and anchored in a little creek. But my friend had seen and recognised me, and after breakfast a boat put off from the "Istar," with a kind note from its owner to go exploring on shore and an invitation to dine on board at seven.

El-Kab is a wonderful region, and I started early to investigate it. Now utterly deserted, it was once an important town. Its parallelogram of walls, 700 feet on each side, still exists, and is forty feet thick. Built of sun-dried bricks, it is thirty feet high, and is in excellent preservation, although of great antiquity. There are apertures for gates, north, south, east, and west,

THE WALLED CITY OF EL-KAB,
Looking through the Northern and Southern gates

and the inclined planes, on each side, by which soldiers and even chariots could ascend to the summit of the fortifications are still visible. Within the enclosure of the ancient walls 10,000 people could find accommodation, and the country round, judging from the number of tombs cut in the rocky hills surrounding it, must at one time have been very populous. Now only one resident, the custodian of the painted tombs, is to be found there. This man proved to be a very intelligent Arab, and, as visitors to El-Kab are rare, he locked up his tombs and accompanied me as guide not only to the adjoining antiquities, but crossed the river next day and conducted me to another deserted city some miles off. I was fortunate in having my servant Achmet, who could translate all his information.

Mr. Somers Clarke had a number of workmen from the opposite bank (where there was a considerable village) engaged in excavating among the foundations of a fine Ptolemaic temple, which was ruthlessly destroyed some eighty years ago, when stone was required by Mehemet Ali's tyrannical governors. Some fine sculptured drums of columns have come to light, their painting brilliant in colour as when it left the artists' hands 2,200 years ago. Mr. Sayce was occupied in deciphering inscriptions of the early Empire engraved on the rocks upwards of 5,000 years ago. I went with my faithful Achmet for a long donkey ride through an arid valley westward. We passed several sculptured rocks, and away among the hills found the object of our search, a lovely temple or chapel of Amenhotep III. (1400 B.C.). It is a little gem of architecture. Its columns are fluted, showing whence the Greeks long afterwards got the idea for the Doric architecture of their temples. Internally the little building is covered with beautiful sculptures and hieroglyphic inscriptions, in many of which the brilliant colours are still found intact.

ROYAL NURSE,
With Prince Uazmes on his knee.
(*Tomb of Paheri, El-Kab*)

On the way along the valley, which resembles the dry bed of a torrent, we met a very splendid gentleman in Arab costume. He saluted us, and we returned his salutation. He was mainly clad in robes of white. His legs were bare, and his stockingless feet thrust into red Arab slippers without heelpieces, but he was quite able to keep them on his feet without laces. As the road or track through the shingly gravel was unpleasant walking, I was puzzled how this was possible. He had a long staff and a voluminous white turban. I asked Achmet who this man could be. He said: " Sir, he must be one great sheikh ; but I never saw such very swell sheikh before."

The sun was getting low, and we came homewards by another desolate " wadi," and visited on the way the celebrated rock temple of the Ptolemies, and then several painted chambers in the rock-hewn tombs of the former great men of Nekheb, the ancient name of the city whose walls I have described. One of these, named Paheri, had been the " royal nurse " to a royal prince of his day (possibly Uazmes), and is represented with a child upon his knee, both looking remarkably happy. (To this day in Egypt native male children are nursed by one of their own sex after they are able to walk.) The walls of this and all the tombs adjoining were beautifully painted, and, where not wantonly destroyed in recent times, in fine preservation. One of the tombs is now fitted with an iron gate, and a custodian has been appointed to show them to visitors.

The tomb which is now locked up is that of " General " Aahmes (who was also a great and brave marine officer, according to his own account), which contains his own and his wife's portraits. "Admiral" Aahmes served from the time of King Aahmes till that of Thothmes III., and had much to do in the struggles against the Hyksos. The tombs were prepared, at great cost no doubt, and the best artists employed, during the lifetime of the occupant. It must have been viewed in progress for several years with great satisfaction by the owner, who depicts his prowess in battle on land and water. After his retirement on his laurels to his native town he seems to have greatly enjoyed his pleasures of the chase, fishing, and other sports. In his hours of ease at home musicians, dancers, and acrobats minister to his pleasures. To show his superiority, the owner of the tomb is always represented on a much larger scale than his dependants, and, while he is usually shown of a clear red tint, his wife, who sits beside him with her arm resting on his shoulder, is always depicted of a fairer colour. Under his seat sits a tame monkey, and his faithful dog is at his feet. The ceiling is represented as the blue sky, with golden stars painted on it. All is cut out of the solid rock, covered with a coating of thin stucco, on which is painted the artist's work in flat colours. Every figure and picture has its description in hieroglyphic characters to prevent any doubt of the meaning. El-Kab was a stronghold of the legitimate line of kings expelled from Lower Egypt for some 500 years by the Hyksos usurpers, and this accounts for evidences of civilisation and extensive population in such a remote district.

The evening was now closing in, and I reached my boat in time for a rest, after the heat of the long ride in the hot sunshine. At the appointed time I dressed for dinner, and found several guests assembled at the "Istar's" hospitable board. I thought I had seen the handsome bronzed face of a gentleman in evening dress before, and we had a laugh over my discovery that the "very swell sheikh" of the morning's ride was Mr. Somers Clarke himself! He visits Egypt every year, and always wears the Arab costume, which he says is absolutely fitted to the climate. In the morning, when a fellah goes to the fields, he has six wraps on. As the sun mounts in the sky he removes them gradually till only one is worn. In the afternoon, and on his return homewards, he gradually restores the whole of his garments. This Mr. Clarke imitates. I visited him the next day on his dahabeah. He was busily engaged making beautiful drawings of the sculptures he had discovered, which are to be published by the Egyptian Exploration Fund. Clad in his Arab costume, with bare feet and legs, he seemed cool and fresh, when in European clothes he would have been overpowered with the heat of the warmest day I had yet experienced. He had two young gentlemen assistants, who were superintending the excavations, while he applied himself to

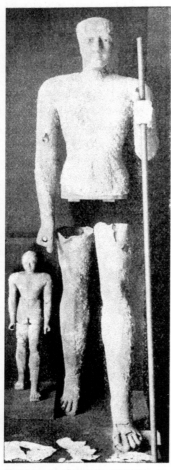

BRONZE OR COPPER STATUE OF
KING PEPI I.

Discovered at Hieraconpolis. The
figure is upwards of six feet high, and
is 2,000 years older than any work of the
kind. Pepi's son, who died in infancy,
stands beside him.

(From a Photograph by Mr. Quibell.)

the measurements, drawing, and descriptions of his discoveries.

Professor Sayce was busy with his translations of the inscriptions, making constant use of his copies from the rocks and of the extensive library (upwards of 1,000 volumes) which adorns the walls of his study in the "Istar." We had a delightful evening, the discoveries, when described and explained by such a man as Sayce, being doubly interesting. The sky was brilliant with stars, as only Egypt can show, and, when I was rowed across to my little vessel, the peaceful scene, with the two great dahabeahs and their lights, the placid-flowing river reflecting the stars, was something never to be forgotten.

Next morning I started early with the guardian of the monuments for a long excursion through a richly-cultivated country to the ancient city of the hawks (Hieraconpolis), now only known by the foundations of its temple, the ruins of its fort or citadel, and the adjacent tombs of its former inhabitants. It would take too long to describe, but is a wonderful experience. There are several tombs cut in the rock some distance off, and beautifully painted. One, in the mounds adjoining the fort, has been the last resting-place of a great priest. He had been a man of terpsichorean taste, for the principal decoration was the evolutions of a corps of dancing girls engaged in much the same exercises as the corps de ballet of our modern theatres of the "Alhambra" type. There were skirt-dancers, we see, in those days, and also dancers without the encumbrances of the draperies. This jovial priest also had representations in his tomb of his vineyard, grape-gathering, and the making and storing of wines in his cellars. He lived possibly in the time of King Pepi (Sixth Dynasty, 3400 B.C.), whose cartouche has been found there.

When I was at Kom el Ahmar (the modern name of the ruins—the red mound) it had never been thoroughly excavated. In February, 1898, the party

TABLET OF SLATE,

With figure of a very early Egyptian king smiting an enemy. About 5,000 B.C.

(*In the Cairo Museum.*)

working for Professor Petrie's "Egypt Research Account" explored the site of the ancient temple. A magnificent bronze and golden hawk was discovered, the head of which was of solid gold, value for upwards of £100 as mere metal. This magnificent work was beautifully modelled, and of great antiquity. The eyes are one solid piece of obsidian, going through the head from side to side, not merely separate bits of stone. It had possibly been buried in time of war, and symbolised the elder Horus, the chief god of the place. This relic is now preserved in the Museum at Cairo.

After I had left El-Kab, Mr. Quibell discovered, at Kom el Ahmar, among the ruins of the temple, a magnificent bronze statue of Pepi, a king who reigned 5,200 years ago. The statue is a fine work, over life size; the eyes, being made of glass, give the old king the appear-

Reduction of design on back of tablet reproduced above.

ance of life. Another bronze statue was found inside it. The mien and attitude are nobly expressed by this ancient sculptor's talent, which carries art of this kind of portraiture back 2000 years. The famous Greek bronze figures of the Naples Museum, the finest hitherto known, are about 2,000 years old. This figure shows how the Egyptians could model such life-size statues 3,000 years earlier. In the same region Mr. Quibell unearthed the records of an unknown king of a much earlier date than Pepi, engraved on a slab of slate in the form of a shield.

It is beautifully carved on both sides. The monarch is depicted smiting his enemies, on one side, and on the back a pair of mythical animals are carved. The inscription shows the struggle to have been with the people of the Delta. The name of the Egyptian king is carefully given, but in hieroglyphics so early and mysterious that it has not yet been read, but one of these days it may be deciphered. It is believed to record the deeds of an earlier monarch than Mena, who lived 4000 B.C.; but every year's discoveries prove that Egyptian art and letters flourished long before this date.

I had to bid adieu to my friends, and proceed on my journey to Thebes. The wind ceased through the day; we made little progress, and we were utterly and

CAPITALS OF THE PTOLEMAIC TEMPLE OF ESNEH.
The lower portion of the columns is underground.

hopelessly inert at last on the river. The next day we seemed to be in much the same plight. In the remote distance, far across the level country, I could discern the minarets of Esneh, the first place I had yet to reach that boasted of a post office and telegraph station. I wanted to write home, and Dahab's daily promises of being at "Esneh to-morrow" seemed incapable of fulfilment. So I sent Achmet ashore to hire donkeys to ride across country (from here there is a great loop in the Nile's course) to reach Esneh before the call of the weekly post-boat. Achmet came back, looking sad:
"There be no donkey, no mule, nothing but camel," said he. "I have got two camel, sar." So we went ashore, and I found a gigantic animal, very shaggy, with great tufts of long hair at intervals decorating his bony, angular carcase. This was to be my steed. Achmet contented himself with a small camel. Being a very large man, I proposed that he should take the greater beast, but Achmet said, "No, sar, the master must always have the biggest camel." And as my dignity must be maintained I agreed. The great creature

was made to sit down on his haunches, and I climbed up. When he rose there seemed no end of his rising; but after abandoning myself to my fate, I was suddenly shot aloft in the air and then securely on his hump, and off he went across country. This was a ploughing camel, and he seemed to like this sort of travel, choosing the fields that needed ploughing most. Our course was far from direct, as the canals came everywhere unexpectedly, and many were too wide to cross. But many were dry, and in that case we had to descend one steep bank and mount another. On such perilous crossing it was hard enough to keep one's seat. I had neither reins nor stirrups. I was sitting cross-legged on the highest point of the huge animal, bouncing about like a ball when his highness chose to gallop. Esneh seemed to move about on the edge of the horizon. However, after some hours of this pleasant exercise a road came in view, and we were at last in Esneh, although I was so stiff that I could barely descend. At the telegraph office I found a Copt who spoke some French and could read English. Here I wrote my letter, completing it just as the post-boat came in sight.

There is no inn in Esneh, so I spent some time in the rude bazaar, and got some interesting scarabs from an old Arab merchant. A fair was going on, and an itinerant dealer had brought a supply of watches. I bought one for Dahab, of whom I became very fond. It was a very fair self-winding watch, costing four dollars, and of Swiss manufacture. Then I visited Esneh's ancient temple, which is mainly underground, the modern town erected on top of its great roof, the courts being used as corn cellars and stables. The mosque of the town has been built over it, and as the Mahometans when their religious places are to be removed demand enormous sums to soothe their wounded faith, so the Government has only bought a small part of the buildings—enough to show the beautiful painted walls that exist below ground. You descend about twenty feet by a ladder, and a vast hall of columns is entered, all perfect and glowing with the brilliant colours of ancient Egyptian art. Every pillar has a beautiful capital of palm and papyrus style, still retaining its original colours. The whole is covered with inscriptions, and the cartouches

INTERIOR OF THE HYPOSTYLE HALL, TEMPLE OF ESNEH.

are mainly those of the Ptolemies and the Romans, but the work has been done by Egyptian artists under them, as all is in hieroglyphs and mostly painted.

The Romans had carried on the work that the Ptolemies had left, and many emperors and others are shown on the walls. A fine figure of Titus, with his name done in hieroglyphics is conspicuous. When the sun is high the light is reflected into the temple from the excavated portion, and the effect is very beautiful, as

PORTRAIT OF TITUS IN
TEMPLE OF ESNEH.

the corridors of columns emerge from the gloom as the eye becomes accustomed to the dark interior.

But one gets tired even of a lovely, cool temple, and I walked down alone to the quay, having sent Achmet back along the river bank to try to communicate with my felucca. As he did not return, I was becoming somewhat anxious, and the sun was high and all the houses shut up to exclude its burning rays. I sought for shelter, and then I recollected that I had a card in my purse of the judge of Esneh, a pleasant native gentleman whom I had entertained at lunch in my hut at Philæ some weeks before. His card was printed in French and Arabic, and I showed it to a policeman, asking where the judge lived. "Hinna," he exclaimed (here), showing his white teeth. I had been sheltering from the burning sun in the outer hall of the judge's house! So I knocked at the door, and handed in my card and his own together. This pleasant gentleman soon appeared, smiling and delighted to see me, for he had made me promise to visit him, when I had entertained him in my little hut at Shellal. I had forgotten all about him till necessity sharpened my wits. At once I was admitted into his sanctum, on the ground floor of the house, which, looking like a strongly-built warehouse outside, was luxuriously furnished within. He was accompanied by his little son, a pretty child of about three or four, carried in the arms of his "nurse," a bright Arab boy of eleven or twelve. Just as I had seen at El-Kab—a prince nursed by a male attendant —so the same habit still exists in this never-changing country. The judge, Ali Feymi, told me that the nurse had been the child's friend from birth, and would be his companion till manhood. I could not help thinking of the picture of the future king sitting on his nurse's knee which I had seen in the tomb of Paheri.

I was fed almost every hour, it seemed to me—delicious coffee and fresh cakes, then sherbet and more confectionery and sweetstuff; lunch, then soup, meat, and vegetables, my host sitting opposite me with his legs tucked under him, chatting volubly in French. It was the Feast of Ramadan, and no good Moslem must touch meat, or indeed food of any kind, from sunrise to sunset.

But a judge, he explained, is exempt from religious fasts; he must be always well nourished, ready for the administration of justice at any time. So there was always meat in his house and cooking to entertain a visitor. I went out to gaze up and down the Nile from time to time, but no tidings of my vessel or of Achmet, who had gone to seek it. Then my kind host insisted on providing dinner, and it was a sumptuous meal, the only trouble being the utter absence of knives, forks, or spoons, as all native gentlemen eat with their fingers, an attendant being always in readiness to pour water over the hands. The Judge

SCENE AT THE LANDING PLACE, ESNEH.

and I had long chats about politics, Egyptian and English. He was sorry he had not spent the time which he had given to French to learn English, which he foresaw would be Egypt's policy to cultivate. He apologised for not asking me upstairs to meet his wife and family. He had but one wife; she was an educated lady, and knew a little French. " We are rapidly advancing," said he. " Now, I dare not ask you to meet my wife (and her parents, who are at present our visitors), but when you come again, no doubt we can all meet together as the family does in Europe. As a judge I cannot set the example; but some day there may be some resident English people here, and we will imitate them, and our domestic civilisation will be complete."

Night came on, and no tidings of my boat, so my host had a luxurious couch prepared for me. I slept soundly, and about sunrise a tap on my window awoke me. I opened the door and outer gate to Achmet. The felucca was at the water's edge in waiting. The wind had been so perverse that my poor fellows had to drag their vessel all the way by a rope from the bank. I parted from my kind host with regret, hoping to meet again. I heard afterwards he was one

N

of the best native judges, utterly reliable and upright, and much trusted by
the censor of the Egyptian Law Courts.   The wind veered round to the south,
and our felucca had a rapid voyage northwards.   We made some stoppages by
the way, visiting El-Gebelen, a strange ruined town with a vast cemetery, on twin
promontories (hence its name) extending into the Nile.   Here some naked,
dirty wretches were digging up ancient tombs, like ghouls.   They offered
me all they had found.   There were beads, scarabs, and fragments of papyri.
The last I reserved for Professor Sayce.   Painted stones were turned up, with
inscriptions, fragments possibly of a temple, but they were too heavy to carry
away.   I was sorry to leave them, for they would undoubtedly be burnt for lime.
Then we visited Erment, where a busy market was going on, and more
scarabs were "found."   The ancient temple of this place was destroyed some
years ago to construct one of Ismail's sugar factories.   Next day we anchored
at Luxor, where I awaited Professor Sayce to get his help to unveil the
mysteries of my treasures, so soon as the "Istar" would arrive downstream.

OFF EL KAB: AT ANCHOR.
The "Istar" in the distance.

CHAPTER XIII.

THE DOOMED ISLAND OF PHILÆ.

THE TEMPLE OF ISIS, PHILÆ: PAINTED COLUMNS IN THE
HYPOSTYLE HALL.

ASSOUAN—THE DESERT ROUTE TO PHILÆ—THE GRANITE QUARRIES—
THE RUINS ON THE ISLAND—
SWIMMING BOYS—BACK BY THE CATARACT.

CHAPTER XIII.

THE DOOMED ISLAND OF PHILÆ.

SUNRISE OVER PHILÆ, FROM MY COTTAGE DOOR.
(From a Painting by the Author.)

WHEN the island of Philæ was threatened with submersion by the reservoir, I thought of studying the locality well, and of visiting everything that was likely to be altered by the coming deluge.

But when I realised that Philæ was doomed, I determined to visit the unfortunate island once more, to reside on the spot for some time, if possible, and provide myself with sketches, paintings, and photographs of its beauties from every point of view. This proved to be not so easy as was expected. The Soudanese War was in the air. Assouan was one vast barrack. Military stores and plant for the far Soudan and desert railway were piled up everywhere, with gangs of chained convicts cheerfully unloading vessels and loading railway trucks. Orders had been given to Cook and Son to issue no more tickets for Halfa or the Upper Nile, and tourists were politely led to know that they were not wanted, as the post-boats were requisitioned to convey troops and stores alone. This might have been awkward for me, for the very place where I wanted to live, Shellal, was Government property, and in the possession of the troops and their stores. So I applied to Sir William Garstin, who had just arrived at Assouan on a tour of inspection. But he said on this occasion the country was under military law, and accordingly he gave me an introduction to the Sirdar, asking him to do what he could for an old friend. The Sirdar, I found, had gone to his bungalow on his island, away on the Nile behind Elephantine. Its many native owners had quarrelled,

THE SIRDAR'S ISLAND, NEAR ASSOUAN.

the irrigation had been neglected, and the island had gone back to nature. A merchant bought up their interests for a small sum for the Sirdar. He has now a little bit of Egypt of his own. He hopes some day, when his fighting is done, to retire there to rest upon his laurels. I had presented myself at head-quarters on the mainland. The bearer of a letter from Sir W. Garstin, I was at once sent across the Nile in the Commandant's launch to the Sirdar's island. I was very kindly received by Major Watson, A.D.C.* Shortly afterwards the Sirdar appeared, a tall, pleasant gentleman, and the letter was read. The Sirdar's manner of receiving a total stranger was charmingly simple and friendly. He took a great interest in my desire to study the threatened island, and told Major Watson to give me every assistance, so I was provided with quarters on a gunboat lying off Shellal. I went down to Philæ at once and took possession of my ship, the *Tamai,* a fine new boat, with all her guns lying on the bank and in charge of two Nubian soldiers, who were told to attend to me. I had secured the permission to remain at Shellal, and got on very well for a time on my gunboat; but one day orders came down to have the guns put in, and my ship, filled with soldiers and stores, steamed off to the front. She afterwards did good work at Dongola and Khartum, and now patrols the Nile beyond.

I should have been homeless, but I had prepared for such an event. I had noticed a little cottage at railhead, quite unlike an Arab dwelling. It had been built by an English engineer of the old railway, a dozen years ago. He had brought out here from England his young wife and infant, and built the cottage with the hope of a happy home. But his wife and child died, and

---

he went away broken hearted. This accounted for such a good house being found in such a wilderness. Being substantially built it still was a pretty place. It was surrounded by a garden, and the whole house was shaded with a creeping plant covered with lilac flowers. The building was in good order and was now owned by an old Greek named Spero. He had tried to establish a little business with the soldiers; they were now gone and he was quite willing to have me for a tenant. I had had no company on the *Tamai* save Nubian watchmen, to whom I could not speak; but I hired a felucca, manned

by two intelligent Nubian lads—a pretty little craft, with one great sail, rather the worse for wear. I spent my time cruising round my island, landing at various points to sketch, and in this way I made many little pictures of Philæ and its temples. I had for attendant a tall, strong, good-looking Nubian, who had been servant to one of the railway engineers, but now was without employment. I liked the look of the man, and, finding that he knew

PHARAOH'S BED, PHILÆ.

some English, I employed him for one day, being really in want of someone to talk to. I had that man for nine weeks. He bore an unpronounceable Nubian name, so I called him Achmet, which did quite well, and I understand has stuck to him ever since. He was a treasure. I would have liked to bring him home with me.

My landlord Spero was an unhappy-looking soul, a man of few words, and those were Greek. His miserable face, Achmet explained, was owing to his being a martyr to rheumatism, which had driven him from his own country and elsewhere, and it was only at this low latitude that he could have any freedom from constant pain and sleeplessness. Spero, for a most moderate sum, undertook to clear and clean out his house and supply me with lodging—two rooms, a fresh Nile bath (in a third room) every morning, to cook my food, and supply an attendant to wait on me alone. He lived himself and cooked in an adjoining building. The cottage having been built by an English engineer accounted for the great bath of concrete, in which one could almost swim about. Spero had used it to store flour in, but for my comfort he restored the tank to its original use. If I was not satisfied I was to leave any day without notice. I remained five weeks. I never was so comfortable out of my own house. I was fed admirably ; so well that I got constant hints from my friends who happened to turn up, that an invitation to lunch would be acceptable, and nearly every day I had visitors from Assouan, which made my time pass pleasantly, for it was so hot that I could not sail or sketch with comfort from twelve till three, and this was the time to rest and have lunch within doors. My house was then perfectly cool ; the walls were thick—of sun-dried bricks—and preserved the rooms at an equal temperature all day. A great ventilator opened from the roof, and pleasantly showed the stars by night. Spero had, it transpired, been a celebrated cook in his early days, hence the excellence of his cuisine. The post-boats were now all armed, in Government service, and laden with soldiers and commissariat stores, and sent off to the front. Before they sailed I had laid in a store of the proper liquors for a warm climate. Fresh bread came from Assouan every third day. Where or how Spero got his meat I know not, but the supplies never failed. Fresh eggs and excellent fowls were purchased from the Arab women in an adjacent village, and from the same source came abundance of delicious milk every morning. The little house was in a grove of date palms at the edge of the river. The view of the temples of Philæ from my door was so lovely, especially at sunrise, that I was able to sketch it often.

At this time Major Lyons, of the Engineers' Department, and Herr Borchardt, of Berlin, were making a scientific survey of the antiquities of the island, and I often joined them. One day Borchardt was fatigued and fell asleep in the shade of a ruined temple. When he awoke he found he had laid down on an engraved slab, on which his experienced glance at once, as he opened his eyes, detected Greek and Latin letters. Thus was discovered one of the most remarkable tri-lingual inscriptions of the Græco-Roman period. Another day Major Lyons found a huge block of blue granite, used as the sill of a door in Roman times. Near it was another stone of similar shape and material. He turned them over—they exactly fitted—and found it was an important decree of the Ptolemies, which had been sawn in sunder and used for the sill and lintel of a doorway. These stones are all preserved in the Museum of Gizeh, near Cairo. This accidental discovery only shows what literary or historical records may be entombed by the impending improvements.

THE ISLAND OF PHILÆ: PHARAOH'S BED AND ROMAN QUAY.

The pylons of the Temple of Isis and the Temple enclosure in the background.

PHILÆ: TEMPLE OF HATHOR, THE EGYPTIAN VENUS.
This will be covered by the waters of the reservoir.

But everything must come to an end, and I had to leave, with great regret, my much-loved Philæ. The weather became unendurably hot, with occasional dust storms, and I had to desert my happy lodge in the wilderness. I have often gone back to look at it, and this year we went again.

Since I thus made the Sirdar's acquaintance he has conquered the Soudan, and secured the control of the Upper Nile to its sources, 2,000 miles away. Nobly has he earned the title of Lord Kitchener of Khartum by avenging Gordon's murder! But Assouan is still under his care, fortunately for the locality. When I went to take possession of my ship, I took the shortest way to Philæ, by the old railway, which was built in Ismail's time, and has not been much altered since. But the proper way is to go, as we did recently, mounted on good donkeys, by the old desert track, through the Arab cemetery and past the famous granite quarries which supplied every obelisk and colossal monument of syenite to the ancient rulers of Egypt for 4,000 years. One of these huge obelisks lies, partially cut out, where Usertesen's architect (possibly making one for Heliopolis in 2755 B.C.) rejected the great block for some flaw in the stone. Later quarrymen have tried to cut it up into blocks, but miserably failed for want of skill, and forty feet of the monster monolith are yet

BISHAREEN TENT.
Scene in their village, near Assouan.

intact. The rest remains hidden by the sand, while the intended apex is still embedded in the virgin rock. When my photograph was taken, a few young "fuzzy-wuzzies" were hanging about, and we got them into the little picture to give it "scale." Then we mounted our donkeys, and wandered across the wide plain of sand, where the great ancient Nile once possibly spread into a lake, making a natural dam

UNFINISHED OBELISK IN QUARRY AT ASSOUAN, WITH BISHAREEN CHILDREN.

and depositing mud at high level, again to be utilized. The Nile had cut itself a deeper channel, and all the flat land had gone back to desert. Then we came to more granite, and several unfinished ancient coffins and tombs for the sacred bulls lie about. One of these the Arabs call Cleopatra's Bath! One of our party seated herself in the huge sarcophagus to give some life to the picture. There are also unfinished colossal statues lying in the quarries. The Arabs call one of them Ramses, but it is more likely the work of Amenhotep III., whose name appears in an inscription near this. Leaving the granite region, the path leads to the Nile past several pretty Nubian villages, and one inhabited by Bishareen, the nearest things to gipsies found in Egypt. They are very dark-skinned, a sort of yellow tint, as if dusted over with soot. To add to their

UNFINISHED SARCOPHAGUS LYING IN THE QUARRIES.

UNFINISHED COLOSSUS IN THE GRANITE QUARRY, ASSOUAN.

attractions they wear the hair in long, spiral, cord-like masses, greased and "perfumed" with castor-oil, which is a common plant hereabout. They do not waste much money on clothes, and the ladies' milliners' bills cannot be excessive, as most of them possess but one garment. Those who followed us were mere children, but their one garment was gracefully worn and never seemed to fall off, though they had no pins or fastenings. A populous village of the Bishareen is passed on the way to the quarries; they seem good-natured creatures, always smiling, and offer little bits of their work for sale.

Farther up the Nile the grown women of the Nubian tribes wear little else but an arrangement of leather thongs, a kind of fringe suspended from the waist. No doubt the inexpensive nature of the women's wardrobe is a direct encouragement to polygamy.

The path by the impetuous, roaring rapids is very picturesque, and the waste of huge granite boulders— red, black, yellow, brown, and purple in tint — is strikingly contrasted with the white, foamy track of of the cataract dashing through them. Then the scene changes suddenly for a while. Patches of cultivated land come in view, with thick fringes of date palms, syca-mores, acacias, and ta-marisk trees, and a vil-lage suddenly appeared

GROUP OF ADULT BISHAREEN.

AUGUSTUS ANOINTED BY
THE GODS.
(From his temple at Philæ.)

among the greenery. Again the desert and another stony waste of huge granite boulders, with the wild river forcing its foamy way through them. Once emerged from this ravine, the lovely green island of Philæ, surrounded with calm, placid blue waters, gladdens the sight. These enormous granite boulders, so striking by their brilliant colours, are quite a feature of the landscape above, below, and at the cataracts. They are piled up forty or fifty feet along the banks, and extend even far into the sandy desert on either side. It is manifest that they are all water-worn and polished by the agency of a river of much greater height, breadth and volume than the present Nile even when at its highest flood. In prehistoric times

TIBERIUS MAKING OF-
FERING TO ISIS.
(Temple at Philæ.)

there may have been greater tropical rainfall, and perhaps the Congo and Zambesi, or even the Niger, in those remote ages may have all been poured into the bed of a prehistoric Nile, which must have resembled in width and volume the Amazon or the Mississippi of to-day. Many of the enormous rounded

granite blocks weighing thousands of tons, bear cartouches and inscriptions on their surfaces, engraved about 5,000 years ago, which shows that the river at that period must have been in much the same state as at present. But vast banks of Nile mud exist on either side and in many parts of Egypt which are far above the present river level, and must have been deposited

PHILÆ: TRIUMPHAL ARCH OF DIOCLETIAN,
Which will be entirely covered by the waters of the reservoir.

SACRED STAIRCASE, TEMPLE OF ISIS, PHILÆ.
The water will reach up to these steps.

by the gigantic Nile of upwards of 10,000 years ago. Part of the work of the new irrigation system now in progress will utilise these immense deposits for purposes of agriculture, for all that is wanted is Nile water of a sufficient height to reach them.

Great changes had come about in a year's time, and more are promised. Where my cool cottage is, sheltered from the burning sun under a lovely grove of date palms, a sheet of water will, in a few years, be spread. More than a mile in width, and over a hundred miles southwards will extend the New African Lake. Spero was still there, but the cottage is now tenanted by several families of the Greek or Italian engineers who are engaged at the new works. The palms had begun to die for want of water, the sakiya having been neglected and broken down. In a very few years there will be nothing but water here, and the palms will utterly perish. The trees on the island opposite have begun to languish, and the excavations necessarily made by Major Lyons for the Government (to ascertain if the temples of Philæ were built on rock or on the Nile mud) have destroyed the undergrowth that was one of Philæ's chief beauties in the olden time. But for three years to come it will be well worth visiting, and should be seen by all who can spare the time. The waters of the Great Reservoir will not be impounded until the huge wall is built. To tempt voyagers to penetrate thus far I give a number of photographs and sketches made a few years since when the whole island was one of the most lovely things of its kind in the world. Let us cross over to Philæ. The most picturesque building on the island is, however, not of Egyptian origin; it is a Roman temple, or pavilion, and was supposed to have been erected in the time of the Roman Emperor Augustus, but now is attributed to Trajan. Whoever was its designer it is a gem of architecture from every point of view. It is in thorough Egyptian style, but more beautiful than anything we know, save perhaps the temple of Queen Hatasu at Thebes. I am much afraid that it will be the first temple to succumb when the waters rise around it. It is, unfortunately, built on the Nile earth. Two of the older temples have their foundations carried down to the rock, but the lovely double colonnade of the Temple of Isis and the little Temple of Nectanebo (B.C. 380) will assuredly perish when the reservoir rises over and around them, having no secure foundation to resist such pressure and infiltration. Nectanebo was the earliest builder here, but he was almost the last king of real Egyptian origin.

The celebrated Nilometer is nearly perfect. It was used to register the rise of the Nile, the joyful tidings of which were transmitted by couriers to the next Nilometer, on Elephantine, and thence full detail sent all over Egypt. The scales of measure- ment, Egyptian, Greek, Roman, and Arabic, are still clearly cut on the steps lead- ing down to the river. This in- teresting build- ing will now ut- terly disappear. I give an illus- tration of the curious idea that the Egyptians had that the Nile rose at the cataracts. The

COLONNADE OF NECTANEBO'S TEMPLE,
Which will all be covered at high water of the reservoir.

rocks shown in the ancient engraving really resemble the boulders of granite. The Nile is represented by a female pouring out water, hidden in a cave, and protected by the sacred serpent. This is carved near the Nilometer. On the wonderful orange and roseate tinted boulders which are piled up in confused masses in the bed of the river north of Philæ are gigantic cartouches cut deeply into the granite of much earlier rulers of Egypt than any names there recorded. On the island of Konosso, a striking mass of yellow granite, is found among other names that of Mentuhotep, of the Eleventh Dynasty, 3000 B.C.

This monarch records that he had subdued thirteen nations, and was a devoted servant of the gods. Thothmes IV. also records his visit (1420 B.C.) and many others do the same. This interesting monument will almost disappear in the waters, and some antiquarians will regret its loss more than Philæ and its "modern" records and Græco-Roman temples.

THE SOURCE OF THE NILE.
(From a carving near the Nilometer on the island of Philæ.)

On the return journey we made the descent of the first cataract. In order to do so it is necessary to engage a boat from the tribe of native Nubians who have monopolised the traffic for many generations. A code of laws and regular tariff for their work have existed for a long time, and a dignified gentleman—the sheikh of the cataract—superintends the making of the bargain, which is maintained scrupulously once the contract is made, though there is haggling enough beforehand. There is doubtless considerable danger in the passage of an open boat down the rapids. The troops of naked black boys who gambol across the stream and tumble down the falls, sometimes lost to view for some seconds, seem utterly without fear, and thoroughly to enjoy their amphibious existence. But when a white man attempts similar pranks he soon feels his utter help-lessness. In the desert, parallel to the cataract, which we had previously crossed, we saw the grave of a young English tourist, who perished in this vain attempt; he was beaten to death before any effort could be made to help him, withal he was an accomplished swimmer. The young native imps who disport themselves do so for baksheesh. The sum demanded (per regulation tariff) is a shilling for the exhibition of their talent in shooting the greatest falls, and this is divided among all the gang of india-rubber gymnasts. Each boy bestrides a piece of wood rounded off at the ends, and sits his steed boldly, sometimes losing hold, but always regaining his wobbling log. They thus form a procession down the roaring stream, and when the great rapids are reached shoot them with great skill, and showing perfect mastery of their logs, keeping proudly erect and gesticulating defiantly at the wild masses of water that would pound a tyro to jelly in a few seconds. Then in the clear pools they will dive for small coins or anything else thrown in. The waters rush at the rate of fifteen or twenty miles an hour. There are two passages down the rapids—one by which large dahabeahs can be taken, requiring many men of experience, and on such occasions the sheikh himself generally accompanies the ship, sitting

GENERAL VIEW OF PHILÆ, LOOKING TOWARDS THE NORTH.
The Barrage wall will be built on the bank of the river in the middle distance. In the foreground are the rocks
on the island of Biggeh, which will not be submerged by the reservoir.

at the rudder beside the steersman, his praying beads in his hands. On the present occasion we took the smaller channel, and made the passage of the rapids in an open boat, with four oars. The rowers were strong men, with scarcely any clothing and nearly black. Not, however, woolly-headed niggers, but handsome Nubians, with straight hair worn rather long. They managed the boat with great skill. We seemed on the point of being swamped many times in the whirlpools, and a spill would have been dangerous enough even to an experienced swimmer. Some large sail-boats were going down the wider channel at the same time, and had an odd appearance, their great white canvas showing like huge giant birds' wings among the reefs of rock, neither hull of the boat nor water on which they sailed being visible. The boulders are piled about in indescribable confusion; there are many ancient inscriptions of different ages in hieroglyphic, demotic, and Greek, a kind of visitors' book recording the names of the tourists of ancient days who risked the rapids. The rounded granite masses are of every hue, from rose-red, grey, orange, yellow-brown, to black. The noise of the water is deafening, mixed with the cries of the Arabs and Nubians—"hourah! hourah! hourah!"—as they enter a whirlpool or a dangerous eddy, or slide down a waterfall. As if to anticipate the coming baksheesh, after each group of hourahs they shout "Thank you!" And when

CHANNEL LEADING NORTHWARDS TO THE CATARACTS BY WHICH WE SAILED TO ASSOUAN.

the last fall is passed, "Hip! hip! hourah! Thank you! thank you!" and we are in quiet water, and the payment begins. On the rocks are seen inscriptions recording the passage by kings and nobles who flourished 5,000 years ago. In the time of high Nile the whole gorge is filled with a turbulent sea, thirty feet higher than now, and the billows of dark, boiling water seem as if they could sweep even rocks down the stream. The cataract traversed, there is a broad channel of several miles of boisterous green water, till Assouan is reached.

The above will soon be ancient history, for since this was written the wide channel of the Nile, the Bab-el-Kibir, has been actually filled up and blocked with

THE TURBULENT WATERS OF HIGH NILE.

great stones tied together with wire. The foundations for the great wall of masonry which is to carry the Reservoir wall have been actually begun. The Mehemet Ali channel shares the same fate. There will soon be no passages of the cataracts such as I have related, and the swimmers and divers may confine their exhibition to whatever rapids may exist below the Great Reservoir.

CHAPTER XIV.

ASSOUAN UNDER LORD KITCHENER.

INSCRIBED ROCKS ON THE ISLAND OF SEHEL.

A SAIL ROUND ELEPHANTINE—AN ANCIENT RECORD OFFICE—
THE NILOMETER—THE RAPIDS BELOW THE CATARACT.

O 2

ASSOUAN, LOOKING TOWARDS THE CATARACT AT LOW WATER, SHOWING THE
RUINS OF THE COPTIC CHURCH.
(From a Sketch by the Author.)

CHAPTER XIV.

ASSOUAN UNDER LORD KITCHENER—A SAIL ROUND ELEPHANTINE —AN ANCIENT RECORD OFFICE.

ASSOUAN is now connected with Cairo by railway, a direct line of some 500 miles, and will one day be a great city, an important station on the Cape to Cairo railway. Even now, under British rule, it is fast becoming one of the most flourishing towns of Egypt. Being still under military law and the excellent if autocratic rule of Lord Kitchener, it has been much benefited by public works being carried on, merely to give employment to the troops who from time to time during later years have been quartered there. Luxor and other towns lower down the river have been left to the native authorities, and are as dirty and ill-planned as native towns in Egypt always are. Assouan has had a broad causeway laid out along the Nile for several miles. This forms a handsome boulevard, lined with trees and flanked by elegant houses and public institutions, each with its pretty garden of roses and orange trees. Bougainvilleas, scarlet, crimson, and brown showers of floral beauty, veil the white walls of the buildings. Date palms, with their golden bloom, rise gracefully aloft. The Sirdar has given ground for an English church, and at least one fine new hotel on an elevated situation is being built.

Opposite the town, across the wide, rapid river, lies the green island of Elephantine. Seen from behind and above Assouan the island is a brilliant

UNLOADING MATERIAL FOR THE DESERT
RAILWAY AT ASSOUAN.

object of beauty in a setting of bright Nile water; for the river has not yet recovered from its exciting rush over the granite reefs and boulders, and is still swift in current, and foaming in its wavy rapid stream. Elephantine is richly cultivated, has groves of tall fruitful palms, and many other trees. Brilliant green crops cover it, fed by sakiyas with their chains of buckets, the wheel driven by oxen, thus lifting the welcome Nile to enrich the coming harvest. Even in March the rye was ripe for the sickle, and wheat was taking its autumn tints. In very ancient days it was a prosperous place, the "ultima Thule" of Egyptian trade southwards. Elephantine is the translation of the old Egyptian name Abu, which goes back to the time when the elephant extended thus far north. On the island were many palaces and shrines. Two exquisite temples were ruthlessly destroyed by a Turkish pasha in 1822 to build one of his worthless palaces on the mainland. The Nilometer of Elephantine he also began to demolish, but the work was fortunately stopped, and much of it yet remains, with its ancient Egyptian scales of measurement intact, and the Roman and Arab measurements added afterwards. The name of Elephantine on the old monuments is expressed by the sign of an elephant.

NILOMETER, ELEPHANTINE.

Assouan enjoys the reputation of being the healthiest place in Egypt at all seasons, and some enthusiasts believe it will yet become the sanatorium of the world. Under British guidance it has made great strides, and there is a fair hotel now and promise of several better. The convicts have made a great quay wall several miles long, under the British engineers' direction. They work in chains,

ENTERTAINMENT ON MY FELUCCA.

and seem a very jolly lot, not encumbered by their badge of office. I was told they were nearly all murderers, the benevolent Khedive having an objection to sign any malefactor's death warrant. The Egyptian native gaols were awful dens of misery and crime. Now the convicts are kept in the open, well fed,

MUSICAL ENTERTAINMENT ON MY FELUCCA.

and made to work, which they really seem to enjoy. However, they are well guarded by native police with loaded muskets. Meanwhile the gaols are being reconstructed, and made healthy dens, fit for wild beasts in durance vile.

I have previously described my adventures on this part of the Nile, when I voyaged in a felucca, below Assouan, and to Luxor

ASSOUAN: VIEW FROM OUR TERRACE, LOOKING SOUTH.

and beyond. My reis (captain) and his good little vessel hailed from these parts. On my visit this season to Assouan, some of my former crew had learned of my return, and one morning I was delighted to find Dahab waiting for me, with welcome written on his handsome black countenance. He had brought a beautiful little sail boat of his own and several of the old crew, and during all my stay the pretty little craft was always at our service. The Nile here flows west and east, and there is mostly a pleasant breeze, morning and evening, enough to carry the little boat against the rapid current of the river at a fair pace, or to make it fly before the wind when its direction is down stream.

Dahab had provided himself with several lads with good voices, and when we lay-to, or were at anchor we were given excellent vocal music, accompanied by the native drum —an arrangement of pottery, gourd-shaped, with a skin drawn over it. One boy's voice would lead the song or story told in musical cadence, and then the whole crew would join in the chorus, sometimes laughing so heartily that they could scarcely sing decorously. Then an improvisatore would recite, musically, a panegyric (in Arabic, of

VIEW FROM OUR TERRACE, LOOKING NORTH.
Banks of pre-historic Nile mud; Dûm palms on the right.

course) on the beauty of the ladies and the merits of the gentlemen of the party, and hearty demonstrations of chorus would follow, the hands being clapped to the time of the melody. Then one of the lads who had been shy, would be encouraged to sing, and some of his performances were almost musical to our Northern ideas. Generally, native Arab melody is monotonous, but the Nubian races, who predominate here, have more music in their souls, and generally are a more interesting people in every way. These boys had sweet voices, and the airs they sang clearly and with evident intelligence. The lads played the tom-tom with skill and effect, producing more music out of their pottery arrangement than any drum seemed capable of giving.

On the hottest days in March (and some were very warm indeed) we always found a breeze coming down from the cataracts. Many creeks, backwaters, and channels thread the numerous granite islets, and here and there the boat could lie still without anchoring. The rocks are of every imaginable hue—yellow, red, black, brown, grey—all granite, polished, and glistening in the sun, reminding one of the boulders above the cataract near Philæ. The rapids (of rushing torrent when the Nile is high) have worn away the hard syenite masses, making them look soft and pillowy in outline and surface. It was very pleasant to let the boat rest in one of these placid creeks and watch the foaming waters hurry past the half sunken rocks. In one of these backwaters, a friend

SWIMMING BOY AT THE RAPIDS.

had found an island with a rocky summit, but firm sandy margin of coast, and rising out of this a terrace of green sward, high up above the restless river. Here we were wont to anchor our boat; the crew carried up cushions, rugs, and mats, and spread them on the sward. Shaded by some rocks from the sun and wind, we boiled our kettle and brewed delicious tea. A tamarisk tree, rising out of a steep bank behind, gave cool shelter.

The Sirdar has established a dairy at Assouan, where the best of milk, cream, and butter can be had. Provided plentifully with these adjuncts, our

INSCRIPTION ON A
ROCK, ISLAND OF
ELEPHANTINE.

little tea parties were a great success. The view from our green platform was superb. The Nile below us, with its tortuous channel, here its course marked out with foam, there a dark, brown, deep, quiet, yet rapid current. Beneath us a maze of rocks, burnished and polished and shining, reflecting the sun, the river forcing itself among them ; here a large, still pool, there a boiling cauldron of disturbed water. The landscape around was weirdly picturesque. Red, barren cliffs, a strip of brilliant green cutting them off at the water level now and then, but mostly rising sheer out of the river bed. The red rocks, varied with outbursts of granite—grey, black, brown, and purple—narrow in the valley to a few miles' width, and patches of yellow desert fill up the gaps in the distance.

The whole space between the hills was the ancient bed of a vast pre-historic river, showing that the Nile in geological periods has left its trace on the rounded polished granite masses, now far above the reach of the highest floods. Through the islets at our feet a winding channel, fit for vessels carefully steered, could be seen. Down this, suddenly emerging from round a corner of rock, we saw a gaily painted boat, with sails and six oarsmen, filled with a company of tourists, who had shot the rapids just below Philæ. As the boat whirled round corners, slid down rapids, shot through a narrow passage, where it seemed scarcely possible to pass with safety, the sailors rested a while for breath, and again and again shouted the usual cries, " Hip, hip, hourra ! " " Thank you, thank you." Then emerged from the rocks and stones a score or more of amphibious naked urchins, each astride a log of wood, making for the unfortunate boat-load of tourists, clamouring for " baksheesh ! baksheesh ! " Away it sped again, followed by the shouting water sprites. Some clung to the boat ; others led the way, many followed for a quarter of a mile or so, swimming vigorously. They were a merry lot, and must make enough money to feed them, for their bodies seem well nourished. When the boat had passed them, they gambolled in the water, tried races, played pranks on one another, utterly fearless of the flood. We were not molested by them, being regarded as residents and frequent visitors, and when the tourists' boat was out of sight they disappeared as mysteriously as they had come.

This network of cliffs, rocks, and islands seems, though utterly desolate now, to have been much visited in ancient times. Nearly every rocky surface suitable for the purpose has been storied with inscriptions, deeply cut in hieroglyph characters, all of them recording the names of ancient visitors, "carved on the rock for ever." Certainly they have endured longer than any other form of record, and are likely to last as long as the rocks

COOK & SON'S TOURIST STEAMER.

themselves. Looking down from our grassy bench, we could see beneath us the large island of Sehel, the richest storehouse of these ancient tales.

Having heard that the stones and rocks of this island were in many places storied with important historical records, a veritable library, we visited the place several times. It had once been partially cultivated, and there is a poor village on it still. But the inscriptions are quite perfect, no wanton injury has been done to them. Some of them are so ancient that the stone (all granite) from great age has scaled off, carrying with it the incised record, but in the main they are in as perfect preservation as when cut. Their date is known by the "cartouches" of the monarchs who reigned at the time, which each inscription bears. Many on Sehel are of the Twelfth Dynasty (2700 B.C.) and some much earlier. Thence there is a regular succession of records for 1,500 years.

One of these becomes interesting at the present time, and refers to the locality. Almost within sight—certainly within hearing—a great reservoir and navigable canals are being made at a cost of several millions sterling. While we were examining the old story engraven on the rocks we could distinctly hear the shots of the blasting of the granite channel now in progress. An inscription here records that 4,200 years ago Usertesen III. made a canal for warships to pass

ANGLO-AMERICAN STEAMER, "THE PURITAN."

the cataracts. Another inscription further relates that Thothmes III. had the canal cleared out and restored to use in his time—3,500 years since. All traces of this canal have been lost. Mr. Fitzmaurice tells me it was certainly not on the western bank, where the new canal is being made. The new canal is to have locks, and is being made on the left bank. It is probable that the ancient one was on the right bank, and that the water flowed by gravitation without locks through a longer channel. I tried to interest the engineers to search on the eastern side for it, but could not make much impression. Their minds are not impressed with reverence for antiquity, *rien n'est sacré à un sapeur* —as the French say—and so much so that one engineer said he had a poor opinion of the science of ancient days. But these old engineers built the pyramids and quarried obelisks and moved the great blocks about with greater ease than we could to-day. When the public records were written on the rocks it implies that everyone could read them; this shows an advanced state of education in those times. How many records of our public works will be handed down for 5,000 years? The oldest British document preserved in our State Record Office is the Domesday Book, which is only 800 years old,·and is not written on such an imperishable material as the granite of Assouan.

We waited till the sun was low, and returned homewards leisurely, past the Nilometer, which was placed here to register the Nile's height below the cataracts, as the one on Philæ was to record the level above them. The great walls now support only a huge sakiya, at work by day and night, with its chain of dripping buckets groaning wearily. Then we sailed under the ruins of the Coptic church and into the almost placid waters of Assouan, as a gorgeous sunset bathed the landscape around. The granite boulders gleamed like molten metal of every shade, from crimson, glowing yellow, and warm plum-coloured brown. The boys struck up a boat song not unlike the Canadian one which was popular forty years ago. We landed here, and walked home under the palm trees' shade, the whole scene being so lovely it was difficult to leave it.

Assouan is rather left out in the military railway arrangements. The new narrow-gauge railway from Luxor to Shellal, near Philæ, does not yet connect with the Assouan railway station, which is a survival of the old line made by Ismail, with broad gauge and carriages of very antiquated pattern. It seems an unwise thing to have broken the gauge at Luxor, when all the railways north of that place were of the British width. But no doubt this will one day be changed, when the traffic demands it; at present the break of gauge is a great annoyance. But it is as well, for tourist traffic, that it is so, for the journey by railway from Luxor to Assouan is a most lugubrious affair, nothing whatever to be seen, and the bare desert, unattractive as it is, is only broken by regions of black earth, which provide clouds of dust that penetrate into every nook and cranny of the carriages. Then, when Assouan is approached, travellers are dumped down on a sandy plain, about two miles from the town. This I mention as a warning to tourists to take passage by steamer from Luxor to Assouan, which will be found to be one of the most interesting parts of all the Nile journey. It has been rather fully described in Chapter XII. Of course all the places possible to be seen when travelling in one's own boat are not open to a traveller by Cook's steamers, which generally visit only the considerable towns, such as Edfou and Esneh. The better class of tourist steamers

ASSOUAN AT LOW NILE, LOOKING EAST.

give also a few hours at Kom Ombo and El-Kab; but these, the most interesting places of all, are quite inaccessible to such as voyage by the "post-boats," as the smaller vessels are called, although they no longer carry the mails.

Just above the little railway station rise the mounds of rubbish which mark the site of the ancient town. These are being levelled to provide space for the new church and other public buildings sanctioned by Lord Kitchener, and certainly no better position could have been found. Mr. Henry Favarger, the English architect, of Cairo, has been selected to build the new hotel. The architect of Mena House is certain to do justice to his task, and the work is already far advanced. In such a wonderful situation, in the best air of Egypt, it will undoubtedly prove as great a success as the great hostelry of the Pyramids. Abundance of water of the best quality will be provided. That has hitherto been the difficult matter at Assouan. The climate of this part of the Nile is, in the winter months, perhaps the best in the world. As the river here runs from west to east, the north wind is kept off, and also the burning air from the south. The whole neighbourhood is full of delightful excursions by boat or by donkey, some of which I describe, and several delightful months can be enjoyed at the very season when the climate of Northern Europe is at its worst. The view from these heights, on every side, is lovely indeed.

ASSOUAN RAILWAY STATION.

Looking across the Nile from Assouan towards green Elephantine, Mount Grenfell towers its sandy slopes, shutting out the landscape to the north. Its summit is crowned by an Arab sheikh's tomb—a white dome glistening in the sun—which attracts the eye from every point. Beneath this, the great ruins of a once flourishing Coptic monastery of the sixth or seventh century occupy the sloping rock, for even this remote part of Egypt was entirely Christian before the Mahometan invasion. The rocky slope of the hill is covered with flesh-coloured sand. In the centre a well-marked line divides Mount Grenfell horizontally. Several clearly-cut angular lines lead down to the river from this rocky shelf; this was the slide on which the mummies were brought up from the water. There are steps at each side of the slide for the mourners to accompany their friends' remains to their long home.

This whole mountain is perforated with ancient tombs—the necropolis of the princes and magnates of ancient Assouan and the once-populous island of Elephantine. The tombs were buried in the all-encroaching sand and lost to view, till Sir Francis Grenfell had them explored and the ancient stairways laid bare. There were many beautifully painted tombs discovered of very early times—Sixth Dynasty (3700 B.C.) and Twelfth (2400 B.C.)—mostly of military or naval officers. In many, the paintings are as fresh as when they left the artists' hands. The hieroglyph writings are so simple, at these early dates, that even a tyro in such knowledge can read many of the inscriptions and decipher the cartouches of the kings under whom the generals served. The sand threatens soon to engulf the tombs once more.

In the recesses of the rocky tunnels the sandy floor is well worth searching for pale-blue beads of turquoise tint, the remains of the decorations of the mummies despoiled by Arabs. These gentry in the hot season rifle the tombs in search of scarabs and other curios to satisfy their craving for gain. In spring time the tourists are as greedy for relics of the poor old-world denizens of the forgotten tombs. I bought many fine scarabs in the bazaar at Assouan which had doubtless come from this cemetery. There are a great number of tombs, many of which have been explored and their inscriptions published. They resemble those of Beni Hasan in style, and are of much the same

ASSOUAN: GENERAL VIEW LOOKING EAST. ISLAND OF ELEPHANTINE, MOUNT GRENFELL SEEN OVER IT TO THE LEFT. (*From a Sketch by the Author.*)

period. One has corridors of Osiris figures and portraits of the deceased in colours fresh as when painted; others have vivid scenes of agricultural life. One relates how the owner explored the Soudan, whence he brought great treasure and a Darga dwarf for his sovereign, Pepi I. (3440 B.C.).

Murray's Handbook gives the best description of these tombs. The ruins of the Coptic monastery on Mount Grenfell show it to have been a very extensive establishment. The monks had, however, no respect for the ancient tombs, and, indeed, seem to have converted them to rather base uses, and to have even wantonly destroyed them.

Many tombs have outer courts with pillars cut out of the rock and building added. They must have been beautiful until the Coptic monks made them into dwellings and destroyed the sculptures as savouring of idolatry. But Grenfell excavated many that had been buried by the sand in Roman and Christian times and so had been spared the destroyer's hand. Arabs had plundered them for treasure. But doors have been put on the best preserved and a custodian keeps careful charge.

We descended the steep path, the sand and rocks covered with skulls and bones so ancient as to be as light as pith. At the river's edge we found our faithful Dahab and his pretty little felucca, and now he had an awning put up to keep off the sun's violence. We landed on the rocks opposite · and spent some time on Elephantine itself, enjoying green fields and rills of water and the palm groves' shade. There were many good curios to be had here, and we bought agate pebbles from the women of the villages. We found where the temple had been, and the inscriptions lately discovered on the rocks, some by Professor Sayce and others by Dr. Petrie, one of which we engrave. Then we took to our boat again, sailed round the Sirdar's island, now abundantly supplied with water-wheels and shadoofs, and rapidly being restored to cultivation and planted with fresh palm and other trees—the white bungalow gleaming out from the rich green plantation. The cool, shady pools were most tempting for a dip. But, after all, the tea which we brewed among the boulders was a wiser refreshment. Then we hoisted our sail, and flew along rapidly till we got again into rough water. So our crew took to their oars, threaded the narrow channels to the western side, and got into the cataract current. We were thus brought

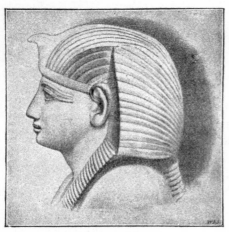

THOTHMES IV.,
Whose records appear at Sehel and on Konosso, and at the Great Sphinx, which he restored (1420 B.C.).

briskly back under the storied cliffs above and opposite the Nilometer. Here the inscriptions are of considerable extent and on a bolder scale than those cut on Sehel island. They are of great historical interest, and the boldly-cut cartouches of Psammitichus and many of his greater predecessors are as clearly carved as when executed. We had another sail and some more musical entertainment from our crew. Then some of us landed on the great rounded granite boulders which are scattered about in the centre of the river here, and photographed or sketched till it was time to return to our comfortable shade in the hotel gardens.

CHAPTER XV.

A TRIP ON THE NILE THROUGH NUBIA.

KALABSHEH: INNER FAÇADE OF THE TEMPLE.

PHILÆ TO WADY HALFA—
KALABSHEH—DENDUR—DAKKEH—WADI SEBOUA—KOROSKO—ABU SIMBEL—
ABU SIR—THE SECOND CATARACT.

WADY HALFA, THIRTY YEARS AGO.
(From a Picture by E. Lear; lent by Miss Griffith.)

CHAPTER XV.

ASSOUAN TO WADY HALFA—THE SECOND CATARACT.

THE recent successful Soudanese campaign gave an interest to the Upper Valley of the Nile such as it had not possessed since the days when British soldiers were sent too late to save the hero Gordon, and the Soudan was lost to Egyptian rule. Travellers who desire to go further south than Philæ have had to content themselves of late years with a visit to Wady Halfa and the Second Cataract, and those who even penetrated so far were comparatively few in number. The First Cataract is still a barrier to the traffic on the great river, and the little railway from Assouan must be made use of to ascend to the higher level of the Upper Nile. The railway ends at Shellal, opposite the island of Philæ, and thence steamers carrying the mails proceed once or twice a week as far as Wady Halfa. Passengers can obtain fair accommodation and excellent attention from Cook and Son, who are entrusted with the management of the traffic, but all the little steamers are the property of the Egyptian Government, and are convertible into gunboats when required. On one of these little vessels a pleasant week can be spent on the voyage.

Wady Halfa, as we see from Mr. Lear's drawing, was a pretty place thirty years since, but war and its accompanying evils have spoiled its beauty. It is now an ugly military cantonment, and possesses no attractions whatever. But it is important as the starting-point of the new military railway to distant Khartum.

Here also we branch off to visit the Second Cataract, which is one of the natural wonders of Egypt. At the time of the high Nile—in August and September—it is possible to sail safely over and above the rugged reefs that form the rapids to which, not very correctly, the name of Cataracts is given. But the torrid climate of those months is not to be endured by pleasure-seekers, and one wonders how the British Army, quartered under such burning skies, could exist at all, let alone fight and conquer native enemies inured to all the tropical terrors of heat, sandstorm, and rainless atmosphere. Now, however, Wady Halfa is garrisoned by Egyptian troops under British officers. It will become an important railway depôt of the great line from Cairo to the Cape. There is no chance of any railway being made between Philæ and Halfa, the engineering cost would be too great. And in time the little town will improve, and perhaps have palms and verdure restored to it by industry and irrigation.

I went to Nubia in the month of March, when the climate was delightful, and still enough water left in the Nile to allow our voyage to proceed at a good rate of speed against the current without grounding on sand-banks; for, although there must be a much greater volume of water here than at Cairo, the river bed is generally much shallower than 500 miles farther down, and the sandbanks are constantly changing their position, which makes navigation difficult. The Nile receives no tributary stream from where it is joined by the Atbara, 1,500 miles from Cairo. The country is rainless, and the quantity of water lost by irrigation and evaporation must be enormous; and yet, strange to say, the Upper Nile is a much shallower river than the Lower Nile.

Before embarking on my Nubian voyage I had made pleasant friendships with several fellow-passengers on the way from Cairo to Assouan, and we agreed to journey together from the First to the Second Cataract. Only seven passengers were in the little steamer. A French professor from the College de France with his two daughters, a Dutch Councillor of State, a Norwegian gentleman, and a bright young English doctor were my companions. We were a very happy family party. The French gentleman and his young ladies spoke English, had visited England often, and were loud in its praises. They had also travelled over the greater part of Europe, which had expanded their views beyond those of the generality of their nation, and they proved delightful associates.

Opposite the island of Philæ was moored our little steamer—our luggage had come on by railway from Assouan—steam was up, and we were soon away, stemming the strong current of the great river, the stern wheel boldly driving us along, leaving a wide track of white and green foam behind. Our first stoppage was at Dabod, where there is a small temple nearly swallowed up by the sand. There is a Greek inscription on it, with names of Ptolemy VI. and Cleopatra I. (not the lovely siren who fascinated Cæsar and Antony, but a much earlier and perhaps more respectable princess of the same name). There are here the ruins of a Roman quay, showing that in their day there must have been considerable trade on the Upper Nile. Other temple ruins are passed; then a bright green region, fringed with tall date palms, with many sakiyas—for the "shadoof" of the Lower Nile is unknown in Nubia—in active operation. The farmers are rich enough to lift the water by sakiya-wheels driven by one or two bullocks or buffaloes. By this apparatus chains of earthen pots are made to lift the water twenty or thirty feet from pits communicating with the Nile. The advance of civilisation is shown, however, by empty petroleum tins being in many places substituted for the picturesque earthen vessels which pour out their crystal flood for the thirsty land's refreshing.

Desert again, and the green margin becomes thinner, and sometimes ceases for several miles; more temples, small and of great antiquity. We refuse to land to inspect anything but a big one. Then sunset comes on, and the steamer anchors for its nightly rest. At four in the morning we are off again. Then we pass barren islands, white as snow with flocks of pelicans, which do not trouble themselves at our approach. The puffing steamer has no terrors for them now; they know all about its harmless mission. In the warm parts of the day we disturb some young crocodiles asleep on a sandbank. They waken up, try to burrow down in the sand like crabs on our seashore, and when they are too large to hide themselves, slide down the bank into deep water, sulkily, lost to view. Flamingoes and many large birds are constantly seen, vultures, eagles, and huge hawks, their pinions spread horizontally against the sky, sailing majestically across the blue with no apparent motion of the wings. Every Egyptian temple has its portal crowned with such a winged form, with the sun in the centre, typical of the flight of the great sun-god across the heavens, the hawk being the symbol of Horus.

Another day passes; wonderful variety of scene, the landscape constantly changing. Here a wide expanse of desert, then red mountain ranges approach from east, now from the west, and again meeting and closing out all view of river north or south. Then a vast mass of ruins appears—the old city of Kalabsheh, with the remains of the largest temple in Nubia. The site of the city is now utterly deserted save by jackals

AUGUSTUS MAKING AN OFFERING OF A FIGURE OF THE GODDESS OF TRUTH TO THE DEITY OF THE TEMPLE AT TALMIS, KALABSHEH, NUBIA.

THE TEMPLE OF KALABSHEH, THE ANCIENT TALMIS.
Restored or rebuilt under Augustus.

and other wild creatures, but it must have been a place of importance as far back as Thothmes III., who lived 15co B.C. The temple itself is of Roman age. The place was known to the Greeks and Romans as Talmis, and Augustus and other Roman rulers are figured here, their titles being expressed in hieroglyphs. The Romans used up the ancient stones to build their "modern" temple, but the design and execution is good, and must have been done by Egyptian artists.

There is a Nubian village by the river where we were besieged by women and naked children with many trophies of the recent war to dispose of. The women had fine figures, and were good-looking although dusky — "black but comely," as the Scriptures put it. Everyone had her baby in her arms or slung on the hip in her mantle. Many had ancient silver bangles on their ankles and arms, and some had earrings and nose jewels. I bought all the personal adornments of one of these dusky belles, and then she offered to sell me her baby! It was a nice little ebony doll, and I was much tempted to buy it, but I doubted if it would be appreciated at home, so I declined the purchase. There

TEMPLE OF MAHARAKA, NUBIA, THE HIERA SYKAMINOS
OF THE ROMANS.

are now and then a mixture of northern types, and another young lady appeared on the scene who was of a pale chocolate tint. She, too, was handsome, and had a pretty infant, which she utterly refused to sell. She was even better caparisoned with jewellery. I bought all her adornments also. One was a beautiful

WADY SEBOUA (THE VALLEY OF LIONS).
The avenue of sphinxes, supposed to be lions by the Arabs.

ancient amber necklace, no doubt taken from a mummy. The bangles and other jewellery were not refused when I laid my purchases before my womankind at home, though I fear the black piccaninny would have been respectfully declined. In this part of the world the ladies do not wear veils as in Lower Egypt, which is considerate. Their northern sisters who hide their visages, no doubt do so for benevolent reasons, for they are ugly enough when seen by chance, although when young their figures are most gracefully shown through their dark-blue robe. The men generally are handsome, whether of yellow or black-skinned race, and the children are frequently attractive little brats, good-naturedly showing their beautiful teeth on all occasions.

In Lower Egypt everyone demands "baksheesh" of the tourists, who have demoralised the people by throwing coins to the children at the landing stages. In Nubia you never hear the word. You are importuned to buy, but not to pay idle wretches to cease molesting you. Then we had a stay and time to sketch at Dendur, a beautiful little temple of Roman work, built in the time of Augustus, in honour of certain Ethiopian heroes. We approach the temple of Dakka, which was begun by the Ptolemies and completed by the Romans. It contains stones of the older building of Thothmes III. and Seti I.

We passed the temple of Seboua (built by Ramses II.), with two granite figures and an avenue of sphinxes, which the Arabs call lions, as the name signifies. In the court of this temple there is a procession of the children of Ramses the Great, in all 111 sons and 59 daughters, but some are now concealed by the sand.

TEMPLE OF DENDUR.
This temple dates from the time of Augustus.

More temple ruins and then Korosko. There is a steep mountain here, and it is the custom for travellers to ascend it to see the sunrise. It is rather hard work, but had to be done. Up at four, and, toiling up a steep, shingly path, after an hour's climbing the rugged summit is reached. We are now in a vast wilderness of great, bleak, rugged, rocky masses, and when the sun suddenly blazes up from behind the eastern cliffs the whole region seems red-hot from a recent volcanic catastrophe. Black, brown, purple, and yellow rocks are all around. The rocks here are red sandstone, but covered with volcanic outbursts. There seems no limit to the mountain ranges eastward.

To the west extends the desert, with the glistening Nile winding through it, bordered with its narrow strip of green verdure and fringe of date palms, then suddenly disappearing altogether round a great corner of rock, and seeming to lose itself in the limitless Libyan Desert. There is a great bend in the Nile at this point. It forms three parts of a circle, and Korosko was the starting-point of the caravan, which struck across the chord of the arc to Abu Hamed. Since the Dervish invasion the caravans have ceased altogether. The celebrated Murat Wells are half-way across, and was held by a strong outpost of Egyptian soldiers. From the top of the mountain we could see the narrow defile, with the path threading it marked out by a white line—the bones of camels and other animals that had died beside the caravan track during a long period of ages.

On a neighbouring height was a square blockhouse, a

KOROSKO: THE LOOK-OUT TOWER.

look-out station, where several soldiers were posted day and night to watch the pass to Murat Wells. The Dervishes were known to be in the vicinity, and the troops lay down every night in their clothes. Next year the Dervishes were driven hundreds of miles further south, and there is now no fear of an attack; but when I was there the town and small garrison of Korosko were in constant dread. The Dervishes had spread terror everywhere, and there were not enough troops to resist them had they penetrated thus far.

We seemed to look down into the cantonment as if from a balloon. The cultivated fields round the little town were like a huge chessboard—patches of brown and green. The barracks began to smoke with the preparations for the

KOROSKO, THIRTY YEARS AGO. (*From a Painting by E. Lear; lent by Miss Griffith.*)

morning meal, and the drill ground was occupied by the soldiers going through their exercises in the cool morning air. We heard the bugles sounding faintly far below us. Then the sun was blazing in full strength, and we came down from our coign of vantage, reached our steamer just in time for breakfast, and pursued our journey up the river merrily.

One of our party who had been too lazy to ascend the hill had bought a chameleon from a boy, and thenceforward this amusing little beast was a great source of interest and occupation for idle moments. I am afraid it was the cause of betting and its accompanying errors, for many arguments and disputes as to its next change of hue were settled by these objectionable practices. The owner of the queer creature constantly asserted that in his cabin it had become vivid green, red, blue, etc. I am afraid I must admit to colour blindness, for to my eyes it seemed to be always an unwholesome greenish grey, rather like a scorpion in tint, and with a curious eye mounted on a swivel arrangement. The eyes acted independently, and one looked at the floor when the other was studiously contemplating the ceiling. The beast had its uses, for when seemingly asleep its long tongue would dart out about two inches to seize a fly or a mosquito that had strayed into its master's cabin. A companion whose only food is flies and mosquitoes would be a welcome one, but chameleons are rare, while the plague of flies has never been removed from Egypt.

The battlefield of Toski, not far from Korosko, is about six miles from the river in the western desert. Here, in 1891, Sir Francis Grenfell defeated the Dervish leader El-Nejumi, and destroyed or scattered his army, taking many prisoners. The desert is still strewn with their skeletons. Their leader was slain on the field. Among the corpses was found an infant, unharmed, the son of Nejumi. He was taken to Cairo, and is now a fine, tall, handsome boy, carefully brought up as a ward of the Government. Let us hope he may not turn out another Arabi. This was the first victory of Egyptian troops led by British officers. Had the Dervishes not been interrupted in their progress the invaders would have sacked and burned Assouan, and after that nothing could have stayed their progress to Cairo, for the people would have joined them had religious fanaticism proved successful. The talent and pluck of the British leader inspired confidence in the Egyptian soldiers, and ever since that day they have never given the slightest cause to doubt their efficiency under proper leadership.

I purchased at Korosko a shield of rhinoceros hide, spears and javelins, a sword, and several daggers that were picked up on the battlefield of Toski. One of the daggers is made out of an ancient bayonet. The sword is a Tübingen blade, about 100 years old. Many of the chief Emirs wore chain mail, dating in all probability from the days of the Crusaders, and helmets which may have been worn by the Knights Templars.

After Korosko we pass more small temples, all on the left bank of the river, some with cartouches of Ramses II. (1330 B.C.), but at Amada we find those of Usertesen III. (2660 B.C.), Thothmes II. (1440 B.C.), and Amenhotep III. (1400 B.C.), all of the Twelfth and the Eighteenth Dynasties, and also traces of Christian worship having been held in these primitive temples of earlier faiths. Then precipitous cliffs rise above the river and an ancient fortress crowns them. This is Ibrim, where we find the name of Tirhakah, the Ethiopian king of Egypt mentioned in our Bible (2 Kings). From an Arab I got a very fine

ABU SIMBEL:
CAST OF HEAD OF RAMSES II.
(British Museum.)

scarab of this monarch, with his name and device legibly inscribed thereon. He seems to have entered Egypt from the south (700 B.C.), from the present Dervish land, and to have conquered the whole country. He and his people called themselves " worshippers of Amon." He became an enlightened patron of religion and arts in Egypt, and restored many ancient shrines.

In the evening of another day we approached the greatest of all Egyptian monuments — that of Abu Simbel. The cliffs seemed to close in upon us. A bend in the river hid it from view, and suddenly the steamer anchored beside the most wonderful of all the temples of Ramses the Great. The façade is 100 feet high and 100 feet wide, and is angled from the river enough to allow a wide open space before the whole. Four gigantic figures of the great king, all originally exactly alike, are seated on thrones forming the front. The whole is hewn

THE GREAT ROCK TEMPLE OF ABU SIMBEL, NUBIA.
View from the western side. The sand is shown again encroaching. When first discovered by Burckhardt, only the heads were visible.

out of the solid rock, each figure being nearly seventy feet high. Three of them are quite perfect ; the head of one has tumbled into the sand below its feet. In the centre is a lofty door leading into the temple and its chambers, which extend 200 feet into the sandstone cliff.

The whole temple outside and inside is covered with inscriptions and pictures describing the life and conquests of Ramses II. (1250 B.C.). His wife, Nefertari, and his eldest daughter are mentioned and depicted. This daughter is believed to have been the lady who adopted Moses as her son. I have scarabs with the names and titles of all these royal personages. Inscriptions of Greek and Phœnician travellers, rudely cut on the statues, show that this marvellous monument was known and visited in or about 600 B.C., but it was utterly forgotten afterwards. Herodotus never heard of it, and Strabo does not mention it.] Burckhardt first brought tidings of its existence to Europe in 1814, but it remained for Belzoni to clear it out of the sands which had well nigh swallowed it up. This was in 1817. We were taken to see the great monument on a starry night. The Southern Cross shone out brilliantly, reflected in the glassy Nile. Orion, overhead, seemed the guardian of the great temple itself; Sirius,

INTERIOR OF THE ROCK-TEMPLE OF
ABU SIMBEL.

glittering in the opposite horizon, threw its light right into the temple doorway. The statues of the great king seemed to glow with life, and the placid countenances appeared to smile with the horizontal light. He has no traces of the parental anxiety on his face, such as might be expected in a father of some 170 children ! Then we penetrated the recesses of the temple, each chamber illumined by flashes of ignited magnesium wire. The bats were awakened up, and gave an eerie aspect with their fluttering wings. The old Egyptians believed that the soul now and then returned from Hades to visit the body, in the form of a bird, and these might seem to give reality to the old creed.

It was late when we returned to our vessel. Early next morning we were awakened to see the interior of the temple illumined by the rays of the rising sun. We penetrated in the almost total darkness 200 feet within the temple to the holy of holies. Suddenly the whole darkness fled. The brilliant rays of the rising sun burst into the wide portal. For a few minutes the whole interior was lit up; the avenue of statues on each side became visible. The roof and lintels disclosed their painted decorations. Ramses in his chariot, with his tame lion underneath it, galloping in fierce charge against the hated Hittites, and on the opposite side the same tyrant crushing the dark sons of Cush. Then, as we wondered at the sudden revelation of the mysteries of the dark interior, the sun rose higher, and we were once more in darkness.

THE ROCK TEMPLE OF ABU SIMBEL, NUBIA (EAST VIEW).

There were four colossal seated figures (one has broken away) representing Ramses the Great. His children are standing about his knees.

THE ROCK-CUT TEMPLE DEDICATED TO HIS GODS
BY RAMSES THE GREAT.
North of the great Temple of Abu Simbel.

Our eyes dazzled with the momentary burning sunlight, we made our way out as best we could, and shortly after started for Wady Halfa. Arrived there we found nothing to interest us. It is a miserable place, surrounded by desert, the sand being only kept back from swallowing up the barracks by a system of walls of sun-dried brick, and full of dirty-looking mud barracks and canteens. But it was a lovely place before the Dervish raids, and to which it may come again with the peaceful times in store for it. I had letters of introduction to the British officers commanding the small garrison, who received me with great kindness.

We desired to visit the Second Cataract, which is some distance beyond the then existing frontier. We were advised to start early in the morning, before sunrise, as there might be Dervishes about. I was to have a guard, and got the rest of the small party included, so we had quite a large escort—six mounted camelmen, fully armed, and six camels (their trappings provided with rifle, pistols, and ammunition) for ourselves.

Riding on a camel is a very extraordinary experience to the beginner. It is sometimes dangerous, and some persons never get the length of enjoying it. But these camels were docile, trained creatures. Their masters were beside them, and encouraged them in Arabic words of tenderness or abuse. Of course, the best of camels swears a good deal when told to kneel down or to rise up, and when once seated on its back it is quite impossible to tell if the beast will use its fore legs or its hind legs first. As a result one of our number was pitched over the beast's head, but was nothing the worse of his tumble, falling in the soft sand. The next time the animal rose, he left himself limp and so kept his saddle. Here the young French ladies eclipsed us all. The girls gently leaped up, the camels knew they had experienced riders, and away they flew like the wind. The young ladies told me afterwards that they had gone to the Jardin d'Acclimation in Paris for six months' training in camel-riding. No wonder they distanced us all and arrived first at the cliff whence the great cataract is viewed. But their father had no confidence in camels, soon dismounted, and came behind on a donkey, arriving long after us, for a trained camel is one of the fleetest of animals on its native desert.

We were fortunate in our guide, the sergeant sent in charge of the camel corps. He spoke English well, having been Gordon's servant at Khartum. His kind master had sent him home to see his sick wife in Cairo a few months before the destruction of the place. When Wilson's corps was sent to relieve Gordon this man got attached to it as a volunteer, but it arrived too late. He saw the flagstaff shot down, and never reached his dear master. The man wept as he told the tale. He also spoke good French, having been page-boy to De Lesseps when the Suez Canal was being made. He was thus able to chat alternately to the young ladies and to me.

Arrived at Abu Sir, we descended from the camels and lunched, hiding from the fierce sun in the shelter of the rocks. The Nile was now very low, yet there was still a wide waste of water extending for many miles before us, foaming over reefs of black, red, brown, and yellow rock, Bab-el-Kibir (the Great Gate) below us, where so many of our gunboats were wrecked in 1882, and again in 1897 a number had great trouble in passing up. The scene is undescribably wild and grand. The air is so clear we could see in the far distance the serpentine course of the open river, with its palm fringes and their green banks. Then a bend of the Nile seemed to carry it to be lost in the desert sands, but it appeared again blue and shining like a vast mirror.

Far away in the extreme distance, more than 200 miles, we saw the peaks at New Dongola. The height of our cliff gave us an uplifted horizon, and we seemed to be able to see to the Equator! We had outstripped our comrades, and the ladies and I had time to sketch the wonderful scene. The muddy Nile was far down below our cliff, the distant blue water of the placid river beyond the cataract, the white, foamy current seen at intervals. These gave bright colours contrasting with the jet black rocks glistening in the brilliant sunshine. Here and there a yellow, red, or brown reef enlivened the blackened

NUBIA: A GROUP OF BISHAREEN.

boulder stones, and flesh-coloured sand filled up all the flat spaces among the great waste of barren, arid, rocky desert. No sign of life could be seen over the vast expanse, save an eagle or a vulture, or now and then a hawk floating across the dazzling blue heavens. The heat was becoming intolerable, and we made the best of our way back to our ship, and, sorry to bid adieu to our kindly escort of the Camel Corps, we soon got under weigh and turned our course towards the north. We had been disappointed as to Dervishes; none came near us, though we found afterwards that they raided a village not far off that day week.

THE SECOND CATARACT, FROM ABU SIR.
View looking south; the hills of New Dongola are in the extreme distance.
(*From a sketch by the Author.*)

We had a pleasant trip back to Philæ, and another charming stay at Abu Simbel, of which one could never see too much. After we had enjoyed Abu Simbel by sunrise, we were fortunate in seeing the wonderful place by moonlight on our return. It was even more wonderful and mysterious. We had the whole interior lit up by magnesium light, and found many chambers we had failed to see before. We also had time to visit the adjoining smaller rock temple erected to the gods for the honour of the great Ramses family. But it seemed hardly large enough to do justice to his manifold progeny. On our previous visit I spoke of the glory of the star Sirius. Professor Norman Lockyer has elucidated that the angle of the central passage leading to the holy of holies was specially chosen to be lit up on a certain night in the year by this star, and by the sun on the same day at sunrise. By this he.

hopes to prove the very day and year on which the dedication of the great temple took place. As if to prove Sir Norman Lockyer's assertion of its influence, the great Dog Star was never in more dazzling splendour than on the occasion of our second visit to this sublime monument.

The railway has now been made from Halfa, across the desert, to far Khartum, but it will be some years ere many tourists will use it. Besides, people of antiquarian tastes will prefer to wend their way by the lonely river, instead of cutting across the sandy waste, a melancholy three days' journey. For by the winding Nile the pyramids of Meroe are to be seen, and the mysterious ruins of Gebel Barkal and other cities and traces of ancient colonies never yet fully investigated. When I go farther south than the Second Cataract I will *not* willingly leave the Nile for any short cut across the desert sands! But there are many cataracts between the one we visited and Khartum, so it will be a tedious river journey when the time comes to undertake it.

Since I made my voyage on the Nubian Nile great events have taken place. The Soudan has been conquered, and Lord Kitchener of Khartum has well earned his title by the exploits of the army led by him to victory. Egypt has been freed from the slave-raider and the fanatical hordes which had threatened her very existence as a nation, and that mainly by her own sons made into good soldiers by the efforts of zealous British officers. Lord Kitchener has great hopes of the future of the Soudan and of its capital, Khartum, becoming a great centre of African civilisation. He has already begun to build his College for the education of the natives, for which the people of England handed him a free gift of £100,000. A hotel has been erected; the house where Gordon died the death of a martyr for civilisation, has been rebuilt as the Governor's residence. Messrs. Cook already announce the programme of tourists' tickets for Khartum! All this, and more, has been brought about by

DUM PALMS AND VILLAGE ON THE UPPER NILE.

The Dûm palm is a branching tree, bearing a yellow fruit with a hard kernel, known as vegetable ivory, yet much appreciated as an edible fruit by the natives.

Q

the self-devotion of one man! But Lord Kitchener says he could not have done the work without the backing he received from Lord Cromer. So all honour to them both!

Let me conclude with a historical parallel. The ancient rulers of Egypt were wont to sculpture on the bases of their colossal statues, two stalwart figures binding the symbols of the River with strong ropes, the control of the Nile being their proudest attribute of sovereignty. To-day we have Lord Cromer personifying the modern rule of the ancient river. The two strong men, represented by the talented engineer and the conquering soldier, join to secure the Nile to restore and enrich the old land of Egypt. For I am safe to say, had the conquest of the Soudan not been effected, the damming of the Nile, now in progress, would never have been achieved.

PATIENT WATER CARRIERS.

CHAPTER XVI.

WATER FOR THE THIRSTY LAND;

THE MODERN "BINDING OF THE NILE."

ABU SIMBEL: THRONE OF RAMSES THE GREAT, SOUTHERN FIGURE.
(A similar group is found on the Colossi of Amenhotep III. at Thebes.)

Two strong men binding the Nile—the cartouche of the king above. His favourite daughter, Amen-mert, stands at his side. (This was possibly the "Pharaoh's daughter" who protected Moses)

ENGINEERS' PLAN

OF THE

RESERVOIR IN PROGRESS

AT THE

FIRST CATARACT.

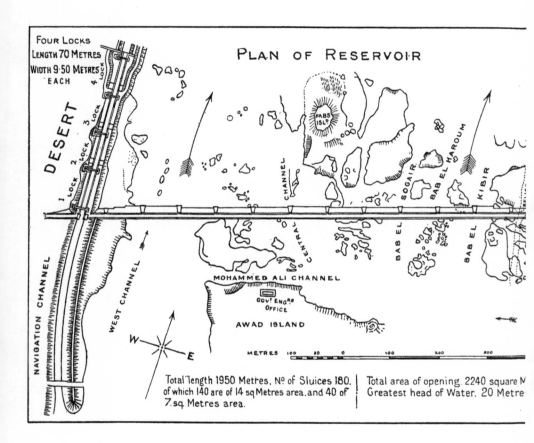

PLAN OF RESERVOIR

Four Locks
Length 70 Metres
Width 9·50 Metres
EACH

4 LOCK

3 LOCK

2 LOCK

1 LOCK

DESERT

HABS
ISLᴰ

CHANNEL

CENTRAL CHANNEL

BAB EL SOGAIR

BAB EL HAROUM

KIBIR

BAB EL

NAVIGATION CHANNEL

WEST CHANNEL

MOHAMMED ALI CHANNEL

GOVᵗ ENGᴿˢ
OFFICE

AWAD ISLAND

W —✴— E

METRES   100   50   0   100   200   300

Total length 1950 Metres, Nº of Sluices 180.
of which 140 are of 14 sq Metres area, and 40 of
7 sq Metres area.

Total area of opening. 2240 square M
Greatest head of Water. 20 Metre

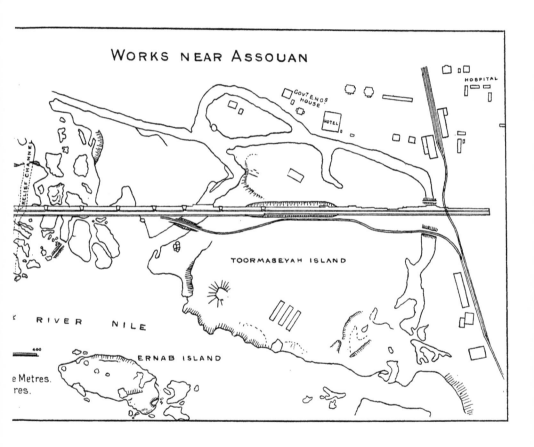

WORKS NEAR ASSOUAN

GOVT ENGS HOUSE

HOTEL

HOSPITAL

RELIEF CHANNEL

TOORMASEYAH ISLAND

RIVER   NILE

400

ERNAB ISLAND

e Metres.
res.

THE ISLAND OF PHILÆ BEFORE THE BARRAGE WORKS HAD COMMENCED.
The perpendicular rock to the right is Konosso, an island when the Nile is high. It is covered with inscriptions, from the time of Mentuhotep (3000 B.C.) to Thothmes IV. (1420 B.C.), and later.

CHAPTER XVI.

I.—THE GREAT RESERVOIR, NEAR ASSOUAN.

It was decreed of another celebrated African locality 2,000 years ago " Delenda est Carthago ! " So the mandate went forth, and Carthage, the greatest naval port of the Mediterranean, was utterly destroyed, never to rise again. The verdict of mankind has ever been that it deserved its doom, and no other course was open to the Romans. But what has lovely, peaceful Philæ done to deserve a similar sentence ? Yet its fate will be the same. It will, at the fiat of modern civilisation, be blotted out, swallowed up by the engulphing waters of the great Nile reservoir, now in course of construction. It is not the conquering Egyptian army that has sent forth the ruthless decree—it is the peaceable, civilising engineer that is the destroyer. The ever-thirsty land calls for water, more water ; the ever-increasing inhabitants of Egypt (for under the present secure government the land under cultivation is doubled every year) must he fed ; the cattle have increased tenfold in recent years—they must have grazing lands.

Egypt is a rainless country, and has but the waters of the Nile to depend on. Wherever the beneficent river is conducted green pastures spring up, and so fertilising is it that in many districts three, and even four, crops in the year can be won from the arid soil by mere irrigation. No manure of any kind is necessary. The Nile overflows its banks for three months of the year. The

SKETCH MAP OF THE NILE DAMS.

flood rushes down, to be lost in the Mediterranean; its muddy waters are discernible for a hundred miles out to sea. This waste will be prevented by damming up the river when in flood, Poor, beautiful Philæ stops the way, and Philæ must go—Delenda est. So say the engineers, and they seem to have proved their case for its necessary destruction. Sentiment says, Why not put the thing somewhere else? But Utilitarianism answers, No place so suitable, so economical; the granite quarries of ancient Syene are on the spot. A splendid foundation exists in the cataracts themselves, which are a natural granite barrier, lifting the water 20 feet already. So the fiat has gone forth, and there will soon be a sheet of fresh water—much more than double the extent of Loch Lomond and much resembling it in shape —seen on the map of the Dark Continent. This will be above Assouan. There will also be another expanse of supplemental reservoir, 200 miles lower down the Nile, vastly bigger than Loch Katrine which supplies Glasgow, but the new African waterworks will meet the wants of five millions of human beings. Not only this, but innumerable live stock will partake of it, and the soil be fed for agricultural purposes along the Nile's banks for seven hundred miles. Millions of acres of desert will be thus rendered fit for cultivation.

The history of the existing Nile Barrage (and the new reservoirs projected for the thirsty land of Egypt for seven years past) has been frequently told. These great new works have been commenced in earnest, and in the spring of 1899, after a ride across the desert to the south of Assouan, I found myself suddenly in the centre of a maze of railway lines, puffing locomotives, gigantic steam cranes, ranges of smiths' forges, the noisy voices of thousands of workmen, Arabs, Nubians, Britons, Savoyards, Greeks—a Babel of confused languages and nationalities. The sharp clink-clink of the tools of the quarrymen makes a musical accompaniment. They are continually piercing the granite for the charges of nitro-glycerine. These blasts, fired each day at noon, dislodge thousands of tons of granite with terrific explosions, which cause old earth to quiver and tremble. Added to this, the roar of the waters, the shrill screams of the

ASSOUAN: EARLY WORK ON THE BARRAGE.
State of the great trench through the granite rock, March 1899.

locomotives—all constitute a pandemonium of noises which it is impossible to describe by words. At first one thinks that it must be a dream, that Harland and Wolff's Works, Crewe Station, Wolverhampton iron forges, the Aberdeen granite quarries may have got mixed, and all have been dropped down together. We are not dreaming! it is stern, noisy reality, but can this be old Egypt, the land of the lotus-eaters? Yes, for there was the mighty Nile, rushing and roaring towards its cataract's first leap, which the bold British engineers are about to grapple with. They will utterly subdue its turbulence, once they fill up and divert the torrent's stream, and will crown their efforts with a granite viaduct 70 feet high and in some places double that elevation, and with a broad roadway along the top.

Pity 'tis that Philæ, of all "old Egypt's piles," should have to sink beneath the flood. As the poet Moore sang, "The towers of other days" may after all be visible "in the waters beneath him shining," but that will be poor consolation for the artist and the archæologist. The highest water level will be up to the floors of the temple of Isis. "Pharaoh's Bed"—the beautiful pavilion

ASSOUAN: GENERAL VIEW OF THE WORKS, MAY 1899.
Looking towards the west channel.

built for Augustus, but completed by Trajan—will gradually crumble, for it is
mainly built on a terrace of Nile mud. Thick slime will engulf the lovely colonnades of Nectanebo, and the wall that supports them will gradually drop away;
it is full of cracks already. The Nilometer steps and its ancient registers of the
Nile's rising will be perennially under water, and no more accessible. The lovely
little temple of Hathor will be drowned out. The temple of Isis, just above the
sacred stair, will be the only bit of dry ground left. The Roman arch of
Diocletian's time will be no more seen. The sculptured rock of Konosso, with
its stories of 4,000 years ago, can then only be viewed from a boat, and part
of its inscriptions will be lost beneath the water. All the lovely date-palms will
die. But Egypt will gain, famine be impossible in the land, and there will
be many (far more ancient) temples left in other parts of Egypt for archæologists
to study and speculate about, though nothing so beautiful for the artist as was
the green isle of Philæ.

Before we inspect the greatest engineering feat of the kind that ever was
attempted, let us glance around the strange scene. In the distance, poor old beautiful

Philæ calmly awaits its doom by drowning. Above all the din, the placid blue sky spreads its glorious vault, across which the vultures and the eagles soar in calm, confident security, already accustomed to the strange devilry of noises being carried on beneath. The hot sunshine pours down mercilessly, the rounded granite boulders, if we touch them, are so hot with the burning sunshine that they singe our skin, and would cook dough into hard bannocks were it spread upon their surface. The iron rails are hot enough to blister fingers incautiously laid on them. Yet the busy multitude of almost naked men—red, black, white, or brown of skin—toil and sweat unceasingly. Astonished camels stray into this weird camp of industry, unwillingly kneeling down to be unloaded. Neat Arab ponies, carrying British engineers who guide and rule this hive of industry, move along the banks. Brisk, 'cute donkeys trot with confidence, carrying us visitors along the narrow edges of the great granite trench, a mile long and 100 feet wide and deep, which already has been blasted out to give footing for the huge wall of Cyclopean masonry.

ASSOUAN: MASONRY, EASTERN CHANNEL, JULY 1899.
The entire section of the great wall is seen in the background.

ASSOUAN : MAHOMMED ALI ISLAND.
Excavating foundations, looking west, May 1899.

The dyke will be 150 feet high in parts, 1,950 mètres in length, and be pierced by 180 openings, every one provided with Stoney's patent sluices. (These sluices are similar to those in use at the Thames at Richmond, and now being fitted to the Clyde at Glasgow.) This wonderful wall will stem the Nile's greatest flood, and hold up the water of "high Nile," whose level will extend back 140 miles into Nubia. All this great, almost-superhuman undertaking has been carried on thus far in the past winter and spring by the energy of Messrs. John Aird and Co., the contractors for the entire reservoir scheme, which will double the cultivable land of Egypt when fully completed. When so much has been done in a few months we cannot doubt but the whole will be at full work within the allotted five years. No money need be paid by the Government of Egypt until the reservoirs are finished and the Nile "held up" sixty-five feet above its present level, at the Philæ dam, and ten feet above the whole Nile width at the supplemental water storage at Assiout. All this and several new navigable canals will be provided.

The cataracts now impede navigation for the greater part of the year. They will disappear; instead there will be a canal and four locks 200 feet long and 30 feet wide, giving constant passage for traffic up and down the Nile. And all this and more also will, no doubt, be done within the allotted time; then the efforts of Mr. John Aird, M.P., and his merry men will begin to receive their well-earned reward. Provided with orders from headquarters, to introduce us to the courteous Engineer-in-Chief of these great works, Mr. Maurice Fitzmaurice, M.I.C.E., we were conducted over the three or four miles of engineering operations. We were then taken across the turbulent Nile in the efficient, swift steam launch, to view, from the little colony of temporary Government offices, the cataract itself, the Bab-el-Kibir (or great gate) of the

ASSOUAN: EASTERN CHANNEL, LOOKING WEST.
Starting masonry, May 1899.

wild whirling rapids, across which the huge granite wall is to be built. It passes belief that piers of 150 feet and more can be safely built right down through the rushing, foamy torrent; but Mr. Fitzmaurice, the able superintendent, and Mr. Blue, the contractors' engineer, are quite confident that it can be and shall be accomplished. A railway has been constructed for excavating and building the canal and locks for several miles and bringing the stone to fill up this "great gate" from the western bank. Millions of tons will be needed to obliterate this gap of a quarter of a mile.

We shelter from the fierce sun of noon in the shady bungalow where the engineers' staff work out their plans and calculations. It stands on the edge of the wildest portion of the famous cataract. After a hospitable rest in the shady quarters of the engineers, we wait outside surveying the scene so soon to be wiped out, and gaze down into the foaming noisy rapids beneath our feet. The tall, handsomely-dressed sheikh of the cataracts appears, emerging from the granite boulders. Two herculean, bronze-tinted, naked athletes follow him, and we secure their willing exhibition of their skill in natation. They plunge headlong into the wild, raging, white and olive-tinted billows. We hold our breath. Have they miscalculated their power, are they not utterly lost, smashed up into fragments? But we see their black, woolly heads bobbing up now and then, like floats of cork. Lost only to sight, with a shout they emerge from beneath the foaming flood, far away down the sloping, boiling waves, and gaily swim, beating the water with each arm alternately, scarcely using the legs at all, except, apparently, as cleeks to grip the billows. The big, muscular fellows crawl up the slippery boulders and are at our feet in a few minutes, vociferating, with no lack of breath, for their well-earned "baksheesh."

Bewildered almost by the din of industry and the war of waters, we bade adieu to our friends, Mr. Maurice Fitzmaurice and his assistants, and, mounting our donkeys, threaded the rails and trucks and puffing locomotives, along the river's brink, towards Shellal, the village opposite Philæ. This part of the journey was along the Nile bank, which will be covered, sixty-five feet over where we are guiding our donkeys, by the summit level

ASSOUAN: PORTION OF COMPLETED WALL OF DAM.
(Photo by Major Hanbury Brown, R.E.)

of the waters of the completed Great Reservoir. I had once lived here in solitude for weeks, not far from a native village of a few inhabitants. Now the wants of 7,000 workmen have caused a populous town and many shops to spring up all over the place.

By the riverside our servants and our lunch awaited us. We had secured a strong felucca to shoot the cataracts withal, and made certain of an experienced crew, but crossed over first to the little island of Philæ and persuaded the custodian to allow us to eat our last meal in the

ASSOUAN : NUBIAN SWIMMER AT THE BAB-EL-KIBIR.

sacred temple of Isis. Here, with the protecting figures of Egyptian faith surrounding us on the painted and sculptured walls, we desecrated the shrine by converting it into a restaurant. We seemed nearly as wicked as those engineers who will smilingly sacrifice the beauties of nature and art to carry out the utilitarianism of a wholly practical age. Wandering round the historic ruins, visiting the Nilometer (which will unfortunately be lost beneath the waves), Pharaoh's Bed, the temple of Hathor the Egyptian Venus, the lovely colonnades of Nectanebo, and the Roman Triumphal Arch, we had time to take a

ASSOUAN: TEMPORARY DAM OR SUDD AT BAB-EL-KIBIR.
Viewed from the opposite dam, June 1899.

lingering farewell of the pretty isle; then, as the sun got low, we took to our
stout felucca and its stalwart crew, made one last circuit of the island, and
boldly rushed the cataracts. It took all the strength of our eight oars to keep us
free from rocks, seen and hidden. There is just enough danger to give zest to
the two hours' descent of the Nile to Assouan.

The excursion by water was delightfully exhilarating, and when we landed
opposite the Isle of Elephantine, in perfectly balmy air, we felt that the refreshing
cup of tea which awaited us in the shady hotel garden was all that was required
to make our day one of the most delightful we had ever spent in Egypt.
Admiration for modern engineering prowess had, I am afraid, made us forget, at
least for a time, our regrets for the coming destruction of the island which we
loved. Some scientific notes have been since supplied by the kindness of Sir Benjamin Baker and Mr. Aird, M.P., under whom the present works are being carried
out. Mr. Fitzmaurice, Major Brown, Mr. Stephens, Mr. de Courcy, and Mr. Aird
have kindly supplied me from time to time with photographs of the great
works as they progressed.

Mr. Willcocks, when in the Egyptian service some seven years ago, was the
Government officer who carried out the reconstruction of Mehemet Ali's Barrage
near Cairo. French engineers had been employed on this great undertaking for

ASSOUAN: THE MASONRY, LOOKING WEST, MAY 1899.
The stone-work is covered with sacking to allow the cement to settle properly in the strong sunshine.

upwards of twenty years. The superstructure was very handsome to look at ; but their (unseen) foundations were so badly done that the work would never hold water. The French custodians ran away in 1882, and British engineers got the job of repairing or destroying the great barrage. Sir Colin Moncrieff and Mr. Willcocks repaired it successfully, and it soon repaid the cost. The original barrage, when made to work, was such a benefit to Lower Egypt that Lord Cromer and his advisers determined to try if similar works were possible for Upper Egypt. Mr. Willcocks was therefore sent to report if he could improve the irrigation of Upper Egypt by similar dams, barrages or reservoirs. He worked as only he can at comprehensive surveys for several years. He provided plans for seven dams or weirs for the storing of the Nile flood which had hitherto been lost in the Mediterranean. Two of these reservoirs were selected by Sir Benjamin Baker's advice, but the French opposition to British efforts (to store the wasted waters for the regeneration of the country they had undertaken to save) made the great works apparently impossible, for the Caisse de la Dette refused all supplies, and the cost was estimated by millions sterling.

At such a juncture the Government might well have been disheartened, but Lord Cromer never despaired. Disraeli said that the unexpected always happens. Mr. John Aird, M.P., and a band of capitalists one day turned up in Cairo and offered to carry out the two reservoirs and a lot of navigation and irrigation canals, for nothing! if Sir Benjamin Baker's suggestions, as approved by Government, were carried out. Mr. Willcocks had left the Government service, hopeless that his beloved reservoirs would ever be made in his lifetime. Willcocks had wanted to raise the Nile dam one hundred and twenty feet; this Sir Benjamin Baker was told to reduce to twenty mètres, to save part of the island of Philæ, the destruction of which the archæologists and the Society of Antiquaries (and Sir Edward Poynter for the artists) had made great efforts to prevent. This offer was accepted by the Egyptian Government. So Sir Benjamin Baker's scheme, now being carried out, will impound the waters only at about sixty-five feet above the mean level of the present Nile.

Willcocks' dam would have been an enormous one, and a greater benefit to Egypt; but the one now in progress is big enough to do a vast amount of good to the land, and the lower level will spare many monuments and tombs in Nubia that the other would have swallowed up. Even the reduced level of sixty-five feet will, however, imperil the existence of the structures on Philæ, and much of the island itself, being composed of Nile mud, will, I am afraid, disappear in the course of a

ASSOUAN: FOUNDATION STONE OF RESERVOIR.
Laid by the Duke of Connaught, 12th Feb. 1899.

few years. Dr. Petrie and his band of archæologists must bestir themselves during the next four seasons. Tourists, if they want to see the most picturesque collection of temples ever gathered together within a few acres, must go there as soon as possible.

I went to Assouan to visit the great works in March of 1899. Sir Benjamin Baker, Mr. Aird, and Mr. Fitzmaurice have given me several months' later

ASSOUAN: THE MAHOMMED ALI CHANNEL (NILE RISING).

L. & G. Windkug

(257)

ASSOUAN: THE BAB-EL-KIBIR.
Temporary dam or sudd to restrain the flood, the Nile rising rapidly. View below stream, July 1899.

tidings of the progress made since.   There were 7,000 men employed at the works
near what has been always known as the First Cataract, labouring by night and
day.   The scene (by electric light when there is no moonshine) is wonderful indeed,
and by day, when a photograph can be taken, the stupendous work is even better
seen and appreciated.   The deep trench in the granite rock, as wide as Regent
Street, has been carried down to where safe foundation for the huge wall can be
found.   There are several "faults" in the bedding of syenite, and intrusive basalt
dykes must be removed, cut out, so as to prevent leakage, and replaced by granite
and cement where rotten or where the heat of bygone ages' eruptive agency has
calcined or metamorphosed the surrounding masses of primary rock.   The shady
palms are gone and the stony plateau itself (where I have often joined in jolly picnic
parties, in previous visits to the lonely spot) is transformed now into a yawning
gorge which has been quarried out for the foundations of the great granite wall.
The masonry has been begun, and will be carried high enough to be safe above
the fierce Nile-flood of the coming autumn. Where I saw the big brawny

IDEAL VIEW OF THE ISLAND
OF PHILÆ

During the high level of the reservoir. The greater part of Konosso, it will be observed, is submerged.

(*See engraving on page* 145.)

Nubians plunge into the boiling cataract, the gorge has now been filled up with huge masses of granite won from the newly-excavated trench hard by. Thousands of tons of rock, tied together with steel wire rope, fill the bed of the " matchless cataract," and the channel of the river has already been diverted. Next year, the building of the Great Reservoir wall (at this point to be at its highest) will be carried on, and soon it will be difficult to realise that here for ages past foamed that " hell of waters " " the Bab-el-Kibir."

Mr. Fitzmaurice told me that he had established a new order of things here with regard to Sunday labour. All over Egypt the English in the service of the Government have to work on Sundays and be idle on Fridays. This did not please Mr. Fitzmaurice, and so he issued a mandate, that the present being a British contract, Sunday should be observed as a day of rest. All the nationalities, whether Mahometans, Jews, Greeks, or English, had to obey, and are quite content with the change. So all the 20,000 workers rest from labour, along with their English masters, on the English Sunday.

NUBIANS SWIMMING THE BAB-EL-KIBIR.

R 2

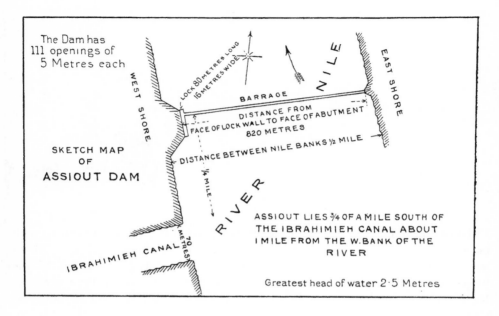

II.—THE ASSIOUT RESERVOIR.

THE subsidiary reservoir (a weir to restrain and hold up the high Nile), 200 miles lower down the river, at Assiout, has also made great progress under Mr. G. H. Stephens, the Chief Engineer. A third of the foundations and a fourth of the whole work has been already done; £270,000 has been spent to date. The land above where the town of Assiout is situated is almost a plain, much of which will be covered with water when the dam is at work. More men could work here than at Assouan (11,500 were employed in June 1899); there are double shifts, and brilliant electric light used every night.

The experience gained by Mr. Willcocks in the saving of the French Barrage at Cairo (which is also built on the strata of ancient Nile mud) led the authorities to recommend the building of the Assiout weir upon the muddy bed of the river itself, with aprons of cement above and below the weir, as had been done for the salvation of the old Barrage. Sir Benjamin Baker's plans are on a surer principle of security, and in many respects entirely his own planning, to avoid from the first the risks that attended the original weak foundations of the French structure.

It was intended to use hard burnt brick, but the Government have now determined to carry out all with stone. This was unfortunate for the workers, for

ASSIOUT: GENERAL VIEW OF THE WORKS, JUNE 1899.

ASSIOUT: DRIVING CAST-IRON PILES TO SOLIDIFY THE CONCRETE
FOUNDATION FLOOR.

the sun's heat is such in summer that the stone had 160 degrees of warmth, and the poor fellows' hands were blistered with lifting and laying the burning blocks. Coffer-dams and huge cast-iron piles are driven on the dry floor of the bed of the old Nile, as shown by the photographs. Mr. G. H. Stephens is the energetic superintending engineer at this point, and is confident all the wonderful works will be accomplished before the promised time. He has sent me some excellent photographs of the progress of the great wall in the river bed, and has recently written me a technical description, which I will give in full, as the work is entirely of a novel character. The foundations are carried down 40 feet below level of high Nile. An immense masonry floor, 87 feet wide by 10 feet thick, has been constructed at this depth. On this floor the superstructure has to be built. At both up and down stream sides of this floor, cast-iron sheet piles are driven down to a further depth of 13 feet, the joints of which are hermetically sealed by cement grout. These piles are to prevent the possibility of percolation below the foundations.

Great efforts were being made by night and by day to have the great weir built, at Assiout, before "high Nile" comes. Now all is safe until next year, when no more coffer-dams will be required. The great dam will extend for

ASSIOUT: COMMENCING MASONRY ON CEMENT FLOOR OF THE DAM.

more than half a mile across the river, and its high level will extend forty miles above the town, filling up the bed of the Nile and covering its banks. Of course, the ancient hills, a couple of miles from the town, with their tombs of the early dynasties, will remain high and dry.

The weir now being constructed at Assiout will "hold up" about ten feet of water; but still this is a great work, the Nile here being over half a mile wide. There will be 111 arches or openings, each fifteen feet wide, all provided with ordinary sluices, always open below, to allow the muddy Nile water free vent, for filtered water, stored up motionless, would lose its fertilising properties, and the valuable mud would soon silt-up the reservoir.

There will be a navigable canal, fifty feet wide, alongside, with gates, affording constant possibilities for the trade up and down the river, which is here very extensive, fleets of gyassas being constantly passing. So in three or four years there will be a placid sheet of water, looking when completed much like the works of the old Barrage, planned by Mehemet Ali, below Cairo. The architectural "elevations" of the new Nile weirs and sluices have not yet been published, but no doubt the style of the roadway and the river front of the existing "Barrage" will be copied to some extent.

There will be no trouble about the money for all these new gigantic works. Egypt will practically pay nothing for them. For all the works now in progress at Assouan, and also at Assiout, the many irrigation canals required to dispense

ASSIOUT: PREPARATIONS FOR MASONRY ON THE CONCRETE FLOOR—DRIVING PILES.

the waters won from the Nile's flood, and all the navigation canals, nothing will be paid till they are at work.   So in about three years hence, £166,666 per annum will be payable, for thirty years, to the contractors—in all £5,000,000. But the increased water supply will bring in much more than double this annual sum.   The contractors asked the British public to lend them (in April 1899) £400,000 at four per cent. for this enterprise, offering no security, only their good name and the faith of certain promises to pay which they would receive from the Government of Egypt, as the work went on: the applications for this contractors' loan within a few hours of its announcement, in London alone, amounted to *eleven millions sterling !*

Verily those who have so much spare cash to invest at four per cent. have now shown their faith in the permanence of the British guidance of Egypt, in the engineers who planned these wonderful works, in the contractors who have, without any guarantee whatever, undertaken the greatest feat of irrigation skill that the world ever saw, and in capitalists who can afford to spread the recoupment of £5,000,000 over thirty years.

Most of the ancient Greek geographers thought the Nile emerged from the bowels of the earth at the cataracts, and perils great and thrilling were the lot of adventurers beyond their rocky terrors.   Herodotus, however, tells of the Nile being fed by great lakes far away beyond the granite region.   The truth of the

ASSIOUT: WALL OF THE NAVIGATION LOCK AT THE WEST BANK.

existence of these huge stores of water has only been proved within the memory of those now living. We now know that the great Victoria Nyanza Lake supplies the Nile with its flood fed by the equatorial rains of a region as far south as Zanzibar. The mountains of Abyssinia contribute their snow waters, which bring down to the Nile the granite detritus, which charges the waters with its fertilizing silt. The Bahr-el-Ghazal brings its peaty discharge from the morasses of Central Africa, adding another element of sustenance for the rich crops of Egypt. In fact the Nile is charged with every chemical product necessary to vegetation. But in years gone by, as in our own time, the Nile's overflow has been known to fail altogether. The earliest record of such a disappointment is 5,000 years old, and is engraved on the rocks near the First Cataract. Again, in the time of Joseph, a like cause produced the famine of which the Bible tells us. The Arabic historian, Elmacin, relates that in A.D. 1106 the "Sultan of Egypt" sent an envoy with magnificent presents to the Emperor of Ethiopia, begging him to remove the cause of the Nile's failure in that year, and so save Egypt from the horrors of famine. The Ethiopian monarch was ultimately persuaded "to suffer a dam to be opened that had turned the river, which, taking its usual course, rose three cubits in one day." The historian records that "the envoy, on his return, received great honours" from the relieved Egyptians.

ASSIOUT BARRAGE, JULY 1899.
Progress with piers built on the concrete floor. Work left at this point till next season.

This year (1899) the same failure of "high Nile" has occurred, but I hear from Major Hanbury Brown that he is confident famine can be prevented by great exertions of the Irrigation Department. The high lands, however, will have to lie fallow for a season.

Mr. Willcocks, in a recent letter to the *Times*, suggests the cause of this unexplained phenomenon, and a remedy. We give his own words :—

"Egypt at the present moment is experiencing one of the worst floods of the century, and that branch of the river which leaves the great Equatorial Lakes seems to have failed completely. This branch of the river (let us call it the White Nile) is completely closed by the *sudd*, and the waters are wandering over the immense swamps which stretch from latitude 7 to latitude 10. The failure of this supply in the summer of 1900 will be serious. Now England holds the keys of the Nile. The waters which leave the Great Lakes are considered never to fall below 18,000 cubic feet per second (see Sir W. Garstin's last report on the Soudan, published by the Egyptian Government). The discharge at Assouan, in spite of the additions of surface and subsoil waters from the Gazelle, the Sobat, the Blue Nile, and the Atbara, has within the last twenty-five years twice fallen as low as 7,000 cubic feet per second, and may again fall as low, or even lower. What becomes of the immense body of water which leaves the lakes? After passing Lado, the White Nile splits up into numerous branches which lose themselves in the swamps. " Divide et Impera." The swamps vanquish the Nile. Now if a very small expedition were to find its way to Lado *viâ* Mombasa and engage labourers among the Bari and Madi tribes, it would be a comparatively easy task to close the heads of the Bahr Seraf and other channels which leave the right bank and confine the water to the Bahr-el-Jebel, which passes by Bor and Shambeh. (Colonel Martyr says the *sudd* is thirty miles north of Shambeh. If he had had a canal engineer with him, he might have cut the *sudd* and come on to Khartum.) Once the waters of the Great Lakes were confined to one channel they would be able to account for any amount of *sudd*. No attempt has ever been made to cut the *sudd* with the aid of the current. This is the true way to do it, looked at from the point of view of the hydraulic engineer. Once the *sudd* is removed, it will be easy, with the aid of a dredger and willows, to confine the water permanently to one channel, because it is muddy for three months in the year. Willows will have to be imported, as none are to be found in the White Nile or the Gazelle river; and very possibly it is owing to their absence from these regions that the swamps have become so unmanageable.

" W. WILLCOCKS.

" CAIRO, *Sept.* 18*th*, 1899."

It is evident that when the Nile was freed from obstruction in 1106 it was done by cutting the *sudd*, as now suggested by Mr. Willcocks. " Sudd " means anything which stops up the river. In this case it is a dense vegetable growth, which, floating on the surface, effectually checks the water's motion.

The great new reservoirs are part of the same scheme which has been at work near Cairo for some years. I have postponed any reference to the construction of the Cairo Barrage till the new works higher up the Nile could be seen and understood. But having seen the vast changes at Assouan and Assiout, the traveller, on his homeward way, should, without fail, visit the original of all Barrages. I subjoin an account of the Cairo Barrage, and the description of this, the pioneer of all Nile dams, will form a fitting *finale* to the story of the modern efforts for " Binding the Nile."

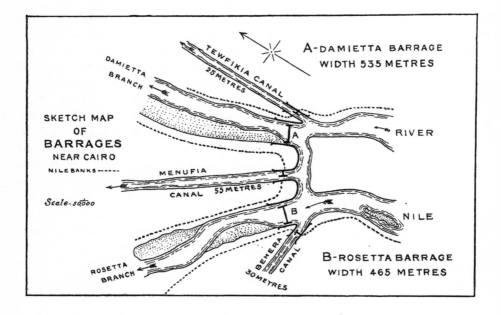

SKETCH MAP
OF
BARRAGES
NEAR CAIRO
NILE BANKS -----

Scale - 50000

DAMIETTA BRANCH

TEWFIKIA CANAL
25 METRES

A - DAMIETTA BARRAGE
WIDTH 535 METRES

A

RIVER

MENUFIA
CANAL   55 METRES

B

NILE

ROSETTA
BRANCH

BEHERA CANAL
30 METRES

B - ROSETTA BARRAGE
WIDTH 465 METRES

III.—THE OLD BARRAGE NEAR CAIRO.

ONE of the pleasantest of many excursions from Cairo is a picnic to the
Barrage. You can go by railway; you might anticipate purgatory by going by
road riding on a donkey or a camel; but a wise man gets invited with a pleasant
picnic party, on pleasure bent alone, and goes by water all the way there and back
in a commodious steam launch. The trip on the Nile is delightful. You run down
stream with the soft olive-green waters brightened by picturesque sailing-boats,
like flocks of giant white-winged birds; the domes and minarets of Cairo, with
its many mosques, recede from view, and the rich fringe of palm groves extends
along the river bank. The Gezireh Palace (one of Ismail's many extravagances),
transformed into an hotel, and a very comfortable one, is now passed. Then
palace after palace of modern shoddy construction, but bright as stucco and
paint can make them, and each in its park-like garden. You start early and
return late, to avoid the burning sunshine. The rapid motion provides plenty of
air, while awning is well supplied to veil the sun at tiffin time, or when the
refreshing cup of afternoon tea appears. It was my good fortune to be invited
to an engineers' picnic. We were about thirty, and the company were mostly
fine, stalwart men, with due accompaniment of fair English ladies in the coolest
and most attractive costumes. It was an official holiday, and some magnates

THE BARRAGE, NEAR CAIRO. UP STREAM, NILE LOW.

from other departments gave us their company. Then we had a prince, a cousin of the Khedive—a very pleasant fellow indeed, who discoursed perfect English, having had much of his education in England. Mr. Willcocks, the greatest living irrigation engineer, who carried out the wonderful works of salvation at the Barrage which we were about to inspect, was on board, as were also Mr. Wilson, whose duty is now to superintend, for the supreme authority, the construction of the two new barrages and their reservoirs, and others of the engineers whose labours are making Egypt one of the most prosperous countries in the world.

My kind hosts landed us at the Barrage, conducting us over the great work. It is upwards of a mile in length, a handsome paved roadway, with embattled walls. We were shown how the sluices operated to stem the current and hold up the great wall of water, twenty feet to thirty feet high, at the proper season. Whirled along on the tiny chair railway, we were shown over the great viaduct. The new sluices, invented by Mr. Frank Stoney, the great engineer, were explained by himself. Lord Cromer and the Khedive were to inaugurate them the next day. A child, by moving a lever, can elevate or depress a mass of solid steel, twenty feet by twelve feet, with all the pressure of the Nile upon it. It is intended to use this clever invention for the Great Reservoir. After a delightful day, when evening approached, we betook ourselves to our little steamer, and rapidly ran back to Cairo. The sun was setting behind the Pyramids in a golden and crimson glory. The old monuments took a rich purple against the fiery sky; the mosque of Mehemet Ali and the citadel of

Saladin borrowed the same tints on the opposite bank; and we landed at Boulak well satisfied with our holiday.

I will try to tell the story of this Barrage as it was told me by my engineer friends. The eagle eye of the great Napoleon, on his visits to Egypt in 1798 and 1799 at once saw what great advantages would accrue to Egypt by dams or reservoirs to store up the flood waters of the Nile. Whether he knew that the ancient Egyptians had done much the same thing thousands of years before his time, whether he knew this or not, to him belongs the credit of suggesting the existing Barrage. The French rule in Egypt was temporary, and Napoleon's career was cut short. But his idea was carried out—or a commencement made —by the founder of the present dynasty in Egypt, Mehemet Ali.

Napoleon had pointed out that where the branches of the Nile bifurcate to form the Delta was the spot to erect a great barrier to be the means of raising the Nile sufficiently to irrigate the low-lying fertile lands comprised between the Damietta and Rosetta arms of the great river. The idea of Napoleon was a wise one, and worthy of its great originator. It had been published as his notion by more than one French author.

Mehemet Ali became Viceroy in 1805, heard of Napoleon's project, and seems to have always contemplated carrying it out. He was a powerful ruler, utterly unscrupulous and tyrannical in his method of governing the country. But withal he was undoubtedly a great man, and when he tore Egypt from the blighting influence of the Sultan he proceeded to make it the great and important Power it has become since, and in some measure to restore its ancient reputation of being one of the leading countries of the world. But he was a selfish, cruel, and domineering ruler; he ground down the unfortunate people, impressed them into his armies, carried on his great works by forced labour, such as the *corvée*, and accentuated all by free use of the kourbash. (Water was needed for Alexandria, and in this way Mehemet Ali caused the great Mahmoudieh Canal to be constructed in one year. Over 250,000 men were torn from their homes, and, unpaid, forced to excavate it without tools, using their hands to fill their baskets of soil. Of these 25,000 died at the work. It is 36 miles long and 100 feet wide. In the same wasteful manner were all the great enterprises of this remarkable tyrant carried on.)

His wars and his own personal expenses were enormous, and he plunged the country in debts which it is still unable to clear off. In order to increase his revenue he began the cultivation of cotton, sugar, and of rice. These crops were new to Egypt, and needed more water than the ordinary Nile unaided could provide. Then he seems to have determined to create the great work

THE BARRAGE, NEAR CAIRO. ROSETTA BRANCH FROM DOWN STREAM.

which Napoleon had foreseen would one day be necessary. Various French engineers were summoned to carry this out. One ventured to suggest a great stone embankment. "Well, then," said Mehemet Ali, "you have those great useless heaps of stone, the Pyramids, use them up, every block, for the purpose." The engineer knew that infamy would attach to his name if he agreed to this proposition, and asked some days to make calculations. His master would only allow him one day. When the engineer again appeared he said the cost of transporting the stone from the Pyramids would be greater than to quarry it anew in the mountains. "Then let the Pyramids stay, and quarry new stone," said the tyrant, and so the monuments were saved. Mehemet Ali planned his barrage in 1833, but the plague came, killed his fellaheen by thousands and thousands, and so even the tyrant had to cease work for several years. It was therefore not till 1837 that the actual work we now see was begun.

The existing barrages were designed and planned by a Frenchman, Mougel Bey, who had been long in the Viceroy's service, and who must have been a man of genius and of considerable artistic taste. It is probable that the foundations of such a talented man would have been properly laid had the designer been allowed to employ skilled workmen, but he had only thousands of poor half-starved fellaheen (country labourers), and when the work was delayed extra thousands were sent down, only to spoil what had been done, or do indifferently anything new. Millions of tons of stones and gravel were thrown into the river bed, and on this cement was poured, often under water. On this unreliable substructure was piled the vast dyke of masonry, pierced by 120 arches, carrying sluices and roadway, and upwards of a mile in length. Skilled labour had to be now employed, and the cost became enormous. Mehemet Ali died in 1848, before it was finished. Under his successors the work went on. At length, in 1861, it was declared completed, but no one ventured to use it to dam up the full pressure of high Nile. The river was only kept back enough to raise the level a few feet. At length, in 1863, it may have been supposed to have been consolidated, and some venturesome engineer closed the sluices and let the water rise. Immediately the unfortunate barrier cracked in several places, and began to actually move down stream! The sluices were immediately opened, and the movement stopped. The extent of its northward progress can still be seen, about 100 feet of the parapet being out of line to this day.

Various experts were called in during the next few years. Some, like Sir John Fowler, suggested spending £1,500,000 more to save it. It had already cost four millions sterling, and would not hold in, for not only did the whole affair threaten to move off to the Mediterranean, but the sills cracked, and springs of water began to boil up everywhere below the arches. Other experts advocated the whole affair being blown up with gunpowder, but even this and

THE BARRAGE, CAIRO. DOWN-STREAM VIEW.

the removal of the vast masses of masonry to free the passage of the Nile would have cost £500,000. Time went on. A costly staff was maintained to keep the sluices always open and constantly repairing the whole work.

Then the events of 1882, and with them the British came on the scene, and Lord Dufferin was sent from Constantinople to report, after several months' sojourn in Egypt, what could be done to save the country after the disastrous effects of Arabi's mutiny. His masterly reports to Lord Granville have been published as State papers, and his advice has undoubtedly saved Egypt from hopeless ruin and insolvency, as all the revenue of Egypt comes practically from the Nile. Lord Dufferin's wise advice to borrow some of our Indian officials and irrigation engineers was carried out, and Sir William Garstin, Sir Colin Moncrieff, Major R. H. Brown, Mr. W. J. Wilson, and Mr. Willcocks, among others, came into power. Sir Colin Moncrieff and Mr. Willcocks were asked if the Barrage should be abandoned and destroyed at a cost of half a million. They spent much time in borings and experiments, and at length Sir Colin Moncrieff reported that for a similar sum he would undertake to save the structure. Lord Cromer backed him up, the work was done, under Mr. Willcocks' superintendence, and soon the Damietta section was

RESTORATION OF THE FRENCH BARRAGE BY BRITISH ENGINEERS, 1889.
Temporary great dam. Repairs in progress.
(*From " The History of the Barrage," by Major Hanbury Brown, R.E.*)

completed and at work. Then the other section was taken in hand. The Barrage has been in full work ever since, and has long ago repaid, in the revenue from the increased water supply, every penny of the money expended on its salvation.

To explain how these British engineers managed to cover the entire bed of the river with aprons of solid concrete, thus plugging up the springs; how they underpinned the piers, which had no foundation to carry them, would be too technical a task for me or my readers. The French engineers, when they found their work would not hold water, all ran away some years before, and carried their plans with them. When the British engineers in 1883 took over the Engineering Department, where such things should be stored, they found everything had been taken away; so in order to repair the piers and understand the nature of the foundations new borings had to be made everywhere. This, however, was a blessing in disguise. A thorough knowledge of the weak points was obtained. The Nile at low water was banked out in sections, the water

s

pumped out, and the bottom left dry. Hundreds of men were employed on the dry bed of the great river to repair any weak spot. This was all done by free workmen (no kourbash—no *corvée*—all paid labour), by night electric light, with relays of men. First one branch, the Damietta, was attacked, and when it was completed and at work, then the Rosetta arm was similarly treated, and in 1890 the whole was in working order as we now see it.

As it now stands, a beautiful light structure, with its slim towers and embattled gates, spanning the mighty Nile, there is no great engineering work at once so dignified, so useful, and so picturesque. Every means are offered for the public to see the beautiful structure. Tiny railways are laid all along the centre to carry wheeled chairs, which are propelled swiftly by fleet-footed Arabs. A pretty little kiosque is built on the central island, where the Chief Resident Engineer lives now, keeping his anxious watch by night and day. This was the palace built for the Empress Eugenie when she went to inaugurate the Suez Canal and to inspect the "completed" barrage, and is a very pleasant place to rest in the heat of the day, especially if you happen to be invited to lunch.

It was accidentally found that poor Mougel Bey, the designer of the beautiful work, was living in poverty, forgotten by his countrymen. The Government took up his case, and a liberal annuity was settled on him. The great work of beneficence that the Barrage has done had already doubled the agricultural produce of the Delta.

Major R. H. Brown and Mr. Brooke, his assistant, are now making a weir across the river above the Barrage, which will add several feet to the storage of water, and enable other canals to be supplied at higher level. I was invited to visit this last addition to the Cairo Barrage in May 1899. There are several novelties in its construction which are worthy of notice. In the first place, it is being entirely done, not by contract, but by the paid labour of the local natives, trained on the spot under two or three English experts. Several thousand men were employed, working day and night. The bed of the river was cleared by diving apparatus and native divers. A huge railway or gantry was projected across the stream, and by this means great boxes filled with stones and concrete were carried to their places, being dropped on the river's bed with perfect precision. These were protected underneath and at the sides with slanting buttress-work, all hermetically sealed with concrete and aprons of cement extending beyond on the bed of the ancient Nile. All went on quietly and steadily, not a rude word used, all seemed intent on doing their work and to know how it should be done. And all these men had been a few months before at work as labourers in the fields. The

CAIRO BARRAGE: WEIR IN PROCESS OF ERECTION ACROSS THE PILE ABOVE THE DAM, 1899,
By native workmen under Major Hanbury Brown and Mr. Brooke, C.E.

stones were conveyed in nets slung on camels that seemed to know their business as well as their masters. The relays of these quaint animals going and returning along the narrow paths among the dams, added a very interesting element to a most picturesque scene of industry. Mr. Brooke was to finish the Damietta branch this season, and next year the Rosetta branch would be given a similar weir.

The sketch map at the head of this paper will show that there are several canals, with locks, for traffic ·as well as those for irrigation, supplied by the great Barrage at Cairo.

In Egypt, when a man has succeeded in doing anything well in his own line he is invariably selected to do something difficult in a totally different branch. Having caulked the old Barrage and planned new ones, Mr. Willcocks was sent to revalue the farms of the fellaheen in Upper Egypt. Speaking Arabic like a native, and a great favourite with the people, even when he had raised their valuations, he never had an appeal against his decisions. This employed him for three years. Mr. Willcocks was then engaged in the service of a French

FRENCH ARCHITECTURE AT THE GATE OF
THE BARRAGE AT CAIRO.

company in providing a supply of pure filtered water for Cairo, and in his leisure hours occupied himself in designing a system of sanitary drainage for the same great crowded city. It has puzzled every engineer up to his time. The constant varying levels of the Nile render it an apparent impossibility, but the man who saved the Barrage may well accomplish what has baffled other scientific men, and he himself is confident of success. Mr. Willcocks is now a director of a powerful company which has taken over from the Government the great private estates of Ismail, the extravagant management of which had, in this tyrant's time, helped to ruin the country. These estates will now bring in a large fixed revenue to the land they helped to saddle with debt. Fortunately, however, Mr. Willcocks is still in Egypt, and likely to remain. His advice would be invaluable on any serious matter of irrigation policy, and he is always ready to give it.

To many of my readers Egyptian Irrigation may be a new subject. Mr. Willcocks (whose holiday library, it is said, consists of the Bible and Shakspere —both works he carries in his pockets) points out in his great book on " Irrigation in Egypt " that Shakspere knew all about it, viz. :—

> " Thus they do, sir ; they take the flow o' the Nile
> By certain scales i' the Pyramid ; they know,
> By the height, the lowness, or the mean, if dearth
> Or foison follow. The higher Nilus swells,
> The more it promises. As it ebbs, the seedsman
> Upon the slime and ooze scatters his grain,
> And shortly comes to harvest."—*Antony and Cleopatra*, II., 7.

INDEX.

LONDON :
EYRE AND SPOTTISWOODE, HER MAJESTY'S PRINTERS,
HACKNEY, N.E.

For EU product safety concerns, contact us at Calle de José Abascal, 56–1°,
28003 Madrid, Spain or eugpsr@cambridge.org.

www.ingramcontent.com/pod-product-compliance
Ingram Content Group UK Ltd.
Pitfield, Milton Keynes, MK11 3LW, UK
UKHW042151130625
459647UK00011B/1289